Cursing the Basil

Cursing the Basil
and other
Folklore of the Garden

Vivian A. Rich

HORSDAL & SCHUBART

Horsdal & Schubart Publishers Ltd.
Victoria, BC, Canada

Cover painting and section-head drawings by Catharine Campbell, Sidney, BC.

Main title courtesy of Susan Anstine, Saltspring Island, BC.

This book is set in New Baskerville.

We acknowledge the support of the Canada Council for the Arts for our publishing program.

Printed and bound in Canada by Printcrafters Inc., Winnipeg, Manitoba.

Canadian Cataloguing in Publication Data

Vivian Rich, 1953-
 Cursing the basil and other folklore of the garden

Includes bibliographical references and index.
ISBN 0-920663-56-7

1.Plants--Folklore. I. Title.
GR780.R52 1998   398'.368   C98-910111-8

Printed and bound in Canada.

CONTENTS

INTRODUCTION

The history of plants and the development of Western civilization are inexorably intertwined. To write of mankind's journey from prehistoric life to the modern, technological world is to write of humanity's dependence on plants: the flowers, herbs and spices which once played an overwhelming role in all aspects of life.

Throughout ancient history, people held the view that their destiny was in the hands of the gods or capricious spirits who had to be kept happy at all times. Plants were important gifts from the gods. Plants helped provide the basic necessities of life, as in the Greek belief that fire was brought from Mount Olympus by Prometheus in the stalk of a giant fennel. Offerings of flowers and herbs, and the burning of spices and incense, helped to appease the gods. Before the advent of modern medicine and before science explained natural phenomena, life was frightening and unpredictable, and mankind's dependence on forces outside his control led to reliance upon magic and superstitious practices in which plants prominently figured.

The advent of Christianity did not significantly change society's dependence on plants. Herbs cleansed the churches, flowers were given as offerings and spices, combined with incense, formed an important part of the ritual of worship. Folk-magic, however, remained, as people grappled with plagues, storms, and other natural disasters. In church people were told to trust their soul to God but it was still necessary to carry an amulet against the evil eye and to hang herbs in the house as protection against lightning.

Plants were the source of everyday necessities and luxuries. They were the primary ingredients of medicine and household products. People relied on plants for their personal needs from toothpaste to facial cleansers to hair restorers, while using them in the home as insect repellents, laundry fresheners and cleansing agents. Herbs and spices were, as now, important culinary ingredients, and flowers were viewed as edible commodities more often than as decorative blossoms.

On a higher level the demand for spices forged important trade links that opened up the world, bringing wealth to individuals and to countries. Plants were used by society as objects of barter in place of hard currency and rent could be paid with a rose or a quantity of pepper.

Political personalities, royal dynasties, countries and wars were defined by specific plants. Members of rival political factions flaunted their affiliations in public with the appropriate flower on their lapels, and levels of antagonism reached such heated proportions that entire plant species were boycotted by nations.

Defining Flowers, Herbs and Spices Through the Ages

Flowers, herbs and spices bring three distinct ideas to mind but putting these ideas into words is difficult. Spices are the easiest to explain. They are the roots, bark, flowers, seeds or resin of plants and are noted for their sharp, pungent taste and strong scent. Almost all spices are native to Asia and the Middle East, the exceptions being vanilla, allspice and capsicum which originate in the West Indies and South America.

Herbs are generally described as plants that die back to the ground after flowering and do not have a permanent woody structure for support as do trees and shrubs. In Europe herbs originated primarily in the Mediterranean region and were brought into northern Europe as a result of the Roman conquests. Whereas the difference between a spice and a herb is clear, problems arise over the distinction between a herb and a flower. There appears to be no simple explanation of a flower. According to the *Oxford English Dictionary* a flower is a "complex organ in phenogamous plants, comprising a group of reproductive organs and its envelopes."[1]

Although enlightening to botanists, this leaves laymen totally confused. In modern, simplistic terms herbs have a practical value while flowers are decorative plants for gardens or indoor floral arrangements.

Historically, a plant could be both a herb and a flower depending upon its use. Plants were considered first in light of their utilitarian benefits. If it was a medicinal, cosmetic or household help it was a herb and roses, violets, carnations and lilies, which are considered flowers by today's standards, have been used as multi-purpose herbs.

Flowers, used for purely decorative purposes, were a luxury grown only in periods of history when there was peace and prosperity. Under the Romans, Italy was free from invaders for over 400 years and this political stability was an important factor in the many ways in which the Romans used plants. Apart from providing food and medicine, plants decorated homes and public buildings, scented clothes and household objects, and perfumed both men and women. Rome was also wealthy, the other important component for the enjoyment of plants purely for pleasure.

There is extensive evidence of plants being grown and used purely for decorative purposes during the period of the Roman empire. Three books — Cato, *De Agri Cultura*, c. 160 B.C., Varro, *De Re Rustica*, c. 36 B.C., and Columello, *De Re Rustica*, c. 60 A.D. — although they are practical manuals on agriculture and farm management, include sections on the cultivation of flowers for pleasure. Imperial Rome saw the proliferation of pleasure gardens within its cities and in country estates. City gardens contained flowers planted in vases, pots or small beds. These flowers were not impressive by today's standards as the majority of "fancy" flowers only began to arrive in Europe from the Middle East and Asia during the 17th and 18th centuries. The Romans planted the familiar flowers of the fields: anemones, cornflowers, crocuses, cyclamens, daffodils, daisies, foxgloves, irises, lilies, violets and roses.

Country estates were status symbols for wealthy Romans and information on their gardens can be found in the *Letters* of Pliny the Younger who lived in the first century A.D. and was the owner of two estates. His Laurentium estate had a decorative terrace planted with violets while a rose garden provided a pleasurable view at his villa in Tuscany. Both villas had separate kitchen gardens and grew violets and roses amid the other culinary herbs and vegetables.

The collapse of the Roman empire was followed by the Middle Ages, a period which is loosely dated from the fifth to 15th centuries. Rome and its Western Empire fell to Germanic invaders in 476 A.D. and life slowly altered to suit the new social and economic conditions. The Germanic invaders were followed by Vikings who raided and pillaged the land. People fled the cities to the relative safety of the countryside and for greater protection built their homes around the manor house of the local lord.

As the remnants of Roman culture disappeared, a new society of illiterate, isolated people was left to eke out its existence in a formidable and frightening land. Without access to cities where food could be purchased in markets and medicines in speciality shops, the family garden became the dispenser of these necessities. Self-sufficiency was essential to survival and there was no room in garden patches for purely decorative plants.

Three documents give an idea of the flower/herb situation during the early Middle Ages. Charlemagne, the Holy Roman Emperor, whose life spanned from 768 to 814 A.D., issued a decree, the *Capitulare de Villis*, which provided a list of plants and trees to be grown on the royal estates. Included among the common herbs such as sage, rue, rosemary and mint were the lily, rose, flag iris and poppy.

From the same period there survives a plan for the monastery of St. Gall in Switzerland. The herb garden is placed next to the infirmary and its plants were for the use of the monk/healer. The plant beds are labelled and include the lily, iris and rose.

The importance of these three flowers in daily life is further confirmed by an informative gardening poem called the *Hortulus* or *Little Garden* composed by Walafrid Strabo, the abbot at the monastery of Reichenau in Germany. The poem, written around 840 A.D., contains the descriptions and uses of 23 plants found in Strabo's monastery's garden.

In his poem Strabo appreciates the beauty of the iris, lily and rose but he does not lose sight of their reason for being in the garden. The iris, with "the beauty of your purple flower" was a multi-purpose herb.[2] Shavings from its root were dried, crushed and dissolved in wine to ease pains of the bladder or added to water to stiffen the monastery's linen and give it a sweet scent. The lily was white like the "white of glistening snow, Its scent the scent of sweetest frankincense" and yet the juice crushed from its blossoms and added to wine was believed to be an antidote to poisonous snake bites.[3] Strabo does get somewhat carried away over the rose, praising it for its beauty and fragrance, calling it "the Flower of Flowers."[4] Still, even this plant was grown because it had so many cures for illnesses that, according to Strabo, no one could remember them all.

Gardens in the early Middle Ages were planted primarily for utilitarian purposes and even the wealthy were more concerned with a sufficient supply of food and medicine than with decorative flower beds. Charlemagne enjoyed the luxury of a pleasure garden at his capital at Aachen, in present-day Germany. However, even the Holy Roman Emperor could only manage a walled garden with apple trees, lilies and roses in a grassy meadow.

As the centuries progressed Europe began to acquire political stability and security with the establishment of kingdoms and the concept of statehood. From the 14th century onwards, the nobility began to plant pleasure gardens which were separate from the kitchen garden. Flower beds became a feature of the pleasure garden and were planted with violets, lilies, daisies, irises, roses, daffodils and other meadow flowers while rosemary, hyssop, lavender, sage and rue were added for their decorative, rather than their practical, qualities.

Mankind's use of plants declined in the West as knowledge of science and technology increased. Quack herbal remedies were proven ineffectual and the growing biochemical industry of the 20th century developed synthetic drugs which, in the minds of most people, provided more effective treatment. Advances in biochemistry opened the way for synthetic versions of every conceivable household product and in the process reduced herbs and spices to a predominantly culinary role, while flowers became decorative adjuncts inside and outside the home.

In the end the question of whether a plant is a flower or herb may best be answered by the Greek scholar Theophrastus who lived in the third century B.C. He was the first person known to attempt to develop a scientific system of classifying plants which he explained in his book *The Enquiry Into Plants*. He came to the conclusion that "one must not make a too precise definition."[5]

Plants carry the collective symbolism of past centuries and civilizations. In the technological explosion of the 20th century, modern society has lost touch with its long, rich history of plants. This book is an attempt to preserve those memories: to remind people of the significance of plants in Western society and allow them the opportunity to see flowers, herbs and spices in a new light. In the words of the 17th-century English poet Robert Herrick:

> I sing of may-poles, hock-carts, wassails, wakes,
> Of bride-grooms, brides, and of their bridall-cakes.
> I write of youth, of love, and have accesse
> By these, to sing of cleanly-wantonnesse.
> I sing of dewes, of raines, and piece by piece
> Of balme, of oyle, of spice, and amber-greece.
> I sing of times trans-shifting; and I write
> How roses first came red, and lilies white.[6]

PART ONE: SPELLS AND RITUALS

LOVE

From the ancient Graeco/Roman period to the 19th century, European and North American girls relied on superstitious practices, such as divination spells, to discover the names of their future husbands and when they would marry. Marriage was important to women because it defined their place in society. A woman was someone's daughter, upon marriage she became someone's wife, and finally she became someone's mother. The identification of women in terms of their husbands and children, and the often negative social stigmas attached to being unmarried, made marriage an important event which consumed both the thoughts and time of young single girls.

Divination spells involving love and marriage had their origins in pagan European culture. They were absorbed into Christianity by monks travelling throughout Europe, intent on making converts. In an attempt to make Christianity acceptable to the

1

Celtic and Teutonic tribes, the monks retained pagan religious dates and many pagan customs. Transition to the new religion was easier when Christian saints' days fell on pagan sacred days and when popular social customs, including the use of divination spells, were retained and put in a Christian context. Divination spells were most effective if performed on certain days of the year and at a particular time of night. Midnight was the preferred hour for conducting these rituals and its importance in this context can be traced back to pagan cultural beliefs involving the division of the hours of the day. In pre-Christian northern Europe the 24-hour day was divided into eight cycles of three hours and the midpoint of each cycle was governed by a specific virtue. Midnight was one of these midpoint hours. It was considered to be a time of regeneration and new beginnings, and since it was believed by the pagans that people who were born at midnight had second sight, the hour assumed the additional association as a time for predicting the future.

The preferred days for performing divining spells were the feast days of Christian saints or the eve before the feast day. The most potent days were St. Agnes' Eve (January 20th), St. Mark's Day (April 30th), St. John the Baptist's Day, more commonly known as St. John's Day (June 24th), All Hallow's Eve (October 31st) and Christmas Eve. These days were believed by the ancient Celts to be spirit nights when the barriers between the real and the spirit worlds were weakened and spirits could roam the earth. In pagan northern Europe, days were measured from sunset to sunset, so the evening and night of the day preceding a sacred day were important, which accounts for the number of holidays where the eve is of special significance.

Pagan influence is obvious in these saints' days which were thought to be the most potent days for divination. St. Agnes' Day (January 21st) was the last day of the month of Beth or birch tree in the Celtic tree calendar, a month which was considered to be a time of new beginnings. St. Mark's Day on April 30th is the eve before May Day and May 1st was the Celtic festival of Beltane, an important celebration to mark the midpoint between the spring equinox and the summer solstice. Fertility rituals were part of its celebration. All Hallow's Eve corresponded to the Celtic festival of Samhain which was celebrated on November 1st to mark the beginning of winter and was the day of the Festival of the Dead.

Midsummer's Day, which was transformed into St. John's Day, was the Celtic celebration of the summer solstice. Midsummer's Eve was considered to be the most potent time for girls to carry out spells to discover the name of their future husbands, and in England girls had a number of rituals for their choosing.

In one spell a young woman would pick 12 leaves of sage at midnight on Midsummer's Eve and as the clock struck 12, the man destined to be her husband would appear before her in a vision. As with so many of the plants used in divination rituals, there is no one reason for the use of sage. From the time of the ancient Greeks to the present day, sage has been used, medicinally, to promote good health and long life, so it is possible that a long-lasting marriage was an underlying idea in the choice of sage. In the 19th century, however, sage was a symbol of "domestic virtue" or the ideal wife. The use of 12 leaves is a probable reference to the 12 apostles, as numbers traditionally throughout Europe have a Christian connection.

In another Midsummer's Eve ritual a young woman would set a plate of flour under a rosemary bush at midnight in the hope that in the morning she would see her future husband's initials traced in the flour. Rosemary was used for a number of possible reasons. It did not become an established herb in England until the Middle Ages and its symbolism would be related to Christian concepts.

Rosemary was associated with the Virgin Mary and, therefore, was a symbol of virginity, being worn by brides or carried in their wedding bouquets. By the Middle Ages it was a symbol of fidelity because a sprig of rosemary would retain its scent for many weeks. It was also used as an aphrodisiac when the flowers were soaked in wine. By using rosemary, the girl was putting her trust in a plant which had strong connotations of virginity (a requirement of a bride), wedding ceremonies for which she was hoping, marital faithfulness from her future husband and a vital love life.

A third Midsummer's Eve spell required the young woman to scatter red rose petals about the churchyard while chanting:

> Rose petals, rose petals,
> Rose petals I strew.
> He that will love me,
> Come to me soon.

Roses were an obvious choice since they were, historically, the flower of love, being sacred to the Greek Aphrodite and Roman Venus, pagan goddesses of love, and to the Virgin Mary. There was also a popular belief in England, from the Middle Ages to the 19th century, that if a young woman dreamed of red roses it was a sign of marriage to a handsome man. Presumably, the use of red roses, as compared to white or pink, had the added benefit of securing a handsome husband.

St. Agnes' Eve, the night before Valentine's Day, and St. Luke's Day (October 18th) were also auspicious times for divination spells in England although they were not considered as spiritually potent as Midsummer's Eve. On St. Agnes' Eve a girl would take a sprig each of rosemary and thyme and sprinkle them three times with water. In the evening she would place one in each of two shoes and place a shoe on either side of her bed. She would then recite the following lines:

St. Agnes that's to lovers kind,
Come, ease the trouble of my mind.

It was hoped that the face of her future husband would appear in her dreams that night. Thyme, like rosemary, was a symbol of fidelity. Its symbolism developed during the Crusades in the Middle Ages when ladies embroidered thyme on scarves which they gave to their knights as a token of endearment.

On the night before Valentine's Day a young woman would take two bay leaves, sprinkle them with rose water and lay them across her pillow. When she went to bed, she would put on a clean night-gown, turned inside out, and in bed she would recite:

Good Valentine, be kind to me,
In dreams let me my true love see.

Bay was associated with love as far back as ancient Greece when, according to legend, Apollo fell in love with Daphne and she was turned into a laurel or bay tree.

On St. Luke's Day girls would take handfuls of marigolds, marjoram and wormwood, simmer them in water over a low fire and rub their bodies with the liquid at bedtime in the hope that they would dream of their future husband. The mixture of the three plants represented three different aspects of love: fidelity, sweetness, and sex. Marigolds denoted faithfulness because of their long flowering period. Their botanical name, Calendula, comes from the Latin *calendulae* which translates as throughout the months, and the implication of marigolds would be long-lasting fidelity. Marjoram represented sweetness in love because of its sweet scent while wormwood was used as an aphrodisiac or "love potion."

In Scotland it was the custom for a young woman to go out silently on Christmas Eve and gather holly leaves which she would tie in a three-cornered handkerchief and lay under her pillow. As she slept her future husband would be revealed to her in a dream. Christmas Eve had double importance as a divination day, being not only the night before an important sacred day in the Christian calendar but also the first day of the pagan Celtic month of Beth, which was considered auspicious for new beginnings.

Holly was used possibly because of its pagan and Christian religious connotations. It was known as the Holy Tree and represented the Crucifixion of Christ with its red berries and prickly leaves which symbolized the blood of Christ and the crown of thorns. In the Celtic religion holly was a sacred tree and its branches were used as charms against evil because it was believed that happy spirits lived within. It is also possible that apart from its religious implications, which would impart strength to the ritual, there was also a practical aspect to the use of holly as there would have been few flowers available in December apart from dried herbs.

These rituals allowed a young woman to see her future husband in a dream without actually having contact with the individual. For those women, however, who wanted more than a dream image or a hint of a name, there were spells which would allow them to see their future husbands in person or to come in contact with potential future husbands.

Again, the English had many rituals to provide the physical presence of a future husband. One spell involved the young woman picking ivy leaves and placing them against her heart while reciting:

Ivy, ivy, I love you,
in my bosom I put you.
The first young man to speak to me,
my future husband he shall be.

Ivy, because it is an evergreen, was, from the Middle Ages into the 19th century, a symbol of fidelity and eternal life. Also, because the ivy needs to cling to something for support, it became a symbol of marriage, attachment and affection.

Another popular spell required the young woman to place a sprig of southernwood or "lad's love" down her back and the first young man that she met would be the one she would marry. There was also a clover spell in which the young woman put a clover leaf in her right shoe and the first man she met would either be the one she would marry or else she would marry someone with the same first name. Clover, which was also known as trefoil, had religious connections to the trinity and, like so many of the plants used in divination spells, it was also a sacred plant in the Celtic tradition.

In the summer an English girl would pick a moss rose, wrap it in white paper and put it away in a secret place. If, in one month's time, it was still as fresh as when it was picked, she would wear it to church and her future husband would come forward and take it from her. The basic spell probably had, like the other spells, ancient pre-Christian origins, but the use of the moss rose in particular occurs in the 18th century. Moss roses are offshoots of the cabbage rose or *Rosa centifolia* and the first written record of their presence in England is in a nursery catalogue from 1727. It would probably have been near the end of the century before moss roses became common in the English countryside but they would have been popular for divination spells because their newness made them special and they also had small blossoms which made them easy to hide.

Given the importance of marriage the English even had a spell to use as a last resort: the unmarried woman would sow burdock seeds on a piece of grass. On a Friday morning, she had to go to a quiet and deserted place, half an hour before sunrise, and say:

> I sow, I sow!
> Then, my own dear,
> Come here, come here,
> And mow, and mow!

She would see a vision of her future husband mowing the sprouted burdock seeds with a scythe. If she was not frightened then the match would take place. By the 16th century burdock was considered to be under the influence of Venus and any connection with the goddess of love would have been an inducement to use the plant. The burdock was composed of many burrs and a popular game, which went back to the Middle Ages and possibly beyond, was for boys to pick off the burrs and throw them at each other. The burrs would easily stick and the boy with the fewest burrs stuck on him was the winner of the game. This popular children's game may also have had an influence on the choice of burdock since the woman, in desperation to find a husband, would have wanted to stick to her "visionary" man like a burr to a child, or have him stick to her.

A variation on this spell consisted of scattering hempseed in a garden or churchyard on Midsummer's Eve. The use of hempseed began in the Middle Ages and it was still carried on at the beginning of the 20th century. The young woman would chant:

> Hempseed I set,
> Hempseed I sow
> The man that is my true love
> Come after me now.

She would then wait throughout the night for a spirit image of her husband to walk by. Hempseed was used to make rope halters and since this was a spell only used as a last resort, the choice of hempseed may have reflected the desire to "rope in" a husband.

Women were not the only ones curious about their future spouses. All Hallow's Eve was the time for young men to discover whom they would marry. The requirements were to gather ten leaves of ivy and toss one away. The remaining nine leaves were placed under the pillow and while the young man slept he would see his future wife in his dreams. Ivy, because of its clinging qualities, had come to symbolize a wife but the use of nine leaves may have had more complex reasons. The number nine was considered an angelic number, for the Bible mentions nine choirs of angels. Nine is also a combination of three times three and, since the time of the ancient Greeks, three was a special number because it symbolized completion, having a beginning, middle and end.

Midsummer's Eve or St. John's Day was the most popular day throughout most of Europe for divination rituals related to marriages, and hypericum, or St. John's Wort (its English name) was the preferred plant to determine the length of time a young woman would have to wait until her marriage. St. John's Wort was named after St. John the Baptist because it was always in bloom on his feast day and *wort* was the Anglo-Saxon word for plant. The blossoms of St. John's Wort are yellow but when they are crushed they produce a red juice which the medieval peasants associated with the blood of the martyred Baptist. This visible connection between the plant and St. John increased its potency in the minds of the young women and men who used it for divination. St. John's Wort was also associated with love through the obsessive love of Salome for St. John which led to the saint's death.

In England, if a young woman picked a sprig of St. John's Wort while it was still wet with dew she believed she would find a husband within a year. Alternatively, she could place a sprig of the plant on her pillow on St. John's Day and if it remained unwithered the next day she would be married within 12 months. St. John's Wort was considered a magical plant in Germany because the strong smell from its blossoms was believed to drive away evil spirits. Young women would gather its flowers during the morning of St. John's Day and if the flowers did not wither by the end of the day the girls would be brides that year. In Denmark two sprigs of St. John's Wort were placed between the rafters in the roof of the house and if the two grew together, the young woman would soon be a bride.

In England, daisies and dandelions were also used to determine how long a young woman would have to wait until her wedding day. Daisies had a medieval association with love, being worn by knights as symbols of fidelity. In the early spring a young woman would find a field filled with daisies and, with eyes closed, she would pick a handful of flowers. The number of blossoms in hand would equal the number of years she would have to wait. When dandelions were in seed the number of puffs needed to remove all the seeds would equal the number of years before marriage.

COURTSHIP

Young women may have dreamed of their future husbands and even determined the number of years till marriage but it was often necessary to attract a young man's attention and keep it until the marriage was arranged. In Wales a young woman would carry a sprig of valerian concealed in her clothes while German girls wore small bags of endive seeds between their breasts. Czech girls wore tiny bunches of fenugreek around their necks. The effectiveness of fenugreek may have been its quality as a good deodorant which was extremely useful when sanitary conditions were poor and baths irregular.

Men also tried various means of attracting the attentions of the village maidens. In France young men went courting with bouquets of vervain, also known as verbena. This plant was dedicated to Venus by the Romans and, in pre-Christian France, it was used in magic and rituals. Bouquets of vervain were presented to young ladies in the belief that the strong magic power of the plant, combined with its associations with the ancient goddess of love, would win over their hearts.

In Northamptonshire, England, the young men went courting during the sheepshearing time which was a major event in the farming calendar. It took place during the early summer and there would be a large selection of wild and cottage flowers available for the young men to make into bouquets. A traditional courting bouquet was composed of cabbage roses, lavender, wallflowers, snapdragons, pansies, honeysuckle, gorse, lad's love and larkspur, tied together with sweet brier and ribbon grass. This is an interesting combination in that the symbolism associated with the flowers covers a wide range of attitudes towards love and courtship.

Cabbage roses were traditional symbols of love but the sweet brier, also known as eglantine, represented love that survived through good fortune and adversity because its beautiful, sweet-scented blossoms were in contrast to its sharp thorns. Lavender, with its sweet scent, was considered to be a token of love while wallflowers were symbols of fidelity. People believed that if they wore a piece of snapdragon, it would make them appear gracious in the sight of others and the young men wanted to appear at their best to the young ladies they hoped to court. Pansies represented the face of the young lady and honeysuckle symbolized her as the clinging vine in need of support. Gorse or broom was a fertility charm because its sprigs carried many blossoms while lad's love was used by young men in a potion in an attempt to cure venereal disease. Larkspur does not have any known symbolic associations and it was probably included in the bouquet to add to its beauty.

Amid all these flowers, lad's love or southernwood was the powerful courting aid. Lad's love, whose botanical name is Artemisia, was named after Artemis, the virgin Greek goddess who watched over women. Women believed that the presence of lad's love in the bouquet would help them decide whether or not to accept a young man's proposal of courtship. If she decided against him she would throw the bouquet to the ground but if she accepted the bouquet they could commence their courting stroll.

Many popular folk names for flowers, like lad's love, had their origins in the plant's association with love and courtship, and most of the names were fanciful, funny and descriptive. There are two very different versions of how lad's love got its name. In one story, lads placed dried southernwood and other sweet-smelling herbs in muslin bags and presented them to their sweethearts. The young ladies would place these bags among their clothes and the southernwood blossoms, which had a long-lasting fragrance, would impart a sweet smell to their clothes and linens and act as a deterrent to moths. The second explanation involves the use of dried southernwood leaves in an ointment to increase hair growth on men with receding hairlines. Young men believed that a full head of hair would make them look more masculine and therefore more attractive to women.

The common wild pansy, or *Viola tricolor*, had an incredible list of names associated with love. According to legend, this pansy, which differs from the modern hybrid, was originally white until it was hit by Cupid's arrow. The flower immediately turned purple, the colour of a bleeding wound. The country people called pansies "heart's ease" because they believed the plant had the ability to cure problems of the heart, especially those associated with love. The pansy was also used in rural love potions and its names included Cupid's flower, cuddle-me, kiss-me-quick, love-lies-bleeding, love idol, call-me-to-you, meet-me-in-the-entry, kiss-her-in-the-buttery, and Johnny-jump-up-and-kiss-me. Another name for the pansy was love-in-idleness which Shakespeare used in *A Midsummer Night's Dream*. Puck, on the orders of Oberon, King of the Fairies, rubs pansy juice on the eyes of Titania, Oberon's consort, making her fall in love with the first creature she sees.

Robert Herrick, the 17th-century English poet, wrote the following verse to pansies which describes their relationship to love:

To Pansies
Ah, cruell Love! must I endure
Thy many scorns, and find no cure?
Say, are thy medicines made to be
Helps to all others, but to me?
Ile leave thee, and to pansies come;
Comforts you'l afford me some:
You can ease my hart, and doe
What Love co'd ne'r be brought unto.[1]

The *Nigella sativa* was called "love-in-a-mist" because its blue flowers were almost hidden among its tangled leaves. For centuries English women would put the fragrant seeds in a muslin bag and wear it between their breasts in the belief that its scent would draw the attention of young men. The seeds were also used to flavour cakes. According to folklore, if a woman ate large enough quantities of the seeds, her breasts would increase in size and make her more attractive to men.

Climbing or clinging plants were associated with love and marriage. The clematis was called the "virgin's bower" and the herbalist John Parkinson in his *Paradisi in Sole* of 1629 reported that country women called the plant simply "love" because it tightly embraced whatever it climbed. The honeysuckle or woodbine was known in the countryside as "hold-me-tight" and people believed that the flower's scent filled the brain with images of love.

Flowers and herbs acquired special significance if they became part of an ill-fated love affair. The wallflower became a symbol of fidelity in love as the result of a love affair in 12th-century Scotland. A Scottish chieftain's son was in love with Elizabeth, the daughter of the Earl of March. The main obstacle to their happiness was the fact that Elizabeth was betrothed, against her will, to the son of King Robert of Scotland. Elizabeth lived at Neidpath Castle on the River Tweed and one day her lover disguised himself as a minstrel and sang beneath her bedroom window. In his song he said that if she wished to elope with him she should pick the wallflower which was growing near her window and drop it at his feet. Elizabeth obliged but lost her balance and fell to her death. Afterwards, her lover always wore a wallflower when it was in bloom.

The basil plant became a symbol of love through its involvement in a dark tale of jealousy, intrigue and madness. The story was first told by Boccaccio in *The Decameron*.

There lived in the Italian city of Messina three rich merchant brothers and their sister, Isabetta. A young man named Lorenzo worked for them and he and Isabetta fell in love. They began an affair which was discovered by the brothers, and fearing for their sister's reputation, they arranged that Lorenzo should go out with them one day. Once they were outside the city they killed him and buried his body in a shallow grave. When they returned they told Isabetta that Lorenzo had gone away on business.

One night, however, Lorenzo's ghost appeared to Isabetta and told her where to find his body. The next day she went to the grave. Unable to return the whole body to the city she took out her knife, cut off the head and returned home. Isabetta placed Lorenzo's head in a herb pot and planted basil over it. She then shut herself in her room where she wept continually, using her tears to water the basil.

Her brothers became suspicious over Isabetta's obsessive devotion towards the pot of basil and they finally took it away from her. Inside, they found the head of Lorenzo and fearing that the murder would be discovered they fled the city. The loss of the pot of basil made Isabetta ill and shortly afterwards she died of grief.

The British poet John Keats based his poem "Isabella or the Pot of Basil" on Boccaccio's story:

She wrapp'd it up; and for its tomb did choose
A garden pot, wherein she laid it by.
And cover'd it with mould, and o'er it set
Sweet Basil, which her tears kept ever wet.[2]

Isabella's passion, grief and madness were captured by the Victorian painter William Holman Hunt in his 1867 painting, appropriately entitled "Isabella and the Pot of Basil," which shows Isabella standing next to a prayer stand, embracing the pot with its basil.

As a result of the popularity of the story of Isabetta and Lorenzo, basil became a love token. In Tudor England it was customary to present little pots of basil as a compliment to someone special while in parts of Europe — Romania, Greece and Italy in particular — men and women would give basil to the person they loved. Italian men took the idea of the love token one step further and suitors would wear a sprig of basil in their hair to indicate their matrimonial intentions. The young man would appear beneath the woman's window and when she saw the basil she could decide if she wished to pursue the romance or have him sent away.

WEDDINGS AND MARRIAGE

Young girls may have had their fantasies about who they would marry but most were probably aware of the realities of how their husbands would be chosen. In ancient Greece marriages were arranged between the bride's father and the groom. During the marriage ceremony the bride wore a wreath of myrtle, a plant sacred to Aphrodite, the goddess of love.

In early Rome only the patricians, who were the aristocracy, could contract a legal marriage. The term patrician quite literally meant someone who knew his father (*pater*) and could inherit from him. It was not until the reign of the Emperor Justinian (527-565 A.D.), under his code of laws, the *Corpus Iuris Civilus*, that Roman marriage laws were finalized and impediments to marriages removed. As an example of the new leniency, senators, who formed the highest class, were now permitted to marry actresses and prostitutes.

A Roman wedding was celebrated with special customs. The bride wore a wedding tunic, a veil on her head and a wreath of myrtle blossoms in her hair. The groom also wore a sprig of myrtle. The use of myrtle was a continuation of the sacred connection between myrtle and the Greek Aphrodite, who had become the Roman goddess, Venus. Both the bride and groom wore parsley and rue in the wreaths around their heads to protect them from evil spirits. Oak boughs were carried during the wedding ceremony as a symbol of fertility and friends sent holly wreaths to the wedding as a sign of congratulations. The wedding was celebrated at the house of the bride's father and the house would be decked with seasonal flowers and boughs from trees.

Special wedding cakes were distributed at the feast. They were called *mustaceum* and a recipe given by the Roman writer Cato includes the following ingredients: a peck of flour with must, which is the unfermented wine or juice from grapes, anise, cumin, bay leaves, lard and cheese. These cakes were baked on a bed of bay leaves which led to the Roman proverb "to look for a bay leaf in a wedding cake." With time this became "to look for a needle in a pyramid" and finally ended as "like looking for a needle in a haystack." Bay leaves were consecrated to the vestal virgins who supervised the worship of Vesta, the goddess of the hearth. The vestal virgins took a vow of perpetual chastity and it is probable that the use of bay leaves in the wedding cake was originally intended as a reference to the bride's virginity.

After the wedding feast there was a public procession to the groom's house and the groom scattered nuts to the crowd as a symbol of fertility. Upon arrival at the house the bride was given a place of honour at the family hearth and then the couple retired to the marriage chamber. Crocuses and hyacinths were placed on the bed for it was believed that these two flowers covered the marriage bed of Jupiter and Juno, two of the senior deities in the Roman pantheon. There was the added significance of Juno being the Roman goddess of women and marriage.

The Christian church was slow to develop rituals of marriage. There appear to have been no Christian wedding ceremonies over the first three centuries of church history. In the East, placing metallic crowns upon the heads of the bride and groom formalized their marriage while in the West, all that was initially required was the consent of the couple and a blessing by the priest. In some western European areas the priest blessed the couple when they were already in the marriage bed.

During the early Middle Ages the Christian church began to insist on the public celebration of marriage and a blessing by a priest. These public marriages were conducted outside the church door and afterwards the married couple entered the church for mass and to receive communion.

Once a marriage had been agreed upon, charms were put to use, as the bride's virginity had to be tested, and rituals performed for the couple's happiness, love, fertility and protection from evil. A virgin bride was extremely important and often young men wanted proof before the wedding night. This would be done with a sprig of basil which the bride-to-be would clasp in her hand; if it withered it was considered a sign that she was not a virgin. This can be explained rationally as a result of guilt which would make the woman perspire and the salt in her perspiration would cause the basil to wilt.

If the bride's family objected to a public virginity test, on the grounds that it was demeaning and insulting, friends and family would make a floral statement regarding her chastity. It was common practice in England for the guests of the bride to hold a piece of rosemary in their right hand when the bride entered the church. Rosemary was associated with the Virgin Mary and its presence was a silent acknowledgment of the bride's virgin status.

Not all brides-to-be were virgins and comfrey was the herb to which they turned for help. Comfrey was used to heal broken bones and skin, and women believed that sitting in a decoction of comfrey would restore the hymen to its original virginal state.

European brides traditionally wore wreaths on their heads as a symbol of maidenhood. Wreaths were initially a Roman custom, associated with feasting and festivities which included weddings, and Christians in the fifth and sixth centuries refused to wear them because of their pagan associations. However, during the Middle Ages brides again began to wear flowers in their hair. In Germany the bridesmaid would buy the myrtle wreath, a symbol of love, for the bride, while a Czech bride would have her wreath of rosemary, symbolic of virginity and protection against evil, woven for her on her wedding eve.

In Normandy the bride wore a headdress comprised of white roses and a small mirror framed in green silk. Afterwards it was laid out on the bridal bed to show that her life as a maiden was ending as quickly as the roses were fading. In Switzerland the bridal wreath was set on fire by the mistress of ceremonies at the wedding feast and if it burned briskly, the couple would have good fortune but if it smouldered, good fortune would not come easily in their future.

Weddings were considered prime targets for witches and fairies; fairies were, until the 19th century, considered unfriendly and potentially evil. Herbs used as protection against witches, and charms to ward off evil were traditionally carried by the bridal party. In Germany the mother of the bride put dill and salt into her daughter's wedding shoes while in Sweden the groom sewed sprigs of garlic, thyme and other strongly scented herbs into his clothing. Salt was considered a pure substance and had a long history of use in religous ceremonies. It was sacred to the ancient Greeks and was mentioned as a religous offering in the rituals of the Jews in the Old Testament. The herbs which were used as protectors against evil acquired their abilities through their odour for it was believed that a strong-scented plant would act as a deterrent to witches and other creatures determined to cause harm to the married couple.

Happiness, fidelity and fertility were important and desirable qualities in the marriage and the bride could attempt to achieve these through the flowers in her wreath or bouquet. Rosemary, powerful by its association with the Virgin Mary, was constantly used throughout all of Europe and sprigs were woven into the bride's wreath or tucked into her bouquet. In England this custom supposedly started with the 1540 marriage of Anne of Cleves to Henry VIII for which Anne wore a coronet of gold and rubies interwoven with rosemary.

Henry's marriage to Anne took place in January, long after the flowering season was over for rosemary. However, there was such a demand for fresh rosemary that it was grown indoors, in pots, during the winter months which would explain the presence of fresh rosemary in Anne's bridal coronet. Regrettably for Anne, the rosemary failed to give her a happy marriage, although she did live a contented life in England after Henry had their marriage annulled. It is, however, likely that rosemary had a long history of earlier use in bridal wreaths in the English countryside, where the people were more superstitious.

According to the English poet Ben Jonson, it was customary during the 16th and 17th centuries for the bride to give her husband, on their wedding day, a bunch of rosemary tied with a gold ribbon. She would then say to him:

> Rosemary is remembrance between us day and night
> Wishing I may always have you present in my sight.

Another 16th-century English custom regarding rosemary was for the bride and groom to dip gilded rosemary twigs into their cups as a lucky charm before they drank their first toast.

The herb vervain was believed by the inhabitants of Celtic and Teutonic pre-Christian Europe to have magical powers. This idea continued into the Christian era and in Germany vervain was an important part of the wedding preparations. It was customary for the bride to start the wedding day with a cup of vervain tea which would ensure fertility. An extra piece of vervain was tucked into the bodice or waistband of her wedding dress and, up until the end of the 19th century, a hat woven from vervain was presented to the bride after the wedding ceremony to guarantee a loving marriage.

Myrtle, until recently, was a popular flower at weddings throughout Europe, initially because it was a sacred flower of Aphrodite, the Greek goddess of love. Long after its pagan Greek origin had been forgotten, brides continued to use myrtle in their bouquets as a charm for a happy marriage. A piece of myrtle was laid in the bride's prayer book on the page of the marriage ceremony and then the book was closed and placed under the pillow of the marriage bed.

It was also a tradition to plant a sprig of myrtle at the bride's new home when she returned from the church. It was the duty of the bridesmaid to do the planting and if the sprig bloomed, the bridesmaid would soon be wed. However, if it failed to bloom, the bridesmaid would never marry. Happily, myrtle rarely fails to bloom when it is transplanted and if the resulting myrtle tree flourished it meant that there would be harmony within the home. When Queen Victoria married Prince Albert in 1840, a sprig of myrtle from her wedding bouquet was planted in a churchyard at Cowes, on the Isle of Wight, the exact spot remaining a secret due to problems with vandalism. Queen Victoria's myrtle shrub flourished and sprigs from it have continually been placed in royal wedding bouquets.

Princess Anne's wedding bouquet, in 1973, included a collection of some of the most popular wedding flowers. Apart from the myrtle, there were 15 white roses, 50 lilies-of-the-valley, white orchids and orange blossoms. Princess Diana, in her 1981 wedding, carried a cascade bouquet of yellow roses, freesias, lily-of-the-valley and a sprig of Queen Victoria's myrtle for good luck.

For centuries European brides have carried lily-of-the-valley, orange blossoms, marigolds and roses in their bridal bouquets. Lily-of-the-valley was popular because it was considered a potent charm to promote love. Orange blossoms were symbolic of fertility and their appearance in bridal bouquets occurred after the Crusaders brought the idea back from the Middle East where orange blossoms were used as aphrodisiacs. Because of their long blooming period and their association with the Virgin Mary, marigolds were a symbol of the constancy of love and were carried by the bride to help ensure fidelity within the marriage. In the Victorian period the rose, as a symbol of love, was given by the groom to his bride on their wedding day. Now the bride provides her own rose bouquet. A modern addition to the bridal bouquet is *Gypsophila paniculata*, better known as baby's breath, which is a popular filler and, as its name suggests, has strong fertility connotations.

In today's society, everyone waits expectantly for the bride to throw her bouquet and then there is a mad scramble by unmarried women to catch it, in the belief that whoever does will soon marry. The idea of throwing the bouquet comes from the old English tradition of "flinging the stocking." This event took place inside the newlyweds' bedroom. The men grabbed the bride, the women grabbed the groom and they pulled the stockings off the newly married pair. The men and women sat at the foot of the bed and took turns tossing the stockings over their heads. If the stocking tossed by a girl fell on the head of the groom she would marry soon and similarly if a stocking tossed by a man landed on the head of the bride the man would be quick to marry. This custom was common until about 1780 when couples began to assert their desire for peace and privacy in their wedding bedroom. To accommodate the revellers, the bridal bouquet was thrown to the women and the bride's garter to the men before the married couple left the banquet.

The groom and his party had their own flowers. White carnations are the traditional flower worn by the groom and ushers and they were especially popular during the Victorian and Edwardian periods in England. White was a symbol of purity and the white carnation was a symbol of the groom's pure love and admiration for his bride as opposed to mere sexual love or lust. Other popular *boutonnières* were gardenias and camellias which were also used because of their white blossoms.

Flower girls are part of the general fertility associations in weddings. In 17th-century Stuart England flowers were strewn along the path where the bride walked into the church. William Brown in his *Britannia's Pastoral* of 1613 expressed this feature of weddings in one of his poems:

> Full many maids, clad in their best array,
> In honour of the bride, came with their flaskets,
> Fill'd full of flowers, others in wicker baskets,
> Bring from the marsh rushes to o'erspread,
> The ground whereon to church the lovers tread.[3]

Until the 19th century it was common for the bridal party to walk to the church along a pathway covered with flower petals and decorated with floral arches.

A non-traditional European wedding was the gypsy wedding in which couples were married by leaping over a broomstick. The broomstick was a branch of green broom which in the right season was covered with strongly scented yellow blossoms. Both the bride and the groom had to jump over the broom which was regarded as a symbol of fertility. There was, however, one catch. If the woman's skirt touched the broom it meant she was not a virgin and possibly even pregnant. If the man's trousers touched the broom it meant that he would be an unfaithful husband. Both bride and groom made an effort to jump high.

The Roman custom of covering the marriage bed with auspicious flowers was still in use in 17th-century England. Culpeper, the herbalist, recommended sprinkling pennyroyal on the marriage bed because the herb was under the dominion of Venus and would act as a love charm. In the country, bridal beds were often covered with rosemary which was believed to be a potent charm against all evil. It was also an emblem of remembrance and signified fidelity.

Fidelity in marriage was an important concern. In Poland yellow marigolds were planted to ensure a husband's faithfulness. The bride would wait until she found her husband's footprints in the soil; then she would dig up the earth which held them and place it in a window-box where she would plant marigolds. As long as the flowers bloomed her husband would remain with her. As the plants aged, new seeds would be planted to keep the window-box full of marigolds.

Brides were also concerned with their husbands' potential for violence. In arranged marriages the groom's temperament was often unknown, as there had been little, if any, time for the couple to get to know each other. If the bride was unsure of her husband, she would bring a sprig of lavender into the house on their wedding day for protection against verbal or physical cruelty and abuse. It was a common belief that lavender had soothing qualities and lavender water was used, from the Middle Ages to the 20th century, to ease headaches. The English herbalist, John Gerard, whose publications spanned the 16th and 17th centuries, recommended a mixture of lavender flowers and spices added to water to help ease "the passion of the heart" and the "swimming of the braine," conditions which might have contributed to violent behaviour.[4]

Just as there were auspicious flowers to have at a wedding there were also plants to be avoided. In northern England it was believed that if a piece of valerian was left in the marriage chamber the couple would quarrel throughout their married life although no explanation has been found to explain this custom. The narcissus also had a bad reputation as a result of the Roman legend of the young man Narcissus and the egotistical love he had for himself. Narcissus blossoms were never allowed at a wedding as it was believed that they would make the bride vain and this would lead to an unhappy marriage.

The peony was a popular wedding flower in ancient China as it symbolized fidelity and longevity. During the T'ang dynasty, which spanned the seventh and eighth centuries A.D., peony plants were placed under the protection of the emperor and the blossoms were exchanged as dowries and, along with jasmine, were embroidered on bridal dresses. In Victorian England, however, cultural differences made the peony a forbidden flower at weddings. According to legend the red peony represented the blushing cheeks of a nymph of questionable virtue and this made the flower too risqué for Victorian tastes.

APHRODISIACS

Aphrodisiacs were used after marriage to promote love and increase fertility, the word aphrodisiac coming from Aphrodite, the Greek goddess of love. Herbalists and doctors recommended aphrodisiacs for couples who had problems during intercourse or in conceiving a child. Aphrodisiacs, however, were more often associated with sexual affairs outside of marriage.

Spices were more popular than herbs because people believed that heat was an important ingredient in an effective aphrodisiac and spices had the more pungent taste. Plants with a hot taste were sexual stimulants while plants that were cooling or considered cold were the oppposite. This idea went back to the times of the ancient Mesopotamian kingdoms of the first millennium B.C. and became so ingrained in Middle Eastern and European cultures that the Puritans, in the 17th century, banned the use of all spices in England in an attempt to control lustful behaviour.

Asafoetida, the gum from the fennels of Iran and Afghanistan, was used as an aphrodisiac in Mesopotamia during the first millennium B.C. The spice is high in sulphur which gives it a foul smell but in small quantities it provides an aromatic flavouring which gives a hot taste to food. The Phoenicians, whose civilization existed from the second millennium B.C. to the first century A.D., used saffron to flavour moon-shaped cakes which were eaten in honour of their fertility goddess, Ashtoreth. They believed that the saffron would make them more potent and fertile.

The ancient Greeks and Romans were noted for their use of aphrodisiacs and in both cultures placing southernwood under the mattress was considered effective once the couple was in the bed. The Greeks chewed the leaves of wild mint as a sexual stimulant

21

and Alexander the Great issued orders forbidding his soldiers to eat mint as he felt it would eliminate their desire to fight.

Ovid, the first-century A.D. Roman poet, recommended eating the white shallots from Megara. Onions were considered a fertility symbol and could, in this capacity, act as an aphrodisiac. They are also rich in potassium, a mineral needed by the body to combat fatigue and loss of libido, which gives a scientific basis to the use of onions as a sexual stimulant.

Garlic was also considered an aphrodisiac and worked probably for the same reason as onions since both are members of the Allium family. It was believed that garlic oil would cleanse the blood, tone up the body organs and increase strength and stamina. However, there was a saying which is still applicable today — if one person eats garlic so should the other.

The Romans associated summer savory with satyrs who were believed to be preoccupied with sex and this led to the herb being used as an aphrodisiac. It was important to use summer savory and not confuse it with winter savory which the Romans believed to be a sexual depressant or anaphrodisiac. Both plants have the same basic chemical composition and are natural stimulants which would indicate that the Romans were incorrect in their assessment of winter savory.

The Romans may have been influenced by the seasons of growth of the two plants. Summer savory would have been considered a "hot" plant and therefore a more effective aphrodisiac, because it bloomed during the summer months whereas winter savory, which is an autumn plant, may have been perceived as a "cold" plant which would have the opposite effect. Another factor may have been the natural habitat of the plants. Summer savory is native to Italy but winter savory was an imported herb which was introduced from southeastern Europe and North Africa and may have initially been viewed with unease.

Nutmeg was prescribed by Arab physicians in the Middle Ages as an aphrodisiac to help increase fertility and it is still occasionally used today. The nutmeg is slowly chewed and, although it causes temporary numbness in the mouth, the aphrodisiacal effect, which is said to last for at least two to three days, apparently more than makes up for any initial discomfort. However, an excess of nutmeg can cause myristicin poisoning which leads to hallucinations and potentially death.

Coriander, with its sweet orange scent, was mentioned as an ingredient of aphrodisiacs in *The Arabian Nights* and it was used in love potions in medieval and Renaissance Europe. Coriander was grown widely in Tudor England and served at weddings in a drink called "Hippocras" which was thought to act as an aphrodisiac. Orange blossoms were associated with fertility and this may have affected people's attitudes toward the plant.

Henry VIII took a glass of mulled wine spiced with caraway seeds before bedtime and Shakespeare's character Sir John Falstaff ate caraway seeds before heading off to bed with his lady. Vanilla was believed to be a potent aphrodisiac in Elizabethan England as the pod was thought to resemble the vagina, the word vanilla coming from the Spanish for little vagina. Elizabeth I used vanilla to flavour her marzipan.

Rose petals dusted with sugar were also considered aphrodisiacs in Tudor England and the 17th-century herbalists John Gerard and John Parkinson also recommended sweet-tasting flowers like tulips. The use of tulips originated in Turkey during the annual Tulip Festival when the Sultan of Turkey would eat tulip roots, chopped and jellied in ginger sauce, to increase his sexual performance. As for other sweetened flowers, crystallized Parma violets were a popular aphrodisiac in Italy.

Rosemary, the seemingly all-purpose herb, was also a popular aphrodisiac in Tudor England. The desired effect could be achieved by drinking a distillation of rosemary water, although the mere smell of the flower was sufficient for some individuals. William Langham in *The Garden of Health*, published in 1579, advised women to carry rosemary with them to make them "merry and well-beloved of all men," to place the flowers on their bed and to put rosemary in the bath to make them "lusty, lively and joyful." There is scientific evidence to back the claims of rosemary as an aphrodisiac for the plant, like the onion, contains high levels of potassium; if people ate the herb or drank rosemary water regularly their potassium level would increase sufficiently to have a noticeable effect on their health, making them more lively while increasing their sex drive.

Rosemary was used in the manufacture of Eau de Cologne, the famous scented water made in Cologne, and Napoleon believed in its reputed aphrodisiacal qualities. He ordered large quantities of Eau de Cologne which he splashed all over his body after bathing, when washing on the battlefield or before entering his wife's apartments. In 1806 the bill from Chardin, his perfumer, showed that Napoleon was supplied with 162 bottles of Eau de Cologne during a period of three months.

Mustard, because of its hot, spicy taste, was another potent aphrodisiac. It was popular with the Romans and retained its popularity until the 20th century. The Prussian king, Frederick the Great, who lived from 1712 to 1786, was so impressed with the effects of mustard that he invented his own drink made from powdered mustard, champagne and coffee.

VALENTINE'S DAY

Valentine's Day is a special occasion for couples to celebrate their love. February 14th has become an institutionalized day for the exchange of love tokens such as red roses, chocolates and sentimental cards, and what began as a pagan Roman holiday has turned into a multi-million dollar business, especially for florists.

In ancient Rome, Valentine's Day was a celebration in honour of Juno, the goddess of women and marriage, and Valentine's Day continued to be celebrated after Christianity became the state religion. The traditional Valentine love token was usually jewellery and the custom of presenting red roses to one's valentine did not occur until the 18th century when, according to tradition, King Louis XVI of France presented his wife Marie Antoinette with a bouquet to honour her as his valentine.

It was not until the 17th century in Europe that valentine cards were used. The first modern poetical valentines appeared in 1667, according to Samuel Pepys the British diarist, and it is from this period that the best-known valentine poem originated.

> The rose is red, the violet's blue,
> The honey's sweet and so are you.

Thou are my love, and I am thine;
The lot was cast, and then I drew,
And fortune said it should be you.

This rhyme is still used, with variations, today although its most common form is:

Roses are red, violets are blue
Honey is sweet and so are you.

In some variations honey was replaced with pinks, while a popular alternative to the last two lines was:

If you'll be mine, I'll be thine,
And so good morrow, Valentine.

Valentine's cards became popular during the Victorian period and were the source of many poetical verses which covered the spectrum of emotions from funny to insulting.

Kiss under a lily
Kiss under a rose
But the best place to kiss
Is under the nose.

There were verses that were plays on words.

Tu-lips in the garden
Tu-lips in the park
But the tu-lips I like the best
Are your tu-lips in the dark.

More serious verses included:

Roses are red
Violets are blue
In my life
There's a place for you.

and

> Roses are red
> Lavender blue
> If you'll have me
> I'll have you.

If the sender of a valentine wanted a change from roses and violets then the following verse made his feelings clear.

> There's a little blue flower
> And in the centre a white, white spot
> It grows in the sunny bower
> And they call it the forget-me-not
> You are the little blue flower
> Your heart is the white, white, spot
> Yours smiles are the sunny bower
> So darling, forget me not.

Of course, there is always the insulting valentine.

> Roses are red
> Violets are blue
> Your mother is good looking
> What happened to you?

The commonly used flowers in valentine poetry are traditionally associated with love. Red roses and forget-me-nots have obvious connotations of love while lavender became a love token because of its sweet scent. Violets were a popular flower and by the Victorian period they represented many ideas, such as humility, faithfulness and modesty, which were considered to be ideal qualities in a Victorian wife. As for violets in the 17th century, they were probably associated more with lust than love since candied violets were eaten as an aphrodisiac.

NURSERY AND SCHOOLING

If the divination spells, courtship rituals, and finally marriage ceremonies were successful then the couple could expect to have a child. Lullabies, nursery rhymes and childhood games would fill the child's early years.

If the child survived infancy then, at least for the boys, school was a concern for the parents. Athenians sent their sons to school from the ages of six to 14 and they were expected to do well both in their studies and at sports. This was not always possible and the young Greek students turned to herbs for assistance. Students wore garlands of mint to stimulate inspiration and improve concentration when they were studying. Rosemary was known for its ability to preserve meat and this led to the idea that it also helped to preserve memory. As a result, Greek students wore rosemary wreaths when taking exams.

Athenian boys used herbs to improve their athletic abilities and this continued into adult life. Olympic athletes ate poppy seeds, from the *Papaver rhoeas*, mixed into honey cakes to give them immediate bursts of energy before competition. Honey was, however, the most important ingredient as it contained both sugar and potassium which improved energy levels. The athletes also ate garlic before races to help reduce fatigue. If the Greek Olympics had been concerned about illegal substances, garlic surely would have been easy to detect.

Chaplets of seasonal flowers were worn by young men on social occasions while leaves and herbs were made into wreaths to signify excellence in studies or sports. There were four major sporting events in Greece and each had its own victor's wreath: laurel for the Olympics and Pythian games, parsley for the Isthmian and wild celery for the Nemaean games.

Laurel or bay leaf wreaths were the most common indicator of exceptional ability. The laurel was dedicated to Apollo who, being a multi-faceted deity, was the god of music and the arts. Apart from their use in the Olympic games, laurel wreaths were also worn by doctors and poets. Apollo was originally the god of healing before he turned this power over to his son Asclepius and poets were under the influence of the Muses, who in turn were subordinate to Apollo. In Britain the official court poet is called the "Poet Laureate." The academic association with the laurel wreath also appears in the word baccalaureate which is the term used for undergraduate university degrees.

The Romans, and philosophers of the early Middle Ages, believed that paleness was a mark of genuine scholarship for if a student spent his time indoors poring over his books he would have little time to acquire a tanned, ruddy complexion. Students who appeared in class with a pale complexion were often given preferential treatment by their teachers, and some scholars consumed large quantities of cumin oil in the belief that they would acquire a pale complexion without having to study.

Childhood was a time for play: for songs, stories and games. The first songs that children hear are lullabies, closely followed by nursery rhymes and fairy tales. The desire to sing to a baby, to soothe it when it cries, or to help it fall asleep seems to be an automatic response with parents and the first lullabies were created by parents to fill these needs.

Flowers appear in lullabies, as in this verse from first-century A.D. Rome.

> Do not want for anything, I will cover you with roses
> I will wrap you in garlands of violets
> Your bed will be filled with hyacinths
> I will make your cradle with lilies
> We will sing thousands of praises to you
> Thousands, and thousands, and thousands.[5]

A lullaby from the late Middle Ages carries on the idea of giving the child good things if only the child would sleep.

> Where was a sugar and pretty?
> And where was a jewel and spicy?
> Hush-a-bye, babe in a cradle,
> And we'll go away in a tricy![6]

From lullabies children progressed to nursery rhymes. The majority of nursery rhymes are folk rhymes that were created by parents to entertain their children and passed down through a long oral history. Anyone who has ever read nursery rhymes to a child knows how quickly the child will correct them if there is any deviation from the original text. Children are the caretakers of the oral tradition of nursery rhymes and while changes do occur, they are mainly due to changes in the spoken language over the centuries.

Nursery rhymes fall into many categories. Some are singing games for fun while others are educational rhymes to help children learn the alphabet and count. Other nursery rhymes are riddles, tongue twisters and street songs. Added to the collection of nursery rhymes, which in North America are referred to as Mother Goose rhymes, are prayers, drinking songs, love songs, and political satires.

The most famous nursery rhyme involving flowers is "Ring around the Rosey."

> Ring around the rosey
> Pocket full of posey
> Ashoo, Ashoo
> We all fall down.

This is probably one of the all-time favourite nursery rhyme singing games that children play and yet it may refer to a very unpleasant period in history. One theory is that it is an re-enactment of death by the bubonic plague.

The bubonic plague, or Black Death, which ravaged Europe in a number of epidemics from the Middle Ages to the 17th century, was a bacterial illness caused by bites from infected fleas. One of the early symptoms was a red rash in the form of a circle — "ring around the rosey." To protect themselves from the plague people carried herbs such as rue and rosemary and these herbs were placed on clothing and carried in a small bouquet in front of the nose to provide clean, healthy scents — "pocket full of posey." A symptom of the plague in its last stages was sneezing — "ashoo, ashoo" — and then the person quickly died — "we all fall down."

This has become a popular theory but more recent research has suggested that the song did not appear until long after the plague had disappeared. The idea of falling down does not appear in writing until the English publication in 1881 of Kate Greenaway's *Mother Goose*. Early versions from the 1700s include:

> Ring a ring a rosie,
> A bottle full of posie,
> All the little girls in our town,
> Ring for little Josie.

and

> Round a ring of roses,
> Pots full of posies,
> The one who stoops last
> Shall tell whom she loves best.[7]

The lack of a pre-19th-century written version of the sneezing and falling-down portion of the rhyme does not mean that it did not exist; only that it is a possibility that an oral version never made it into print before this time.

On a less sombre note, brothers were teased with being made from "frogs and snails and puppy dogs' tails" while their "superior" sisters were made of "sugar and spice and all things nice." Other taunting rhymes which implied that one child was better than the other are:

> Little girl, little girl, where have you been?
> Gathering roses to give to the queen.
> Little girl, little girl, what gave she you?
> She gave me a diamond as big as my shoe.

and

> My Mill grinds
> Pepper and Spice
> Your Mill grinds
> Rats and Mice.

The duo of Simon and Garfunkel, in their song "Scarborough Fair," used as their refrain the following lines:

> Can you make me a cambric shirt,
> Parsley, sage, rosemary and thyme,
> Without any seam or needle work?
> And you shall be a true lover of mine.

This refrain is part of an eight-verse rhyme which uses parsley, sage, rosemary and thyme as a constant refrain in each verse. Those herbs were thought to have magical and medicinal properties and it has been suggested that the refrain was either a witch's incantation or an excerpt from a housewife's recipe in which the four herbs were used constantly.

> Nose, nose, jolly red nose,
> And what gave thee that jolly red nose?
> Nutmeg and ginger, cinnamon and cloves,
> That's what gave me this jolly red nose.

This was a mirth or drinking song which was first printed in 1609 in a book entitled *Deuteromelia*. It was used in the same year by the playwrights Beaumont and Fletcher, who were contemporaries of Shakespeare, in their play *The Knight of the Burning Pestle*. In the play the accent on the word ginger was placed on "gin" and, by dragging out the accented syllable, the song suggested that alcohol, not spices, was the cause of the red nose. This song made its way into popular nursery rhymes and first appeared in children's books in the early 19th century. Children, however, did not accent "gin" and the verse was turned into a pleasant song about spices rather than alcoholic imbibing.

The yellow daffodil was the source of many popular songs which have come down over the centuries. The term daffy-down-dilly was first used to refer to a daffodil by the garden writer Thomas Tuser, around 1573. Two variations on the nursery rhyme are:

> Daffy-down dilly is come up to town,
> In her yellow petticoat and her green gown.

and

> Daff-a-down-dilly that grows by the well,
> My mother's a lady my father can tell.

Many childhood games recreate the pastimes of young adults. The plucking of daisy petals — "He loves me, he loves me not" — later becomes a courtship ritual. Most daisies, however, have an odd number of petals so the questioner will most likely end on "he loves me." In the English countryside the daisy was called the "measure of love" because of this game.

One of the pleasures of childhood is blowing the seeds of the dandelion and watching them bob in the breeze. However, there was an old English saying that children had to be careful to leave some of the seeds on the stalk or else their mothers would no longer want them.

Buttercups placed under the chin was another centuries-old spring pastime. Children would search the lawns and fields for buttercups and then hold them under each other's chin to see if they liked butter. The sun would cause the yellow of the petals to be reflected on the skin and the child would be pronounced a lover of butter.

In rural England a popular childhood game was the same as an adult courtship ritual. Quantities of cowslips were pressed together into a ball and the child would juggle it from hand to hand while reciting:

> Tisty tosty, tell me true
> Who shall I be married to?

The child called out names of likely boys in the neighbourhood until the ball fell and the last name called indicated a future boyfriend. The ball was then repaired and passed on to the next child.

> *I Call and I Call*
> I call, I call: who doe ye call?
> The maids to catch this cowslip-ball:
> But since these cowslips fading be,
> Troth, leave the flowers, and maids, take me.
> Yet, if that neither you will doe,
> Speak but the word, and Ile take you.[8]

FAIRY TALES

The best-known collection of fairy tales is that of the brothers, Jacob and Wilhelm Grimm, who gathered their stories in Germany in the early 19th century by having storytellers come to their home and tell their tales. If people expect flowers to figure prominently in fairy tales they will be disappointed. Although flowers occur in the fairy tales of the Brothers Grimm, the stories themselves do not focus on any flowers as the main subject.

Flowers make up the names of main characters. The correct name of Sleeping Beauty is Briar Rose while Snow White is a name which appears in two stories. One is the well-known story of the beautiful princess and the wicked stepmother. The other, however, is called "Snow White and Red Rose." Through her kindness to a bear (who is really a prince under a curse) and a bad-tempered dwarf (who has put the prince under the curse) Snow White marries the prince and Red Rose marries his brother. It is the classic tale of a poor beautiful girl marrying a handsome prince and living happily ever after. The interesting aspect of the story is in the character of the two girls. Snow White is portrayed as gentle and quiet with a preference for staying at home. Red Rose, however, is lively and vibrant and prefers to spend her spare time running through the fields and meadows, looking for flowers and chasing butterflies. Their personalities are summed up in how the colours white and red are perceived.

Flowers may not be the main characters of children's fairy tales but they have other roles in the stories. They are often the catalyst for events such as in the "Twelve Brothers" or they provide protection through transformation. In "Foundling," "Sweetheart Roland," and "The King's Children" the main characters escaped death or persecution by being turned into flowers. In these transformation tales the individuals always return to their original shape.

Possibly flowers perform a secondary role in fairy tales because the original stories were meant to make a moral statement and involve people as the main characters. Character can be indicated by using a flower as a name. Briar Rose suggests a gentle person like the sweet pink flowers which grow on the country hedgerows while Red Rose suggests a more out-going personality.

Fairies became an important part of childhood in the Edwardian period when they were changed into playful, harmless, childlike creatures, the opposite of their traditional roles as wicked, spiteful, deceitful child-stealers. The newly transformed fairies were subjects of sentimental poetry, stories and paintings, and children easily began to identify flowers with fairies.

Certain plants had a long history as fairy plants. Foxgloves were given their name by their fairy association; the blossoms were said to be gloves for foxes made by naughty fairies. These gloves allowed the fox to steal quietly around at night and get up to no good raiding the chicken coop. The little flecks on the blossoms were the fingerprints left behind by the fairies. On a more sinister note, it was believed that fairies used the juice of foxgloves when exchanging human babies for unwanted changelings.

The forget-me-not was used by fairies as a magic key to their hidden treasure and the yellow primrose or cowslip was called "fairy cup" because fairies took shelter in its blossoms on rainy days. In Ireland, lilies-of-the-valley were called fairy ladders because their hanging blossoms were thought to resemble miniature steps.

The dandelion, which is regarded chiefly as an annoying weed, is said to have its origins with the fairies. The name dandelion comes from the French *dent de lion* or lion's teeth because its leaves supposedly resemble the teeth of lions. According to English legend, when the world was filled with fairies, gnomes and elves, the first humans could not see them and unintentionally kept stepping on them. To protect themselves the elves hid behind rocks and the gnomes went underground. However, some of the fairies, who loved the sun, dressed in yellow and became dandelions. In English folklore, if a dandelion was stepped upon another would spring up, as the plants contained the spirits of the fairies.

Some flowers even allowed humans to see fairies. Potted marigolds let people see fairies dance in front of them. However, given that fairies until recently did not have a good reputation people often preferred to avoid meeting them. Bluebells served as a warning that the area where they grew was a place of fairy magic and enchantment and therefore best avoided.

Fairies were a source of fun in pictures and books for children. One of the best artistic creators of fairies was Cecily Mary Barker who was born in South London in 1895 and died in 1973. She combined fairies, flowers and poetry, and her first book of flower fairies, *Flower Fairies of the Spring*, was published in 1923. Her books were extremely popular and after her death, members of her family compiled her unpublished poems and paintings into the *Flower Fairies of the Garden*, *Flower Fairies of the Winter* and *Flower Fairies of the Trees*, all of which were published in 1985.[9]

Cecily Mary Barker's books were designed for children but she was meticulous in ensuring that the flowers, which she transformed into fairies, were botanically accurate. Although her representation of flowers as people can be linked to J.J. Grandville and his *Fleurs Animées,* her flowers are fairy children, not floral adults, and her poems are fun without being moralizing.

Lewis Carroll provided whimsical flowers in *Alice's Adventures in Wonderland* in 1865 and *Through The Looking-Glass and What Alice Found There* in 1871. In *Alice's Adventures in Wonderland* the famous flower scene occurs near the end of the story when Alice comes across the playing cards painting the white roses red. A white rose tree has been planted by mistake and if the Queen of Hearts discovers it the gardeners will lose their heads.

Through The Looking-Glass has a more personal encounter between Alice and the flowers. When Alice wishes aloud that the flowers could talk, the tiger-lily replies, "We can talk ... when there's anybody worth talking to."[10] The rose explains that it is merely a question of manners: it is impolite for a flower to speak first.

Once the flowers begin to talk to Alice they are critical of her poor appearance. The rose thinks her face does not look clever although it has the right colour. The tiger-lily feels her hair should curl more and the violet thinks Alice is the stupidest person she has seen. No wonder Alice is glad to escape their company.

THE LANGUAGE OF FLOWERS

The language of flowers was an elaborate method for two people to declare their romantic interests. It had its origins in the Middle East but became very popular, especially in England, during the mid-Victorian period. The 18th-century English poet Leigh Hunt accurately described the courting customs of the language of flowers in his 1837 poem "Love Letters Made of Flowers."

> This curious art of writing billet-doux
> In buds and odours, and bright hues!
> Of saying all one feels and thinks
> In clever daffodils and pinks.[11]

The language of flowers was a romantic means of passing messages to one's beloved. The idea was not new but what made the language of flowers unique was its thorough and complex use of flowers. Not content with a few flowers to say "I love you," the Victorians assigned a sentiment to every popular flower and covered a wide range of emotions from love and hate to indifference and danger. It required its participants to use code books and to have a good knowledge of horticulture. A mistake in the choice of flowers could have serious repercussions.

The language of flowers began as a simple idea. The individual would decide upon a message and then consult his or her code book for the appropriate flowers. Once the flowers were arranged into a bouquet, it was dispatched to the loved one who would consult a code book and decipher the message. As the language of flowers gained in popularity, code books multiplied and the system became more complex. Soon the positioning of the ribbon and the number of its knots were also significant. Miscounting the number of knots in the bouquet's ribbon could drastically alter the message. Life and love were not quite so simple as it may have seemed.

The basis of the language of flowers was Islamic poetry which is rich in floral symbolism. The *Rubaiyat* of Omar Khayyam, which is well known in the West, contains many verses full of floral allusions.

> I sometimes think that never blows so red
> The Rose as where some buried Caesar bled
> That every Hyacinth the Garden wears
> Dropped in her Lap from some once lovely Head.[12]

Floral symbols had become a substantial element of Islamic poetry starting in the 11th century with the appearance of a mystical group of Muslims called Sufis who expressed intense mystical religious ideas in the form of love poetry. From the sacred it was very easy to apply the same symbolism to secular love poetry. Throughout the Islamic world a vast repertoire of poetic imagery, which included the flower, became standardized.

Of all the flowers, the rose holds the highest place in Islamic thought. It is believed that once a person has achieved perfect inner peace with God no harm will befall him or her. In the Qur'an, Nimrod, the King of Babylon, cast Abraham into a burning pyre. Abraham refused help from the angel Gabriel, preferring to rely on his own faith, and as a result, Allah turned the fire into a bed of roses.

According to legend the rose was created from perspiration which fell from the brow of the Prophet Muhammad. Later, it was believed that when Muhammad saw a rose, he kissed it and pressed it to his eyes, and said that the rose was part of God's glory. The red rose became the symbol of the divine beauty and glory of God.

The rose has a number of other attributes. The red rose is also the symbol of the healthy, red cheeks of the beloved while the yellow rose symbolizes the pale cheeks of the lover pining for the one he loves. The majority of Islamic love poetry is written from the man's perspective. The man is the lover and the woman, the beloved.

The narcissus and the tulip follow the rose in popularity. The narcissus with its large white petals and yellow or orange centre is used to describe the large, beautiful eyes of the loved one.

The tulip has many meanings. Because of its shape, it is referred to as the Cup of Jemshid. This cup, which belonged to a legendary king, had the power to reflect within it the whole world and confer all knowledge onto anyone who drank from it. Following this idea the tulip became the symbol of the wine cup in general. Although wine is forbidden in Islam some mystical religious sects believe that through intoxication from wine they can become closer to God.

The red colour of the tulip is seen as a reflection of the splendour of the glowing cheeks of the one who is loved while the black streaks at the base of the petals symbolize the wounded heart of the lover longing for his beloved.

> As then the Tulip, for her morning sup
> Of heav'nly Vintage, from the soil looks up,
> Do you devoutly do the like, till Heav'n
> To Earth invert you — like an empty Cup.[13]

Many flowers represent parts of the face of the loved one. Apart from the rose, narcissus and tulip there are also the violet, hyacinth and jasmine. Violets are a reference to dark colours. In a verse by the 14th-century Persian poet Hafiz — "The violets around thy lips are fresh" — the violets refer to the fine dark hair on the upper lips of women. Because the violet is a low-growing plant it is said to grow at the feet of the rose and therefore it becomes the image of the lover worshipping at the feet of the one he loves. The violet also represents a lowly person: the humble penitent before God. The hyacinth with its small, curled blossoms is the symbol of the hair of the beloved while the white flowers of the jasmine represent the flawless complexion of her skin.

The lily is often used in Islamic poetry. It stands for silence even though it is said to have ten tongues with which the flower continually praises God. Its tall, sharp leaves resemble a sword, giving it the name "sword of Allah."

The floral symbolism which developed between the 11th and 14th centuries in Islamic countries remained part of their culture and when the Europeans arrived in Turkey they discovered a symbolic code which had been in place for centuries.

Why did the language of flowers become the rage among English society's fashionable in the 19th century? One of the main reasons was that it fit into the lifestyle of the upper classes. Women in this station of life were not expected to work beyond the demands of supervising a household. Servants attended to the running of the house, leaving the lady with time to fill. The same applied to the young men. What separated a gentleman, a member of the nobility, from his lessers was the fact that he did not work. He may have needed money but having a career or profession was not the way to get it. Instead, he was expected to find a wealthy heiress and marry for money.

These ideas on the unsuitability of work left both men and women of Victorian society with time on their hands. For women, horticulture was considered an acceptable hobby along with drawing, needlework and playing a musical instrument. Men, between riding horses and attending shooting parties, also found plenty of time to study horticulture.

This passion for flowers spilled over into all aspects of Victorian life. Conservatories and greenhouses were built to house exotic tropical and sub-tropical plants from overseas. The Victorian house was filled with potted plants and terrariums. Flowers decorated the house from the table to the stair bannisters when company was invited. Floral designs decorated everything in the house including chairs, fire-screens, china, silverware, clothes, linens and much more. The excessive use of flowers in daily life made it easy for the language of flowers to flourish amidst a leisured society.

The language of flowers was introduced to Europe through the unlikely combination of an exceptional (some would say eccentric)

English gentlewoman and a mentally unstable Swedish king. Lady Mary Wortley Montagu, who lived from 1689 to 1763, although she was the second of the two to reach Turkey, was the first to send word of the language of flowers to England. Lady Mary was the eldest daughter of the Marquess of Dorchester and destined for a life of wealth and leisure. However, she was a remarkable woman in many ways, and her refusal to follow society's accepted rules for ladies of good breeding changed the path her life would take.

Lady Mary was determined, strong-willed to the point of being obstinate, and romantic: attributes which contributed to her marriage to Edward Wortley Montagu, the grandson of the Earl of Sandwich. Their courtship was acknowledged in 1708 but her father refused to give his blessing to the union. Instead of meekly accepting her father's decision, Lady Mary eloped with Edward in 1712. An elopement was cause for serious scandal and she was considered an outcast from her family and many of her social equals. However, it was her marriage which was instrumental in bringing the language of flowers to the attention of high society in England.

In 1716 Edward Wortley was appointed ambassador to Turkey. He and Lady Mary were installed at Pera, the European enclave in Constantinople and Lady Mary indulged her passion for languages and literature by learning Arabic and falling in love with Arabic poetry. Blessed with a strong curiosity and a refusal to be restricted by the social conventions which kept most European women in Pera isolated from the Turkish community, Lady Mary happily ventured forth and took "great pains to see everything." She made friends with members of the Turkish aristocracy and soon had access to their harems where she spent many hours reading poetry and learning about the lives of Turkish women. This happy period ended with the abrupt recall of Wortley in 1717.

Considering her interests in languages and literature it is not surprising that Lady Mary made an effort to learn Arabic so she could read first-hand the poetry she heard recited in the harems. Through her contacts with these women she learned that they often sent floral messages to their lovers. When her friend back in England, the poet Alexander Pope, who had previously requested a Greek slave, asked for a sample of a Turkish love-letter, Lady Mary was more than happy to comply. The love-letter consisted of a box containing a variety of items, each of which conveyed a message. The contents of the box were a pearl, clove, jonquil, paper, pear, soap, coal, rose, straw, cloth, cinnamon, match, gold thread, hair, a grape, gold wire and pepper. The message was:

> You are the fairest. I have loved you for a long time. Have pity on me. I faint every hour from love. Give me some hope. I am sick with love. May I die and all the remaining years of my life be yours. May you be pleased with me and may all your sorrows be mine. Allow me to be your slave. You are priceless. My fortune is yours. I burn from love. Don't turn away from me. You are the crown of my head. My eyes are to see you. I am dying — come quickly. Send me an answer.[14]

A letter such as this soon became the talk of high society and that is where it remained: an exotic idea shared among a few select people. If Lady Mary planted the idea of the floral letter (her letters were published in 1763, after her death), it was left to the French to firmly establish the idea in England.

The French connection was a result of the wars of King Charles XII of Sweden. His early successes against Peter the Great of Russia led him to make the fatal error, an invasion of Russia. Any invasion of Russia is difficult but Charles made matters worse by marching in the middle of winter. It was a winter which, even by Russian standards, was considered one of the severest in memory. Charles and his army were defeated and, finding himself no longer welcome in his own country, Charles fled to Turkey where he remained in exile from 1709 to 1714.

Accompanying King Charles was a Frenchman, Aubry de La Mottraie, who, during his stay in Constantinople, learned the language of Turkish love messages. Upon his return to France he published a book on this floral code in 1723. The Turkish term for this language of flowers was Sélam.

The French were the first to take a serious interest in flowers as a form of code. M. Hammer in his nine-volume *Annales des voyages de la géographie et de l'historie*, published in 1809, included a section on the language of flowers with a glossary of the Turkish floral code. This floral code was acknowledged in the 1835 edition of the *Dictionnaire de l'Académie français*.

Between 1810 and 1811 three books which are considered the pioneering code books for the language of flowers were published. These three were works on flower lore but they also included glossaries of the meanings of flowers, which were derived from mythology, literature and French folklore. They were Madame de Genlis, *La Botanique historique et littéraire* in 1810; Madame Victorine Maugirard, *Les Fleurs, rêve allégorique* in 1811; and F. Delachénaye, *Abécédaire de Flore ou Langage des fleurs* also in 1811. All subsequent French language-of-flower dictionaries were based partly on these works and the Turkish Sélam.

In 1824, Aimée Martin, under the pseudonym of Madame Charlotte de Latour, published *Le Langage des Fleurs*. It was extremely popular in France. The book was into its third edition in 1827 and its sixth edition in 1844. It was translated into English in 1830 and became a bestseller in England. With this book the English fascination with the language of flowers began.

The popularity of the English translation of Charlotte de Latour's book was an incentive to British authors to begin writing their own code books. There were a number of popular British writers whose code books reflected their "Britishness" and also their personal quirks and fancies.

One of the earliest and most prolific English writers on the subject was Robert Tyas. His *The Sentiment of Flowers or Language of Flora* was into its ninth edition by 1842 and it was followed by *The Handbook of the Language and Sentiment of Flowers* in 1845. In *The Sentiment of Flowers* Tyas acknowledged using Aimée Martin as the basis of his book but he enlarged the list of plants and applied his own form of censorship through "the rejection or alteration of those passages which were not suited to English taste."[15] His *Handbook* was advertised as the complete list of every flower to which a sentiment was assigned and Tyas acknowledged the Eastern origins of the custom although he professed that his sentiments were derived chiefly from ancient mythology and history.

Tyas, like many Victorian writers on the language of flowers, took a sentimental approach to flowers. It is interesting to note that the majority of writers on the subject were men. Tyas considered plants to be spontaneous products of the earth and evidence of God's benevolence towards mankind.

The next major writer on the language of flowers was Thomas Miller whose *The Poetical Language of Flowers or the Pilgrimage of Love* appeared in 1847. Unlike Tyas, Miller rejected the work of Aimée Martin and announced that he had created his own language in which he was guided in his choice of sentiments by the works of Chaucer, Spenser, Shakespeare, and Milton. He filled in the gaps with his own ideas or, as he so delicately put it, "adding here and there a blossom to the beautiful wreath they left unfinished."[16]

Miller coyly attributed the origins of the language of flowers to Cupid who set out to discover the language which had been spoken by the flowers before the coming of man. Believing that the language still existed, Cupid spent many weary days listening to the flowers but heard only the breathing of the blossoms. Finally, exhausted and sad, he sat down in a rose bed and wept. The rose came to his aid and taught him the language of the flowers. Cupid decided to give this knowledge to women and flew to the "burning East" where the language of flowers was restored.

Miller's idea that the flowers had their own language before the coming of man was not new. A French floral manual, written by an anonymous author and published in 1821, idealized flowers by relating them to the innocence of Paradise. According to the author the language of the flowers was first choice among early primitive man.

Another theory about the origin of the language of flowers was developed by Captain Marryatt of the Royal Navy, author of *The Floral Telegraph or Affection's Signals* published around 1850. Captain Marryatt comes as a surprise for his explanation of the book contains a sentence unexpected from a man of the navy:

> This little book, which I, with an adoration that trembles while it burns, lay at your feet, is the offspring and the proof of a gentle supernatural agency.[17]

His book tells the story of Sir Horace Honeycomb who goes to visit his friend Sir Aldobrand Belamour at his country seat in Devon. While strolling through his host's garden he comes across a crumbling wall and upon questioning the gardener is told ". . . the enclosure had been the favoured Flower-Garden of his master's grandfather; that it had been closed up on nearly a hundred years, mortal foot, for that space, never having invaded its solitude."[18] The gardener did not think that Sir Aldobrand would allow Sir Horace to enter but Sir Horace is overcome with curiosity and when no one is looking he enters the garden.

The neglected garden, to Sir Horace, is equal to Paradise, like Eden before the fall of man. In a contemplative state Sir Horace sits down on a fragment of a broken column and speaks aloud his thoughts. This brings his presence to the attention of the sylph Floribel, who has the job of looking after all the flowers on earth.

Floribel explains her presence in the garden, which is both a penance and a punishment. It is an involved tale about the planned marriage of two cousins and the disastrous intervention of Floribel which resulted in three deaths. Floribel, as punishment for her role in the romantic tragedy, is forced to remain within the deserted garden until someone enters and she decides to invent a secret form of correspondence. The forces that keep her within the garden allow her to make a pilgrimage to the East and it is here that Floribel learns the language of flowers. Since then she has been waiting for someone to enter her lonely garden so she could pass on her information and gain her freedom. Sir Horace becomes the possessor of her knowledge and it is this information that Captain Marryatt presumes to pass on to the public.

The language of flowers was not confined to Europe but made its way to North America. There were numerous American floral code books but the most interesting was by Sara Josepha Hale who wrote *Flora's Interpreter* and 16 years later added *Fortuna Flora* to her newly revised and enlarged edition. *Flora's Interpreter* was a typical code book that listed the "mystical language of flowers." Following the sentimental approach to flowers she referred to them as the "sweet messengers of nature."[19]

Fortuna Flora was a departure from the traditional language of flowers. In this book Hale devised a complicated means of ascertaining people's character and probable success in life based on flowers connected with their birthday. Hale believed that these messages would serve as "warnings or encouragements" to help individuals make decisions affecting their lives. She also believed that through flowers "Heaven gives us opportunities; their improvement or neglect is our own work."[20]

There is no scientific basis for any of Sara Hale's floral fortunes but they must have provided plenty of amusement for young ladies with time on their hands. She may have been serious about the potential of her floral fortunes to help mould young lives but the majority of people who used the book probably viewed it on the level of a parlour game.

The most popular of all the language of flowers books in both Britain and North America was a simple code book printed in 1884. It consisted of two lists: the flowers with their meanings followed by the sentiments with their matching flowers. Unlike the other language-of-flowers books, it contained no sentimental or romantic stories of cupids or fairies flitting about the Middle East. What it did have was beautiful illustrations by the artist Kate Greenaway which made it an immediate and long-lasting success.

The language of flowers was a fanciful illusion played out to add a touch of romance and excitement to life. Secrecy was its most important ingredient although, by the late 19th century, the language was so well established that there were few who could not read the messages in the most frequently used flowers. The language of flowers was not a simple code. The number of flowers could range from 200 to 700 and the messages attributed to the flowers varied according to the different authors, as did the methods of interpretation. Therefore, if two people planned to converse through the language of flowers it was essential that they use the same book or awkward misunderstandings could arise.

Large numbers of flowers were necessary to cover the growing seasons. More than one flower was used to impart important sentiments such as "I love you" for it would have been difficult to carry on secret conversations if the required flowers were not in bloom. Four flowers were used to say "I love you" and they cover all the seasons. The tulip was in bloom in spring. The myrtle was a summer blossom while, depending on the species or variety of rose, their blooms were available through summer to mid-autumn. The chrysanthemum blooms in late summer and autumn but it could also be grown in conservatories or greenhouses during the winter.

The language of flowers was about love, and no flower has been more closely associated with love than the rose. Its colours, varieties and general condition all told a tale. The red rose, the colour of a blush, stood for bashfulness while the white rose meant "I am worthy of you." No young woman or man, however, would have been happy to receive a yellow rose which was an accusation of infidelity.

Each species of rose also had a message. A Damask rose complimented a woman on her brilliant complexion while the Japan rose signified that beauty was her only attraction. The Carolina rose, rather pragmatically, warned that "Love is dangerous." The development and condition of the rose were further factors to be taken into account. Red rosebuds spoke of purity and loveliness, a full-blown rose placed over two buds urged secrecy, a withered white rose symbolized fleeting impressions while a dried white rose made this melodramatic statement — "Death is preferable to loss of innocence."

Once the declaration of love had been made, or if the young man wished to impress the young lady, then a number of complimentary messages could be sent. The American cowslip declared her a divine beauty; the jasmine, an amiable personality; bluebells and violets both referred to her faithfulness; and orange blossoms called her pure and chaste.

If the floral courtship proved to be successful, a proposal of marriage could be made through flowers. The young man would present a pink to his intended and if the feeling was reciprocated a pink would be returned. However, if his proposal was rejected then a carnation was sent instead.

When being presented with a floral marriage proposal it was important that the woman know the difference between a pink and the much larger carnation. This problem was addressed in a poem by Louisa Anne Twamley in which the heroine, Lady Edith, overjoyed upon receiving a pink from Sir Rupert, promptly sent him the largest blossom she could find and inadvertently sent him a carnation. Sir Rupert took his broken heart off to war and Lady Edith was forced to travel after him, only to have him die in her arms. However, like all good Victorian moral poems, it ended with an important message for all potential brides:

Now, Lady — when a Cavalier
Presents a chequered PINK,
'Tis time to ascertain my dear,
His rent-roll, you may think;

And then — provided his estate
Don't meet your approbation
It cannot, surely, be too late
To cut — with a CARNATION.[21]

The language of flowers provided for all contingencies in a relationship including lovers' quarrels, and the prettiest, in the physical sense, of insults could be traded. The narcissus was symbolic of egotism while the seemingly innocuous pink larkspur was an accusation of fickleness. The columbine called a person foolish. If the argument heated up there was the African marigold with its accusation of vulgar-mindedness or the scarlet auricula which signified avarice and greed. When the quarrel became truly bitter and hostile, basil could be sent to declare hatred, followed by the trefoil for revenge. Of course, if all was resolved, hazel was sent as a sign of reconciliation.

The language also dealt with the problem of unreciprocated love. The first step would be to send a posy of snowdrops to ask if there was hope or a bouquet of jonquils to convey the message "I desire a return of affection." If the object of one's adoration did not wish to continue the relationship then several floral choices were available to indicate that a love affair was not possible. A bouquet of yellow tulips meant that it was hopeless. Candytuft or mustard seeds conveyed the message of indifference while a bouquet of asphodels meant "My regrets follow you to the grave."

A rejected man would hide his feelings while a woman would wear a variety of flowers to publicly express her feelings. The geranium announced that she was melancholy, the marigold, grief-stricken and the garden anemone, forsaken. If she became completely disheartened there was hemlock to declare, "You will be my death."

Not every "blossoming" relationship had parental consent and if the unacceptable suitor was suddenly discovered by an outraged papa, a bouquet of oleander, rhododendrons and pennyroyal —

"beware, danger, flee" — could be counted on to resolve the immediate problem.

Messages were usually passed on in bouquets called "tussie-mussies." The main idea was conveyed by the central flower with additional sentiments expressed in the flowers which surrounded it. However, the presentation of the bouquet was also an important part of the message.

The manner in which a bouquet was handed to a person had to be carefully observed. According to some code books, if the person delivering the flowers inclined them to the right of the body it meant the message was about the giver but if they were inclined to the left it applied to the receiver. A bouquet handed upside down indicated that the message meant the opposite. However, other code books merely indicated that flowers presented by the right hand stated a message while those presented with the left meant the opposite of the floral message.

The most complicated system was devised by Captain Marryatt. His floral vocabulary was divided into three parts and the flowers were assigned a meaning according to their section of the vocabulary. Any flower could have three different meanings and it was the number of knots in the ribbon which told one where to look in the code book.

A typical Marryatt bouquet would consist of a number of small bundles of flowers tied together with one ribbon. When this ribbon was untied the bunches of flowers would be laid out. Each bunch of flowers was also tied with a ribbon and by counting the number of knots on each ribbon one would know which part of the vocabulary to use.

The language of flowers, in which one grew one's "choice words and fancies/In orange tubs and beds of pansies," may not be used any more but the memories of many of those floral messages remain.[22] Roses are still symbols of love, orchids signify a beautiful woman, violets represent humility and pansies are for thoughts. It was a charming pastime while it lasted and it fit in well with the Victorian passion for flowers. It was a hobby for young women who were expected to be genteel and young man who were expected to be discreet.

The language of flowers had an impact on art and literature in Europe in the 19th century. One of the most interesting books to

47

emerge utilizing the vocabulary of the language was *Les Fleurs Animées* with text by Taxile Delord and illustrations by J.J. Grandville.

The book is famous more for its illustrations than its stories which are based, to a degree, on the code given to the flowers in the language of flowers. The premise of the book is that the flowers visit the Flower Fairy and complain that they are tired of their lives as flowers. They wish to be allowed to assume a human form so that each of them may judge for themselves whether the virtues or vices which man has given to them are accurate.

The Flower Fairy tries to talk them out of it by pointing out what they will be missing: diamonds made of dew, conversations with the breezes and last but not least kisses from the butterflies. The flowers, however, are adamant. The Marvel of Peru complains that the dew makes her cold; the rose is bored to death by the songs of the breezes which have not changed in a thousand years; while the periwinkle accuses the butterfly of being so selfish as to not recognize his own mother.

There are 52 illustrations ranging from exotic garden flowers to familiar wild flowers and weeds. The flowers, in the spirit of French Romanticism, appear in balletic postures and are accompanied by beetles, butterflies, caterpillars and other insects found in the garden.

Grandville, who died before the book was published, injected considerable humour into his illustrations of these "humanized" flowers. The commentary by Delord is not particularly inspired but he also finds humour in the flowers. The tulip is described as a beauty with no brains, the rose is enthroned and receives homage from the beetles while the pink is portrayed as a latter-day Marie Antoinette with an adoring centipede carrying her train.

Grandville's illustration of the forget-me-not records an interesting event in history. Robert Fulton, the American engineer, spent the years from 1797 to 1806 in Paris, working on the development of steamboats. In 1802 Fulton built his first steamboat and conducted experiments with it on the River Seine in Paris; Grandville has noted the Paris occasion by showing the forget-me-not waving good-bye to a steamboat in the distance.

DEATH

And come he slow, or come he fast,
It is but Death who comes at last.[23]

These words by Sir Walter Scott sum up what most people
prefer not to think about: inevitably all who are born must die.
The rite of passage of death has been marked historically and
culturally in many different ways, with plants retaining strong
funereal associations.

Ancient Egypt, with its pyramids and mummies, is thought of
today as a civilization obsessed with death and the afterlife
although this strong interest in death was the result of the desire
on the part of Pharaonic Egyptians to achieve immortality. The
preservation of the body was important because within the body
was the spirit, or *ka*, which would return to the tomb to visit the
body. The need to retain a well-preserved body for the *ka* led to
the continual advancement in the process of mummification.

The methods of mummifying bodies varied greatly over time
but one principal method involved removing the viscera, cleaning
the body with palm wine and spices, filling up the cavities with
myrrh, cassia, cumin, anise, marjoram and cinnamon, and sewing
up the incision. The body was then treated with natron, a desic-
cating agent, washed, and anointed with cedar oil and other
ointments such as myrrh, or cinnamon. It was then wrapped and
wreaths of seasonal flowers were placed on the head.

The widespread use of flowers in Egyptian burials is demon-
strated in the tomb of Tutankhamun, a young pharaoh who died
in 1327 B.C. at the age of 18. There were floral tributes on the
coffins and in the tomb. On the outer coffin, or second coffin,
which is in the shape of the mummy with a painted image of the
young man's face, there was a wreath of cornflowers and water-lily
petals draped over the two symbols of Egypt, the cobra and the
vulture. A four-banded garland lay on the chest area: two of the
bands were composed of olive leaves and cornflowers, the third
band of cornflowers and water-lilies and the fourth band of wild
celery leaves and cornflowers. On the inner coffin, which
contained the mummified body of Tutankhamum, there was an
impressive floral collar of nine rows which contained palm leaves,

nightshade blossoms, pomegranate leaves, willow leaves, blue water-lily petals, cornflowers, and ox-tongue (*Picris radicata*) blossoms. Outside the burial chamber were found similar collars of cornflowers and nightshade blossoms.

Live flowers were used to make the floral collars, which were sewn together at the time of the pharaoh's death, and their blooming period has established the time of Tutankhamun's burial as between mid-March and mid-April. The flowers in the tomb, with the exception of the lotus, did not have specific religious meanings but were cultivated plants noted for their strong fragrance. The importance of the flowers would be their familiarity to the pharaoh's *ka* when it visited the tomb. The cornflower was the most popular flower in the tomb and there does not appear to be any special significance except that it was an imported flower, which might have given it more importance. However, it is entirely possible that the reason for its repeated use was nothing more than that Tutankhamun liked the flower and it was in season when he died.

The ancient Greeks thought that after death, eternity was spent in the fields of Elysium, where perfumed rivers constantly filled the air with sweet odours. This led to the belief that pleasant smells, including those of flowers, were present in the afterlife.

The Greeks, like the Egyptians, wreathed their corpses in flowers as part of the burial ceremony. Bay and parsley were often placed around the head of the deceased while marjoram was used to scent the winding-sheet. Bay leaves were sacred to Apollo who presided over the deaths of men who died of natural causes or of illness while parsley was revered as a sacred herb of Persephone, goddess of the Underworld, and also of Archemorus, the forerunner of death. As a baby, Archemorus, whose name means beginning of doom, was carelessly laid, by his nurse, on a bed of parsley leaves and was bitten and strangled by a snake.

Corpses were sometimes consumed on a funeral pyre of burning juniper wood and afterwards aromatic spices and oils were mixed with the ashes before they were put into urns. However, burial was the most common method of sending the dead to the Underworld.

The Greeks planted flowers on graves and their choice was determined by an association with a deity or the flower's fragrance. If marjoram grew on a grave it was a sign that the deceased was enjoying eternal bliss and happiness. This gave rise to the herb's botanical name, *Origanum,* which means Joy of the Mountain. Parsley was planted due to its connection with Persephone and Archemorus while other popular flowers like amaranth, myrtle and roses had dual connotations. Amaranth, in Greek, means not fading, because the flowers do not fade as the plant dies, and it became a symbol of immortality. The amaranth flowers and their juice are red, a colour which has historically signified blood and death. Myrtle and roses were planted because they were aromatic flowers and both were sacred to Aphrodite, the goddess of love. While the fine scent of the flowers signified the Elysian Fields where the loved one had, it was hoped, found peace, the flowers were also a reminder that the dead person was loved. The early Romans believed that the souls of the dead dwelt underground or near their burial place in the bosom of Mother Earth from whom all humans were supposed to have descended. This idea gave rise to the imagery of the bones or the ashes of the dead acting as a form of fertilizer for flowers, as reflected in this tomb inscription from Rome:

Here lies Optatus, a child noble and dutiful.
I pray that his ashes may become violets and roses and that the
Earth, who is his mother now, rest lightly on him, who in life
weighed heavily on no man.[24]

To prepare the body for its funeral was a solemn religious duty for the surviving members of the family. After the body had been washed and anointed with oils, a wreath was placed on the head. The flowers in the wreath could correspond to the individual's achievements in life, such as laurel for a general who had earned a laurel wreath for a specific military action, or they could be those associated with death such as columbines, roses or violets. Once the body was prepared it was placed on a couch, surrounded by flowers, to lie in state until the time of the funeral. Branches of pine or cypress were placed on the door of the house as a warning that the house was polluted by death.

The Romans either buried or cremated the body. If it was to be a cremation, the couch was placed on a wooden pyre which contained large amounts of spices and perfumes. The wealthier and more important the family, the greater the amount of aromatics, as in the cremation ceremony of the Emperor Nero's wife Poppaea in 65 A.D., when Nero burned a year's supply of cinnamon on the pyre.

The body or its ashes found final repose in a tomb, preferably within a garden. The tomb was a necessary part of the Roman cult of the dead in which food, drink and flowers were given as offerings at the altar in the tomb. The gardens around the tomb not only provided fruit, flowers and wine to honour the dead but were seen as a reflection of the Elysian Fields where the dead spent eternity. These tomb gardens also provided comfortable surroundings when the family came to visit on specified religious days, and often the gardens were very elaborate with trees, flowers, fountains, benches, covered arbours and summer houses.

There were four main times of the year when a family would visit the tombs of their ancestors. The Parentalia was a memorial festival which lasted from February 13th to 21st and people would bring, among their gifts to the dead, offerings of violets. The burial day of the deceased was commemorated annually, again with gifts and flowers, in particular roses and violets. The Violaria, a festival at the end of March, and the Rosalia, a festival in May, were important occasions when violets and roses were laid upon the graves or heaped over the urns of the dead.

The two most important flowers in the Roman rituals of commemorating the dead were the violet and the rose. Ausonius, a fourth-century A.D. Roman poet, wrote an epitaph in which roses were regarded as pledges of eternal spring both in life and in death.

> Sprinkle my ashes with pure wine and fragrant oil of spikenard:
> Bring balsam, too, stranger, with crimson roses.
> Tearless my urn enjoys unending spring.[25]

There is no specific reason why violets were used but since they are a spring flower it is probable that their significance is the same as that of the rose; both were seen as symbols of eternal springtime which is how the Romans perceived the Elysian Fields.

During the Middle Ages in Europe people believed that ordinary death did not come as a surprise, but gave advance warning of its arrival, often by the presence of a ghost in a dream or by a premonition of impending death. By the 17th century, Europeans were divided on the subject; the educated people did not believe in harbingers of death while the common people did. In the 16th and 17th centuries in England, if a bay tree died it was considered a serious omen of death and disaster which Shakespeare referred to in *Richard II*: "'Tis thought the King is dead; we will not stay, the bay trees in our country are all wither'd."[26]

In Europe, during the Middle Ages, people believed that if a person was unjustly executed, white lilies would spring up from the grave to proclaim his or her innocence, while flowers were also believed to grow of their own free will on the graves of lovers. In the European legend of Tristan and Iseult, ivy grew from their graves and entwined above, a symbol of their union in death and the constancy of their love.

Christianity developed its own funerary flowers separate from the Graeco/Roman world. Whereas the Romans placed roses on their graves the early Christians banned roses because of their association with paganism. Roses were seen to represent the voluptuousness and debauchery of Roman culture which was everything the early Christian church stood against.

St. Jerome and St. Ambrose objected to the use of flowers at funerals, considering them a waste of money. St. Jerome compared the cost of the violets, roses and lilies that a husband would place on the urn of his wife with the works of charity that could be achieved with the same amount of money. This idea had its origins in the New Testament where Judas objected to Mary Magdalene using expensive unguents or perfumes to massage the feet of Christ. There was the suggestion from the church, although never strongly put, that it was better to spend the money on good deeds and helping the poor rather than wasting it on flowers which would soon wither and die.

Violets and lilies, symbols of the Virgin Mary, were considered acceptable by the church and by devout laymen. The rose, however, could not be kept out no matter how hard the church tried. By the early Middle Ages the majority of people had forgotten its pagan associations and they wanted roses on the coffins and graves of their loved ones because they were beautiful, sweet-scented flowers. The church was forced to accept the rose and to give it credibility, the theologians made it symbolic of Jesus and the Virgin Mary.

The most important plant in Christian burial rituals, until this century, was rosemary. This herb was believed to be endowed with mystical powers which were strong enough to guard the church, the dead and the living from all evil and to allow the soul to rise to Heaven unhindered by the devil. Rosemary was presented to mourners attending the funeral as they left the house, for up until the 20th century the coffin was kept at home until it was transported to church for the service. The mourners would clutch the rosemary in church, and at the burial site each would drop the sprig of rosemary onto the coffin after it had been lowered into the grave. Apart from being a protector against evil spirits, rosemary also symbolized remembrance, friendship and fidelity.

The poet Robert Herrick referred to the use of rosemary as both a bridal wreath and a funeral flower in these lines:

> Grow for two ends: it matters not at all
> Be't for my bridall or my buriall.[27]

Rosemary and sage were both believed to help alleviate grief and there is an extensive herbal history going back beyond the Middle Ages for rosemary. Europeans believed that eating sugared rosemary blossoms would comfort the heart but there is no herbal evidence that sage had any connections with grief. Sage, however, had an equally long history as a multi-purpose cure-all; there was not a single illness that could not be cured or improved by eating the leaves of sage. Possibly this idea that sage was a cure for everything was carried over to make it a cure for a broken heart.

Sage was often planted on graves and rue would be planted nearby to guard the sage from being eaten by toads. This combination planting does work but not in the way that pre-20th-century Europeans thought. Toads do not eat plants but rather the insects, especially beetles, which eat the plants. Rue has a strong smell which discourages insects from coming near the plant, something that European country farmers did not understand. The smell of the rue deterred the beetles from coming near the sage and without any beetles, there was no food for the toads so they would go in search of another plant with beetles.

The association of violets with death was still a common idea in 17th-century Europe. In *Hamlet* Ophelia says to Laertes:

> I would give you some violets
> but they witherd all when my father died.[28]

When Ophelia dies Laertes hopes that violets will grow on her grave.

> Lay her i' the earth, and from her fair and unpolluted flesh, may
> Violets spring.[29]

By 1863 gardening books and magazines were commenting on the fashion of planting flowers on graves, a practice which had been rare 20 years earlier. The major criticism of the writers was the choice of flowers rather than the actual planting of flowers. Scarlet geraniums and yellow calceolarias were the flowers of choice, leaving the critics to level accusations of tasteless gaudiness at the graveside flowerbeds. Even the royal family was not exempt from criticism. When Prince Alexander, the youngest son of the Prince and Princess of Wales, died in 1871, his parents, the future King Edward VII and Queen Alexandra, had his grave edged with rows of red geraniums and verbenas which ranged in shade from pink to scarlet.

The garden writers had a list of recommended flowers which they considered suitable for grave sites. Socially acceptable flowers were white roses, crocuses, tulips, narcissus, hyacinths, daisies, primroses, pansies, lilies-of-the-valley, forget-me-nots and anemones. It was considered the epitome of good taste to edge the grave in blue scillas with snowdrops planted on the grave. Snowdrops were a practical suggestion since they grew profusely in most church graveyards.

Another suggestion by horticulturists of the Victorian period was to plant both blue and white periwinkles on the grave while white lilies, in pots, could be sunk into the ground to form a border. If the grave site was large enough then dwarf rose bushes were acceptable, even though they were considered somewhat ostentatious. There was a difference between urban and rural England over the types of flowers that were used in mass planting on the grave. Yuccas were often used in the countryside while lilacs were popular in the cities.

The choice of the flowers that were sent to the family of the deceased was determined by the sender's status and relationship to the dead person, and there were etiquette books solely on the subject of behaviour following a death and the subsequent mourning period. Relatives and friends sent wreaths of white flowers or immortelles. These latter flowers were also known as everlastings or helichrysum and they dried very well, making them easy to preserve. Circular wreaths of flowers were hung on the front door and placed in the grave in the belief that the spirit of the dead was enclosed within the circle and could not return to earth.

Close family members were allowed to strew flowers on the floor of the room where the coffin rested and they were also permitted to lay flowers in the open coffin. Placing flowers within the coffin can be traced back to the Middle Ages when rosemary was placed inside to protect the soul of the dead. In the Victorian period, however, the flowers were chosen less for protection and more for their symbolic effect. When Queen Victoria died on January 22, 1901, the royal ladies arranged lilies and white orchids around her body.

The Victorians went one step beyond planting flowers on the grave. They had flowers in the form of bouquets, garlands or a single bloom carved on the gravestone as a lasting tribute to the deceased. These flowers were for the Victorians the "last words" that would carry on the eternal memory of a beloved family member.

Modern cemeteries have changed dramatically in character since the 19th century. Today's cemeteries are vast expanses of grass filled with mass-produced, easily maintained gravemarkers. Flowers are still the most popular symbol to grace contemporary graves but the variety has been reduced as society forgets the meanings that were once attached to individual flowers. Today, in Canada, carved grave decorations are usually limited to the rose, maple leaf and provincial flower with an occasional carnation or lily. This, however, was not the Victorian way.

The Victorians were fascinated with flowers and their symbolism, and the flowers on gravemarkers were chosen with care. Either planned by the individual before death or chosen by relatives afterwards, the flowers were a message to be read and understood by all who passed. These were more than pretty decorations. They told of love, happiness, beauty, devotion and, of course, sorrow. There were even flowers to indicate a person's social status within the community.

Flowers were a vital part of the early Christian concept of Paradise. In art and literature Paradise was a garden, a place of eternal spring where every known flower and tree was in continuous bloom, and a place of rebirth and salvation. All flowers were regarded as symbols of Paradise and when engraved on a gravemarker they were an indication that the individual had achieved salvation and been reborn in Paradise.

While flowers in general symbolized Paradise, each individual flower also had a specific meaning which added to the "message" on the gravemarker. The Victorians chose their flowers from a number of sources. One was traditional Christian symbolism of flowers such as roses, lilies and violets while folklore provided ideas which had remained in popular memory. Another important source of floral symbolism was the language of flowers. With this mass of symbolism at their disposal, Victorians could leave floral messages on their gravemarkers to remind future generations of the personality of the deceased.

The fern was used in its Christian context. According to church theologians the fern, because it grew in solitary places, was a symbol of humility. Humility was considered by many churchmen to be the most important of all virtues that a person could possess and therefore if one was truly humble one would achieve salvation and a place in Heaven. The fern appears on the gravestones of women more often than men, an implication that Victorian men considered it an appropriate and desirable quality for their wives to possess.

Ivy was often used on the graves of women. It was the symbol of marriage and fidelity and Victorians liked to compare a husband and wife to a tree and ivy or a wall and ivy. The tree or wall was the husband who was the source of support to which the ivy or wife would cling for survival. Other climbing vines such as the morning glory and the honeysuckle appear to serve the same purpose and were interchangeable with the ivy.

The lily was popular on the graves of women. Apart from its associations with the Virgin Mary as the mother of Christ, the lily also symbolized her innocence and purity. Victorian men wanted their wives to be innocent and pure in thought and the lily was one means of expressing this on a woman's grave.

The rose is the most popular of all flowers found on gravestones. It comes with a double meaning of both love and death. The white rose was originally the flower associated with love and was sacred to the Greek goddess Aphrodite and the Roman Venus. The red rose was created at the death of Adonis, Venus' mortal lover, and became a symbol of death.

In Christianity the white rose became the symbol of Mary's love for her son Jesus, and ultimately the symbol of love in general while the red rose became the symbol of the Crucifixion, martyrdom and death. Engraved roses were uncoloured and could be seen as symbols of love or death or possibly both. It was common in Victorian cemeteries to have a husband and wife buried next to each other with the gravemarker of the wife showing a hand holding a lily while that of the husband showed a hand with a rose. Rosebuds, as symbols of innocence and chastity, were the preferred flower on the gravemarkers of young children. Often the stem of the rosebud was carved as broken to suggest a short life.

The lily-of-the-valley was a favourite flower of the Victorian period in spite of its unpretentious appearance. It was considered to be an accommodating flower for it could be left to grow outdoors in beds and in some places, such as Scone Palace in Scotland, it would cover an entire acre with minimal maintenance required from the gardeners. The lily-of-the-valley is one of the first flowers to bloom in the new year and as an early spring flower, it became associated with Easter and a symbol of the Resurrection. Placed on a gravemarker it was a declaration that the deceased had gone to Heaven. This association was further emphasized by the flower's folk name in England, "ladder to heaven."

The lily-of-the-valley, like most flowers, acquired a number of different symbolic connotations over the centuries. According to French legend the flower was created from the blood of a dragon which was slain by St. Louis of France; wherever the dragon's blood fell on the ground, tiny white flowers sprang up. In Christianity the dragon is symbolic of the devil and on a more advanced level, St. Louis killing the dragon is a story of a man overcoming worldly temptations; the lily-of-the-valley became a symbol of the purity which resulted from such actions.

The lily-of-the-valley was, due to its white colour, dedicated to the Virgin Mary. When the lily-of-the-valley was carved on the gravestones of married women it referred to the purity of their thoughts while in the case of unmarried women it was a reminder of their virginity.

Pansies are commonly associated with remembrance. They are members of the Viola family and the name pansy comes from the French name for the flower, *pensée*, which means thought. Another popular flower with a similar meaning was the forget-me-not, whose name says it all.

For the rich and the famous there could be no better flower for their gravemarker than the passion flower. It was the distinctly Victorian decorative plant which came to symbolize wealth and social prestige. This was not, of course, what the Jesuit priests had in mind when they first discovered the passion flower in the jungles of Brazil in the 16th century. For them it was the flower seen in a vision by the 12th-century mystic St. Francis of Assisi, and it was filled with religious and moral symbolism.

The passion flower arrived in Britain during the 17th century as a hot-house exotic which graced the conservatories of the aristocracy. However, by the mid-19th century it was becoming affordable for the middle class. Shirley Hibbert, a popular 19th-century writer on horticulture, decreed that no middle-class home could be considered decorated in good taste if it was without a passion flower.

The passion flower may have evoked deep religious sentiments in some people while for others it was a flower of upper-class, ostentatious wealth. However, neither of these ideas was sufficient to justify its prominence on Victorian gravemarkers. It needed the ultimate arbiter of fashion, Queen Victoria, to make it "the" socially desirable funeral flower.

The queen started the trend in 1865 when she arranged for a wreath of passion flowers to be sent to the funeral of Abraham

Lincoln. The passion flower was, according to Queen Victoria, the only acceptable flower for funerals. In many ways, it was the ideal plant to decorate a gravemarker. Being a climbing vine, it was carved with its tendrils and leaves delicately curved around the arms of the cross, while its stem, heavy with exotic blossoms and laden with fruit, cascaded down the front.

What Queen Victoria started others immediately copied. Gravemarkers with designs of the passion flower are divided into two categories: those in which the passion flower is the only decoration on the gravemarker, usually entwined around a Celtic cross, and those in which the flowers form part of a larger bouquet or garland.

The passion flower was expensive to engrave. The blossom is intricate, and to be done well it could not be produced in a hurry. Crosses covered with delicate passion flower blossoms indicate a family with money. According to the language of flowers, the passion flower represented religious superstition which would suggest that by the mid-19th century it was no longer sincerely viewed as a religious symbol. Instead, it is more likely that the passion flower was engraved on gravemarkers because it was a beautiful flower and its cost would indicate that the recipient was wealthy and held a high social status within the community.

GARDENING LORE

To plant a herb or flower was not merely a matter of digging a hole and placing the seed or young plant in the ground. Many plants had superstitious planting rituals which had to be carefully followed if the plant was to flourish in the garden.

Basil appears to be surrounded by more superstitions than any other plant. Pliny recorded that basil degenerated with old age into wild thyme and its purple flowers turned pale at the rising of the Dog Star. During Greek and Roman times people believed that basil caused madness, lethargy and liver troubles. The Greeks considered basil to be a symbol of hatred and misfortune, a concept that may have derived from the idea that madness was often a misfortune inflicted upon mortals by the gods, especially the Furies, who were the spirits of justice, revenge and retribution.

It was a popular belief, developed in the Middle Ages, that pounded basil leaves left under a stone, or basil laid under a pot, would breed a scorpion and should a person smell basil up close it could cause a scorpion to grow in the brain. Furthermore, if a man ate basil and was bitten by a scorpion on the same day he would die. Herbalists from Roman times to the 18th century could not agree on the benefits of basil. Nicholas Culpeper, the English herbalist, summed up the general attitude of herbalists towards basil, with the comment that they "rail at one another, like lawyers."[30]

The herbalists and linguists could not even agree on how the plant was given its name. One theory is that basil means kingly herb, from the Greek, an abbreviation of *basilikon phuton*. A second theory is that the name comes from *basileus*, the Greek for king, because the plant smelled so sweet it was fit for a king's palace. There is also a third idea that basil is derived from *basilicus* or *basilisk*, the mythical dragon whose single glance could kill a person on the spot. The basil plant was supposed to be an effective antidote for anyone unlucky enough to catch the eye of the basilisk.

The Greeks believed that basil would not grow unless the gardener shouted curses and abuse at the plant. The Romans also believed that basil had to be cursed to make it grow. This idea lives on in the French phrase "sowing basil" (*semer le basilic*) which means to rant. The reputation of basil improved a little in the Middle Ages when, despite the ideas connecting basil and scorpions, it was also believed that basil could only be successfully grown by a beautiful woman. Poverty, however, was illustrated in medieval and Renaissance art as a sad, ragged woman with basil by her side, a reflection of misfortune.

Culpeper, in his 1653 herbal, *The English Physician, or Herball*, continued to propagate the negative attributes of basil. Basil was under the influence of the astrological sign Scorpio, the scorpion, and Mars, the Roman god of war, two influences which accounted for its virulent character. Culpeper also noted that basil and rue would not grow together or near each other as rue was an enemy of poison and basil was associated with poisonous creatures. Basil and rue do not, in fact, grow well together but only because their similar requirements for nutrients from the soil retard the growth of both if they are in close proximity.

Parsley was another herb which had to be planted with care. To transplant parsley would bring bad luck into the home and this would account for this gardening rhyme from the Middle Ages:

Plant Parsley fair on Lady Day [March 25th]
Away from Rhubarb and from Tare,
Remember! — Say The Lord's Prayer.[31]

The Lord's Prayer would protect the household from any bad luck that would be generated from the planting of the herb.

In the Middle Ages parsley seeds were planted very deep in the ground for people believed that the seeds must visit Hell three or seven times to obtain permission from the devil to grow on earth. This helped to explain the long germination period of the parsley seed.

Sage was supposed to grow well only where a woman ruled in the household. It was an important medicinal and culinary herb which was grown in every herb garden and it must have been embarrassing for husbands whose wives grew a good crop of sage. If there was a particularly successful patch of sage in the garden it was not uncommon for husbands to sneak out during the night and uproot some of the plants to preserve their reputations within the village.

Tarragon, like basil, had some wondrous characteristics and Gerard in his 1597 herbal had strange tales to tell of this herb which was "cherished in gardens." According to Gerard, to obtain tarragon, a seed of flax was put in a radish root or an onion and planted in the ground. When the plant sprouted it would have turned into tarragon.

The planting of flowers also came with superstitions, most of which go back to the Middle Ages. It was not advisable to split a clump of snowdrops unless the person told the plants that they were going to be moved. Failure to inform the snowdrops meant that they would wither and die after the transplant. Peonies were also believed to take being transplanted personally. The plant considered being uprooted an affront to its dignity and it would refuse to flower for several years while it supposedly got over its mortification. Daisies were never to be planted in a cultivated garden. They were to be left to grow in the wild and if anyone should be foolish enough to transplant them into their garden then bad luck would follow. It was believed that lilies would only grow well for a good woman. This belief was probably a result of the association between the lily and the Virgin Mary who was viewed as the ideal "good" woman.

Seeds watered with wine rather than plain water were thought to produce stronger, healthier plants and this idea remained popular from the Middle Ages down to the 19th century. Also, if a plant was not faring well in the garden, either drooping or dying, the gardener would plant chamomile nearby, for it was considered to be the physician to plants, having the ability to cure any plant in close range.

Gardening rhymes were developed by monks in northern Europe, dating back to the 11th century, and were intended to be used as guides to when and how to sow certain plants. These rhymes were taught to farmers who handed them down from father to son and they remained in popular usage in Britain until the Industrial Revolution of the 19th century. Apart from the previously quoted rhyme for growing parsley, other rhymes include advice on the planting of lavender, anemones and borage.

> For Lavender, bushy, sweet and tall,
> Tend upon the feast of Paul. [June 29th]

> Anemones in at Simon and Jude [October 28th]
> Bring forth colours contra prude.
> Do not fret about the yield
> They are Our Lord's lily of the field.

> Philip and James on 1st of May
> Plant good Borage and let it stay.
> T'will liven up the Claret cup
> To drink with the hazel nut.[32]

The rhymes combine two ideas: knowledge of the best planting times for individual plants and the belief that by planting on a saint's day the plant would acquire additional merit which would help it flourish.

Planting based on the astrological calendar is a very ancient idea which has been followed by gardeners and farmers into the present. There are references to the early Egyptians using the phases of the moon to determine when to plant and it is probable that other earlier civilizations also planted on the basis of astrology. It was believed that plants would acquire specific characteristics depending upon their relationship to the phase of the moon and astrological signs. Each day of the month is under the influence of one of the signs as the moon moves through the zodiac chart.

According to an article in *Park's Floral Magazine* of 1886, it was best to plant flowers when the moon was in the signs of Cancer, Pisces and Virgo if abundance was desired. If, however, it was beauty that was required of the plants, then they were to be planted as the moon passed through Libra. Sturdiness came from planting when the moon was in the Scorpio phase and hardiness during the phase of Taurus.

Part Two: TRADITIONAL FOODS, HYGIENE AND MEDICINES

Food and Feasting

Flowers, herbs and spices played many different roles in their association with food. They flavoured and preserved food, stimulated the appetite, and were used to prevent hangovers after drunken revelries.

Two of the oldest flavouring ingredients are garlic and onions, which have historically been classified as herbs. Garlic was the staple food for slaves in Egypt, especially those who constructed the pyramids, and Roman soldiers were given a daily mixture of garlic and cloves to sustain their strength. The word garlic comes from the Anglo-Saxon *gar* meaning lance, a reference to the shape of its stem, and *leac* meaning pot herb.

Onions are one of the oldest vegetables known to man, with a recorded history going back some 3,500 years. They were a favourite food of the Egyptians and when the Israelites left Egypt for the Promised Land they mourned the loss of Egyptian onions. It was the Romans who gave the plant the name by which it is known today, calling it *unionem* or *unio*, in reference to its single bulb.

The Egyptians flavoured their food with a variety of herbs and spices. Herbs were grown in the family garden plots or picked in the wild while spices were bought at the markets. Herbs were common and the cost of spices was sufficiently low to allow even the peasants access to a wide variety of flavourings.

Parsley and coriander were the main flavourings used for meat. There was also a species of celery which was considered a herb rather than a vegetable and was one of the main ingredients in Egyptian cookery. This celery was found in the tomb of Tutankhamun which would suggest that it was of sufficient importance to be considered necessary for his enjoyment in the afterlife.

Cumin seeds were sprinkled on dough before it was baked into bread while the ground seeds were probably used to flavour meat. Pepper was not imported into Egypt until the Graeco/Roman period, in the fourth century A.D., so cumin would have been the main aromatic seasoning during the Pharaonic period. A basket filled with cumin seeds was included in the tomb of the architect Kha, who died around 1500 B.C.

Fenugreek has been found in tombs south of Cairo and dated to about 3000 B.C. while a black-seeded variety of mustard has been found in New Kingdom tombs which date from 1500 to 1000 B.C. Poppy juice was used for its medicinal value and the seeds for flavouring in cooking.

There are other herbs and spices which historians assume the Egyptians used but written records are unclear on their names. Rosemary grows naturally in Egypt and it is probable that it was used as a flavouring although written records are sketchy on identification. Mint, dill, chervil and fennel are also believed to have been used in Egyptian cooking, although the translations of their names causes some difficulty. However, leaves from mint and sage have been found in tombs from the Late Pharaonic period, which covers the first century B.C. to the second century A.D., and it is generally accepted that these herbs were used long before then.

The Roman civilization was the first in the West to use flowers, herbs and spices extensively in cooking and in the external decorations of the meal or feast. By the time of the emperors, in the first and second centuries A.D., trade was well established between Rome and the Arab middlemen who imported the spices from India and China.

The Romans generally ate three meals a day. Breakfast was a light meal of bread and fruit or onions. The midday meal was also a light meal as it was considered vulgar to eat large quantities of food in the middle of the day. This meal consisted of fish, eggs, cold meats, vegetables and bread. The evening meal, called the *cena,* was the main meal of the day. It began around 4:00 P.M. and continued into the night. The *cena* made up for the light meals of the day. It consisted of three parts: hors d'oeuvres, main dishes and dessert. The main dishes would be from three to seven in number and even more if it was a banquet. These dishes included fish, shellfish, poultry, game, meat, and stuffed animals cooked whole.

Dining rooms were decorated in varying degrees of ostentation depending on the wealth of the owner. The dining room would be furnished with couches, and strewn with flowers such as myrtle, anemones and crocuses, which had sexual connotations. Myrtle and anemones were associated with Venus while crocuses signified the love of Crocus for Smilax and had adorned Juno's wedding bed.

The Romans believed that certain herbs could increase appetites and when huge feasts were given, the host and hostess wanted their guests to have hearty appetites. Mint was commonly used for this purpose. It was rubbed on the tables and strewn on the floors where its scent would be released when stepped upon. Its aroma symbolized hospitality.

Nero, who reigned from 54 to 68 A.D., had a special ceiling built in the dining room of his palace, the Golden House. The ceiling was made of moveable ivory squares and when the squares turned, flowers and perfumes fell onto the guests. Roses were the favoured flowers to be dropped from the ceiling at banquets. Heliogabalus, whose reign was from 204 to 222 A.D., had the misfortune of killing some of his guests at a particularly drunken banquet. As the evening was ending he had roses, which were suspended in nets on the ceiling, released onto the guests. Sadly, many were in a drunken stupor and as the rose petals piled up to a height of 18 inches a number of the guests suffocated.

Guests were greeted at Roman banquets with garlands and wreaths of roses. This may be viewed as a hospitable gesture but there was an underlying purpose behind the flowers. The Romans believed that roses, parsley and marjoram could prevent drunkenness if any of these three or all three together were woven into wreaths and worn around the head. Roses were placed in wine glasses as another means of preventing the guests from becoming inebriated. Bunches of parsley were also placed on the banquet tables as the Romans thought that intoxication was caused by the fumes of the wine and the spicy aroma of the parsley would absorb the fumes.

After the banquet, the Romans would sleep on saffron-filled pillows as a backup system in case the roses, parsley and marjoram failed. If, upon waking, they found that these remedies had all proved ineffective then an infusion of chamomile flowers and oil of roses or violets poured over the head was supposed to help ease the morning-after headache. Wreaths of ivy were popular as they were cooling to the head and had no strong fragrance. Myrtle wreaths were thought to dispel the fumes of the wine which the Romans believed to have lingered and to be the cause of the headache. Rose wreaths were thought to have sedative qualities which were effective against hangovers and, like ivy, they were believed to have a cooling effect. Gillyflowers, however, were to be avoided as they excited the nerves of the head and would make the condition worse.

One of the earliest books on cooking is the *Deipnosophistae* or *The Sophists at Dinner* by Athenaeus, a native of Egypt who lived in Rome at the end of the second and the beginning of the third century A.D. The characters in the book discuss a wide range of subjects while dining and there are numerous conversations on food and its preparation. Inevitably they come to the flavouring of food and all agree that anise, capers, coriander, cumin, fennel, garlic, leeks, marjoram, mashed raisins, must, mustard, onions, rue, sesame seeds and thyme were the important herbs and spices.

These herbs and spices are comparatively few in number compared to the flavourings used by the famous Roman chef Apicius, who lived during the first century A.D. In his book *De Re Coquinaria [On Cooking]* Apicius lists the seasonings which no household should be without. The list is extensive and would presumably be applicable only to the wealthy. His essential seasonings are as follows: almonds, anise, bay leaf, cardamon, caraway seeds, celery seeds, cloves, colewort, coriander, costmary (a herb with large leaves), cumin, dill, damsons, dates, elecampane (a herb also known as scabwort), fennel, filberts, garlic, gentian roots, ginger, honey, juniper, lovage, marjoram, mint, myrtle berries, oregano, onions, parsley, pennyroyal, pepper, pine nuts, pomegranates, poppy seeds, raisins, rue, saffron, sage, sesame, shallots, spikenard (an aromatic root of the valerian family) and thyme. In addition to these basic ingredients Apicius also used cinnamon, chervil, mustard seeds, nutmeg, saxifrage, wormwood and mastic which is the gum or resin from the mastic or pistachio nut tree.

In the *Deipnosophistae*, Athenaeus offers the description of a procession by King Ptolemy Philadelphus of Egypt, in the third century A.D., when Egypt was a province of the Roman Empire. The king provided a pavilion where soldiers, artisans and tourists were entertained and fed. It held 130 couches and the floor was entirely covered with a wide variety of flowers. The procession included the display of 300 pounds of frankincense, 300 pounds of myrrh and a combined 200 pounds of saffron, cassia, cinnamon and other unmentioned spices.

The Romans consumed a large number of dishes during their feasts. The fictional Trimalchio's Feast from the *Satyricon* by Petronius, who lived during the reign of Nero, gives a good example of the extent of Roman festive cooking. Trimalchio's Feast consisted of the following dishes:

Hors d'oeuvres
White and black olives; damsons and pomegranate seeds; dormice sprinkled with honey and poppy seeds; grilled sausages; *beccaficos* [unknown] in spiced egg yolk; honeyed wine.

Main Dishes
The main dishes were foods of the zodiac. There were chickpeas for Aries, beef for Taurus, kidneys for Gemini, myrtle for Cancer, African figs for Leo, a sterile sow's womb for Virgo, scales supporting tarts and honey cakes for Virgo, scorpion fish for Scorpio, eyefish for Sagittarius, lobster for Capricorn, goose for Aquarius and two red mullets for Pisces. Apart from the foods of the zodiac there were also roasted fowls, sow bellies, hares, roast of whole wild boar with dates, and a boiled whole pig stuffed with sausage and black puddings.

Desserts

Fruits and cakes; pastries stuffed with raisins and nuts; quince and
pork disguised as fowls and fish; oysters and scallops; and snails.

A Roman feast ended with dishes to aid digestion. Cakes, called
mustaceae, were made primarily of flour, anise and cumin, anise
being considered a digestive. Ginger was also served after the feast
as a digestive aid. It was wrapped in bread and, over time, the
herb became an ingredient in the bread, thus leading to the evolu-
tion of gingerbread.

The Romans enjoyed foods which were very sweet and also
highly spiced. Seasonings were of enormous importance in Roman
cooking; and the discovery of Asian seasonings, around the first
century B.C., revolutionized Western cooking. Pepper became the
most important seasoning in Roman cooking; before its advent,
the Romans used ground myrtle berries. Pepper was used in the
preparation of almost all meats, vegetables and fish and it was
sprinkled on cooked dishes just as they were ready to be served.
The herb lovage was equally important in Roman cooking. Its
seeds, roots and leaves were used almost as frequently as pepper
in Roman recipes.

Asafoetida is the spice made from the hardened sap of the giant
fennel plant of Asia. On its own it has a terrible taste but mixed
with other foods and spices it takes on a delicate onion flavour.
The ancient Persians called it the food of the gods while in Rome
it became so popular that it was depicted on coins.

The Romans developed mustard into a seasoning. The name
mustard comes from the Latin *mustum ardens* or burnt must. The
Romans mixed mustard seeds with grape must to form a paste
and they also ground the seeds and sprinkled them over food,
much as pepper is used today. The development of mustard, in
its contemporary form, began in 1720 when Mrs. Clements of
Durham, England, invented a powdered mustard, appropriately
named "Durham Mustard" and made herself a fortune. Prepared
mustard, the familiar yellow paste sold in stores today, is a
mixture of ground mustard seeds, salt, vinegar and spices, with
turmeric added to give it its bright yellow colour. Prior to the
development of prepared mustard, Europeans ground the seeds
between two stones called a *querne* which were specially designed

for that purpose. As John Parkinson, the 17th-century British herbalist, recommended: mix the ground seeds "with some good vinegar" and serve.

European food was greatly improved by the use of spices. Cooks had to contend with the problems of a total lack of refrigeration which resulted in main ingredients rotting, and the need to overcook food to compensate for dental problems which resulted from the lack of dental hygiene. Pepper was the preferred spice for meat preservation and flavouring although cloves were also used to help prevent meat spoilage. The ability to improve flavour and reduce spoilage made both these spices worth their weight in gold.

Both garlic and onions were favourite flavourings in the Middle Ages as they were used to disguise the taste of rotting meat before the large-scale importation of spices. For the poorer people who subsisted mainly on pottage, a thick vegetable stew which was boiled for hours until the vegetables turned into a puree, onions and garlic added a pleasant tang to an otherwise extremely bland dish.

Sugar made its first appearance in Europe during the third century B.C., when it was brought back by Alexander the Great from his campaigns in the Middle East and India. It became extremely rare in Europe during the early centuries of the Middle Ages and was reintroduced in the 11th century, through contact between Europeans and Muslims in Sicily and Spain. The earliest record of sugar in England is from the 14th century.

Initially, sugar was considered a medicinal ingredient but soon it was used to flavour many dishes, including fish and meat. A popular dessert was made by encasing caraway or anise seeds in as many as ten coats of molten sugar and they were served as the final course at a banquet to aid digestion. Sugar was classified as a spice because it was imported from the East; it was sold in powdered form, in a conical block or as a two-pound loaf.

In Gerard's herbal he describes sugar cane as a "pleasant and profitable reed." Its juice was used to make "infinite confections, confectures, syrups and such like."[1] It was also popular for conserving roses, violets and rosemary flowers which were eaten as desserts. Cinnamon was another favourite flavouring for sweet dishes but people were warned of its constipating effect.

The taste for fennel changed over the centuries. The Romans ate the entire plant; its leaves and stem were served raw in salads, its root was cooked as a vegetable and its seeds were used to flavour bread, cakes and soup. By the 17th century, fennel had been reduced to a culinary flavouring and Parkinson, in his herbal, recommended using only the seeds to flavour pippin apple pies and give bread a better taste. In the Middle Ages fennel seeds were chewed to alleviate hunger as illustrated in the behaviour of the poor man in *Piers Plowman*, written in 1362.

In Puritan New England fennel seeds were called "meeting seeds" from the church services, called meetings, which could last as long as three hours. There are two theories on the use of fennel seeds by the Puritans. One is their ability to act as an appetite suppressant during the long hours in church. The other theory is that some parishioners drank whisky before going to church and as this was strictly against church belief, imbibers chewed fennel seeds to disguise the odour of alcohol on their breath.

By the 14th century, spices were associated with licentious behaviour, as seen in the actions of Gluttony, another character in *Piers Plowman*. Gluttony is tempted into a tavern on his way to church but it is not so much the good ale and gossip which acts as a temptation but the promise of hot spices such as pepper, peony seeds, garlic and fennel seeds. The association between spices and immoral behaviour was still prevalent in the 17th century in England when the Puritans objected to the use of all spices, including fennel seeds.

Sauces made of herbs and spices mixed with vinegar or wine were considered bad for an individual's health according to some schools of thought during the Middle Ages. Maino de'Maineri, an Italian physician, wrote a treatise on the effects of sauces, *Opusculum de saporibus*, in the first half of the 14th century and he asserted that sauces were developed by gourmets for the sake of enjoyment rather than regard for health. Maino contended that sauces had a negative effect on health as they induced people to eat more than was good for them and disguised the taste of rotten meat which could lead to food poisoning.

In medieval medicine it was believed that herbs and spices had an impact on specific parts of the body and therefore what people ate could influence their health. Maino believed that people in good health should eat sauces sparingly, as each ingredient had a medicinal value and could upset the natural harmony of the body.

He did, however, acknowledge that sauces could be beneficial in stimulating a poor appetite and aiding digestion. Hot spices were to be avoided in summer but increased in winter.

Maino did not favour the total absence of sauces in cooking but recommended comparatively simple sauces such as the "green sauce" which was popular throughout Europe. This sauce consisted of parsley, rosemary, bread crumbs, ginger and cloves, mixed with vinegar. An even simpler sauce was cinnamon and small pieces of bread mixed with vinegar or wine.

One of the earliest cookbooks from the Middle Ages is the *Forme of Cury [Manner of Cookery]* written around 1390 at the request of the English King Richard II. It includes 196 recipes which were prepared by the best chefs in the country. The cookbook, however, gives a misleading look at English cooking at the time. The recipes are for dishes prepared for the nobility, and they are not representative of the majority of foods eaten by the average person. However, it does give an insight into the use of spices at the highest level of society in the country.

Some of the recipes from Richard's cookbook include:

Boiled Garlic. — Peel garlic. Cast it into a pot with water and oil, and boil it. Add saffron, salt and strong powder. Serve it forth whole. [Strong powder is ginger or a blend of cinnamon and mace.]

Stuffing for a Goose. — Take sage, parsley, hyssop, savory, quinces, pears, garlic and grapes and fill the goose with it.

Baked Herb Eggs. — Take parsley, mint, savory, sage, tansy, vervain, clary, rue, dittany, fennel, southernwood. Chop them and grind them small. Mix them with eggs. Put butter in a baking dish and put the mixture in it. Bake it and serve it in portions.

The cooks during the time of Richard II liked to disguise food by using herbs and spices as colouring. Roses or sandalwood were used to create the colour red. Saffron and dandelions tinted food yellow, and mint, parsley and mallow gave food a distinctive green colour. Heliotrope produced blue food and violets created a purple colouring. Individual plates were uncommon and large slices of bread called trenchers were used instead. These were also coloured and could be eaten after the meal.

Herbs and spices were used to aid digestion. During the time of Shakespeare, baked apples with caraway seeds were considered a good digestive and in the play *Henry IV*, a meal ends with a pippin apple and a dish of caraway seeds. Ginger was thought to be good for digestion and it was used in sauces for meat. Pepper was considered beneficial in softening hard-to-digest food.

Lavender was thought to increase a person's appetite. It was used as a flavouring in dishes and in powdered form was sprinkled on food from condiment dishes set on the table. Queen Elizabeth I loved conserve of lavender which was always on her table. She was also very partial to coriander seeds coated in multiple layers of hardened sugar.

Parsley has a long history as a breath freshener after a meal. The Romans began munching parsley at banquets and Europeans continued to eat parsley after meals. The historical trail leads to the parsley garnish on the side of the plate in restaurants today. There is scientific backing for the use of parsley as a breath freshener for it contains a high proportion of chlorophyll which is the "clor" in Clorets and one of the active ingredients in Certs.

Flowers have been more than just a decoration at banquets; they have also been considered food. Cooking with flowers reached its peak during the medieval and Renaissance periods. Crusaders in the 11th and 12th centuries liked a stew made of roses and prim-roses, and flowers were an edible delicacy in Elizabethan England. Flower blossoms, buds, leaves and stalks were used in salads while the blossoms were sugar-coated, candied and pickled. They were also ingredients in sauces for puddings, and in tarts and cakes. Two recipes from the 15th century which use flowers as the primary ingredient are:

Red Rose Pudding
Take roses, boiled, pressed and ground, cooked in milk or almond milk thickened with rice flour and sweetened with sugar.
Hawthorny
Take hawthorn flowers, boil them, press them, grate them small, mix with almond milk, and mix it with flour, grated bread, rice flour; add enough sugar, or if none then honey, colour it the same colour as the flowers are and serve.

The Complete Housewife or Accomplish'd Gentlewoman's Companion, written by Mrs. E. Smith and published in London in 1753, shows the extensive use of flowers in cooking. Her recipes include how to pickle nasturtium buds, candy angelica and many sorts of flowers, make a conserve of roses or other flowers, make sugar of roses, pickle broom-buds, and make syrup of flowers. Mrs. Smith and other writers of the period made it clear that not just any flower was suitable. Fragrance, appearance and, of course, taste were important. Of these three qualities, fragrance was the most important. A flower that did not smell good was not worth eating.

Flowers were to be suitably arranged. Cookbooks and household handbooks encouraged the woman of the house or the cook to arrange the flowers on plates as they appeared in nature. Gervase Markham in *The English Housewife* of 1675 recommended that "you may set [on the plate] ... some full bloom, some half blown and some in bud, which will be pretty and curious."

The preservation of the flower's natural colour was also important. The anonymous writer of *A Closet for Ladies and Gentlemen or the Art of Preserving, Conserving and Candying*, from the 17th century, included a recipe "To Candy Violet Flowers in Their Natural Colours."

Take your Violet flowers which are good and new, and well coloured .... Take the flowers with the stalkes, and wash them over with a little Rose water, wherein Gum-Arabic is dissolved, then take fine (serced) sugar, and dust over them, and set them a drying on the bottom of a sieve in an oven, and they will glisten as if they were Sugar-candy.

Individual flowers went through phases of popularity. Carnation recipes abounded in 17th- and 18th-century England and they also enjoyed popularity in France and Spain. The preference was for the spicy petals of the small dianthus.

To Make Syrup of Clove-Gillyflowers
The Queen's Delight, 1671
Take a quart of water, half a bushel of flowers, cut off the whites, and with a sieve sift away the seeds, bruise them a little; let your water be boiled and a little cold again, then put in your flowers

and let them stand close covered twenty-four hours; you may put in but half the flowers at a time, the strength will come out the better; to that liquor put in four pounds of sugar, let it lye in all night, next day boil in a gallipot, set it in a pot of water, and then let it boil till all the sugar be melted and syrup be pretty thick, then take it out and let it stand till it be thoroughly cold, then glass it.

Roses and violets were always popular and candied violets remained favourite sweets into the late 19th century. It is not as easy today to cook with flowers. The old-fashioned varieties of roses, including the wild rose, are considered the best for cooking as modern hybrids have tougher petals and are less fragrant. The scent of the rose is considered an important part of the charm of eating it and this is lost with modern varieties. The sweet violet or *Viola odorata* is the preferred violet with the best taste and most fragrant blossoms.

Queen Victoria was extremely fond of violet flavouring. Her favourite sweetener was a violet syrup made from violet flowers, sugar, gum arabic and dried orris-root powder. The ingredients were boiled in water, left to cool and then bottled. The mixture was diluted according to its uses which ranged from a refreshing, although sweet, drink to syrup for ice cream. Queen Victoria may have inherited her taste for violet flavouring from her mother, the Duchess of Kent, whose favourite drink was violet tea made from an infusion of dried violets in a cup of boiling water.

Marigold blossoms, dried and ground, were the poor man's pepper, although the blossoms were also used extensively in cooking. The *Calendula officinalis*, which is native to Europe, is the edible flower referred to in recipes, not the French or African marigolds which are native to Mexico.

The nasturtium, *Tropaeolum majus*, was another popular spicy flower. It is a member of the cress family and has a flavour similar to watercress but less peppery. Its blossoms, stems and leaves were eaten and provided a delicate spicy addition, mainly to salads.

Primroses, cowslips, angelica, rosemary, daisies, chicory, dandelions and squash flowers also appeared in recipes, especially in salads. Gerard, the 17th-century herbalist, noted that there were two places for the salad in the menu, depending on what was required of it. It could be eaten first to start the meal or served after the meal to prevent drunkenness.

John Evelyn, a prolific British author noted for his in-depth study of British trees, took time out to write *Acetaria, The Grand Salad* in 1699. He recommended aromatic flowers, on the basis that they were generally endowed with all the goodness of herbs but "in a more intense degree."[2] These healthier flowers could be eaten alone, unlike herbs, or could be added to salads. Evelyn's book lists the plants as individual ingredients and leaves it up to individuals to create their own mixture to achieve the required results, especially in the area of "hot"and "cold" plants and their effects on health.

Common belief held that hot illnesses were cured by cold plants and vice versa. Each plant was described in terms of temperature which would determine the combination of plants used in each salad. Violets and primroses were cold and moist, carnations were temperate, while balm, fennel, parsley and sage were all hot and dry. Evelyn did have one word of advice about garlic — "we absolutely forbid it entrance into our Salleting, by reason of its intolerable Rankness ..." and it was definitely not for "Ladies' Palats."[3]

During this period salads became more complex. In 1596 Thomas Dawson in *The Good Huswifes Jewell* gave only two salad recipes; one for lemons sprinkled with sugar and the second for greens and cucumbers. By 1675, Gervase Markham listed five categories of salads; simple and plain, compound, boiled, preserved, and salads for show. Preserved salads included violets, primroses, cowslips and carnations pickled in vinegar and he recommended distilled vinegar to preserve the colours of the flowers. Preserved salads of more than one flower were intended to be decoratively arranged.

Other authors included flowers in their equivalent of Markham's simple and compound salads. John Murrel, in his *Two Books of Cookerie and Carving*, in 1650, describes a salad of rosebuds and carnation blossoms while Robert May in his *The Accomplisht Cook or the Art and Mystery of Cookery* has a watercress and violet-blossom salad.

Candied flowers were extremely popular. One of the oldest recipes for a candied flower is in an incomplete 15th-century cookery manuscript which is found in segments in the British

Museum, London and the Bodleian Library, Oxford. It recommended boiling violet blossoms and adding them to sugar or
honey. By the 16th century, recipes for candied flowers were
becoming common. Dawson included this one.

To Make Conserves of Roses, and of any other flowers
Take your Roses before they be fullye sprung out, and chop off
the white of them, and let the Roses be dried one daye or two
before they be stamped, and to one once [ounce] of these flowers
take one once and a half of fine beaten Suger, and let your roses
be beaten as you can, and after beat your roses and Suger together
againe, then put the conserve into a faire glasse: and likewise
make all conserve of flowers.

CHILDBIRTH

The ability to conceive a child has always been an important
part of a woman's life. Contemporary women are just as determined to have children as their predecessors and for today's
women who find themselves unable to conceive, modern medical
technology has provided a variety of treatments including fertility
drugs, corrective surgery, artificial insemination, and in vitro
fertilization. Before these modern techniques were developed,
however, a woman with a fertility problem was limited in her
choice of procedures, of which the majority involved special plants
and spells.

Mandrakes (*Mandragora officinarum*) were considered the most
potent aid to fertility. The ancient Egyptians called the plant the
"phallus of the field" and the name Mandragora comes from the
Greek meaning hurtful to cattle. The Greeks believed that the
mandrake belonged to the powerful witch, Circe, who used it in
her potions to make men love her. However, she could also turn
men who had rejected her, or men whom she considered enemies,
into animals with a similar potion. In Gerard's 17th-century herbal
he refers to the plant as "Circaea," a variation on the name Circe.

The mandrake is native to the southeast Mediterranean and the
Himalayas and is highly toxic with narcotic, hallucinogenic and
aphrodisiacal properties. Its aphrodisiacal quality was probably
the reason why the mandrake was used as an aid to conception

although its association with Circe would have increased belief in its potency.

Mandrakes had to be imported into northern Europe and they were often confused with briony, a native plant in the north of Europe. In England mandrake and womandrake were country names for the male and female briony. Women herbal healers used briony roots, as if they were mandrakes, in spells to increase a woman's fertility. Ground briony root was sprinkled on food to induce conception but this was a dangerous practice for the entire plant is poisonous and causes extreme irritation of the stomach and intestines.

The mandrake proper is best known in the Old Testament story of Jacob and his two wives, Leah and Rachel. Because Leah was the unwanted and unloved wife, the Lord made her fertile and she bore Jacob six sons. Rachel, the beloved wife, was made barren. During the wheat harvest, Leah's eldest son, Reuben, found some mandrakes and gave them to his mother. Rachel asked for them and Leah gave them to her only on the condition that Jacob would spend that night with her rather than with Rachel. The mandrakes do not seem to have helped Rachel for Leah gave birth to two more sons and a daughter before Rachel had her first child, Joseph.

Both the ancient Greeks and Romans had small families and as long as the wife produced a male heir there was little need for mandrakes or other herbal aids to conception. In Greece, as the result of inheritance laws under which the family property had to be divided among all male heirs, there was a strong incentive to have only one son in order to keep the property intact. Daughters, in both Greece and Rome, were usually unwanted as their wedding dowries were a drain on the family income.

There was, however, a strong interest in female-health issues in ancient Greece, and a collection of medical treatises called the *Hippocratic Corpus*, written by several anonymous authors, has survived from the late fifth and fourth centuries B.C. The majority of the works are devoted to the subject of illness in women, which would suggest that women formed a large part of any doctor's practice.

The Greek doctors had no real knowledge of female anatomy and many absurd ideas abounded. One of these was called the "wandering womb" syndrome. This condition was based on the idea that the womb was an animal living within the woman and it must be satisfied with children. If it was not satisfied it would become restless and begin to move around the woman's body, causing physical pain and illness. The obvious solution to the problem was for the woman to become pregnant. However, until this happened, the condition was treated with a pessary dipped in perfumes of myrtle or marjoram.

The Greeks believed they could test a woman's ability to conceive based on the idea that a woman was an empty vessel through which incense should be able to pass. The woman was wrapped in a cloak and incense was burnt underneath her. If the smell of incense was detected in her nose and mouth she was declared capable of conception.

If a woman failed to conceive she resorted to doctors. It apparently did not occur to Greek men that they might be the cause of infertility in marriage. The medical approach to infertility was to try to soften and open the entrance to the womb, primarily through the use of fumigations from the smoke of laurel leaves, myrrh, wormwood, and garlic. There were also ointments made of goat fat, cyclamen juice, fig juice or cardamon seeds which were rubbed into the vagina.

Greek physicians thought that one of the underlying causes of infertility was a moist and slippery womb which would prevent the male seed from fertilizing the woman. Sage wine was given as a tonic to dry the womb and the fourth-century B.C. physician, Hippocrates, prescribed it for all Greek women, after a war or an epidemic, as a means of replenishing the country's population.

Once the woman became pregnant there was the ever-present prospect that she and/or her child could die during childbirth. Hera was worshipped as the goddess of childbirth although she later passed the function over to her daughter, Ilithyia. Offerings of a variety of flowers would be made at their temples for a safe delivery.

Midwives hung garlic and cloves around the birthing room to protect the baby from disease and witchcraft but the garlic was not always successful. The mortality rate of Athenian infants, based on grave inscriptions, may have been as high as 30% to 40% in the first year of life. Every parent could expect to bury at least one child and given the young ages of the mothers they, too, often died in childbirth. Eight days after a birth in ancient Greece, the family would hold a special ceremony to announce the birth and the sex of the child. A crown of olive leaves was hung on the door if the child was a boy and a band of wool if it was a girl.

The Romans had their own ideas on conception. Pliny the Elder in his *Natural History* states that the planet Venus was the cause of all things born on Earth. It was commonly believed in the first century A.D. that during the morning rising of the planet and its appearance in the evening sky a genital dew was scattered over Earth which stimulated the contraceptive organs in humans and animals. Roman women also prayed to Juno Lucina, who was a combination of Hera and Ilithyia, to make them fertile.

The most influential writer on childbirth during the Roman period was the Greek physician Soranus who practised at the beginning of the second century A.D. His book *Gynaecia* or *Gynecology* was an important guide on pregnancy, childbirth and child rearing. To check a woman's ability to conceive, Roman doctors recommended a fumigation of resin, rue, garlic and coriander and if the ingredients could be smelt on the woman's breath then she would be fertile. Soranus, however, did not believe that this was an effective method of predetermining fertility.

Soranus concentrated on the care which must be given to the woman once she was found to be pregnant. His first and probably most important advice was to find a good midwife. Soranus' book on gynecology was intended for knowledgeable midwives who could read and also for male physicians who treated female patients. His book was the Roman equivalent of Dr. Spock as it also provided advice to the expectant mother and on how she should treat her newborn child.

According to Soranus, once conception occurred the mother must immediately change her diet and eat only neutral food. Garlic, onions and leeks were to be avoided because they produced flatulence which was believed to cause miscarriages.

Morning sickness was dealt with in a number of ways. If the woman suffered extreme nausea, her stomach was rubbed with oil of roses, quinces, myrtle and spikenard, or the ingredients could be bound around her stomach with wool. Plasters were also placed on the woman's stomach. Dried dates, apples or quinces boiled in a tart wine or diluted vinegar formed the basic plaster but to make it stronger and more effective, aloe, roses, and saffron were added. Women were often given a tea made of the leaves of birthwort (*Aristolochia clematitis*) to ease the pain of childbirth and Soranus recommended holding pennyroyal leaves mixed with vinegar under the woman's nose if she fainted during labour.

Once the baby was born it was wiped with salt, washed in warm water, swaddled and placed in a bed with coverlets which some mothers had scented with sweet bay or myrtle leaves. To announce the birth of a child a crown or garland of flowers was placed on the outer door of the house.

The Christian belief that every act of sex must be open to procreation led to an increase in the number of births. By the 16th century infant and child mortality was high with as many as one-third to one-half of all children dying before the age of five. The child was at risk before and during birth as well as in infancy.

An important source of information on medieval childbirth and the raising of children is the *Rosengarten*, written in 1513 by Eucharius Rösslin. It was the first printed manual for midwives and became the basic guide during the 16th and 17th centuries for all female-related medicine, covering gynecology, childbirth and child care. There is little contemporary literature on the subject between the Roman period and the late Middle Ages or early Renaissance and it is thought that medical writers, who were male, paid little attention to pregnancy and childbirth because it was outside their area of expertise. Traditionally, pregnancy and childbirth were the domain of women: the midwives, and healers who were knowledgeable in the use of herbs.

Rösslin, a physician from the city of Frankfurt, believed that ignorance on the part of midwives and expectant mothers was the major cause of infant death. He listed 18 circumstances which could lead to a difficult and painful birth, including eating foods which would cause constipation. For this reason marjoram, crab apples and dried berries were on his list of foods to be avoided.

To make the delivery easier Rösslin recommended a number of alternative treatments. The midwife could make the mother sneeze by using pepper or hellebore. She could lubricate the vagina and uterus with lily oil, or barleycorns saturated with saffron or musk oil, or she could apply wool nets soaked in oil made from rue leaves. There is some validity in the use of rue, as chemicals in the leaves act upon the uterus and were used as an abortifacient.

In the same period in England information gathered from diaries, letters and other sources indicates that the expectant mother was taken to a warm birthing chamber which was scented with olive oil, herbs and wine and, if the family was wealthy, rose water. After the birth, the baby was washed in warm water with oil, and salt or rose petals.

Once the child was born, magical charms were put in place to ensure its safety. Garlic, the traditional means of warding off evil and witches' curses, was placed around the room and, along with cloves, hung over the baby's cradle. In northern Europe the root of a peony was hung round the infant's neck to prevent illness.

Later in the 16th century the *Haussbuch* by Coler was published in Germany. It was a guide for fathers and included everything from estate management and household repairs to what to do during a wife's pregnancy. This book was first printed in six parts between 1591 and 1605 and ended as a work of encyclopedic size which was still being consulted into the 19th century.

The *Haussbuch*, although intended for husbands, gave advice to the expectant mother. She was to bathe often during the weeks before birth, making sure she washed with mallow and chamomile. In the days before she was to give birth, Coler recommended that she eat crushed aniseed (licorice) and avoid strong purgatives such as saffron, cabbage and celery.

In 1651 the English herbalist, Nicholas Culpeper, wrote *A Directory for Midwives* with the sub-title, *A Guide for Women in Their Conception, Bearing and Sucking their Children*. It filled a need for useful information and was reprinted 17 times, the latest edition in 1777. Culpeper had a personal interest in the subject of child-birth and development for of the seven children borne by his wife, only one survived beyond infancy.

Culpeper made recommendations for the diet of the pregnant woman. The mother-to-be was to avoid any food that could start her menstrual cycle and in this category he listed garlic, onions, olives, mustard, fennel, pepper and all other spices. He did, however, suggest that cinnamon be added to the woman's diet in the last months of her pregnancy.

He was aware of a woman's concern about stretch marks and advised her to place on her stomach a cloth soaked in a combination of oils of almond, jasmine, and lily. This would help loosen the skin and allow it to stretch with greater ease as the pregnancy progressed.

If problems arose during labour, Culpeper recommended rubbing the woman's stomach with a mixture of oil of almonds, lilies and wine. After the birth he advised that, providing the woman did not have a fever, she be allowed to drink a mild wine or cinnamon boiled in water for the first few days. A week after the delivery, to close and fortify the womb, vervain was to be boiled with her meat and added to drinks. When the woman was going to make her first appearance in public after the birth, Culpeper suggested she first bathe in a decoction of lily roots, elecampane, mugwort, agrimony, borage, rosemary, chamomile, fenugreek, linseed and citrus peel.

If the woman had problems producing enough milk and did not want her child to have a wet nurse, Culpeper's book provided two remedies. One was to swallow a mixture of fennel roots, smallage roots (a species of wild celery), parsley seeds, dill, basil, anise and rocket. The other was to make a compound from fennel seed, anise and rocket seed and mix it in a broth.

If the mother's milk had a bad taste then the baby would not feed properly. To prevent this the mother was to avoid fried onions, salted and spiced meats, garlic, leeks, onions and mustard. The temperature of a mother's milk could be regulated by salads. If her milk was too hot she was to eat a salad of endive, succory (also known as chicory), lettuce, sorrel, pulsane and plantain, all of which were considered cold plants. However, if her milk was too cold then a mixture of hot plants such as borage, bugloss, vervain and cinnamon was to be eaten.

Advice for the care of the newborn child and cures for some of the basic medical problems the child would encounter in its early years were important information, especially for first-time mothers. Teething was a problem, no matter what the century. Soranus recommended poultices of fenugreek or linseed be applied to the baby's gums. Tonsilitis was another problem facing parents throughout history and Soranus prescribed a poultice of roasted cumin seeds mixed with water be wrapped around the child's throat.

The ultimate problem with every baby was diaper rash. Rösslin recommended a powder of myrtle, roses and mandrake or a salve of rose oil, frankincense and camphor. Coler's approach was somewhat more unusual although probably effective. He suggested dusting the rash with the powdered wood produced by the death-watch beetle which inhabited the wooden houses of the period.

One area of child care which saw little change from the Middle Ages to the Victorian period was the method of stopping babies from crying. Up until this century it was comparatively simple — just dose the child with opium. The 16th-century solution provided by Dr. Rösslin was to make a paste from poppy stems or flowers, poppy seeds, poppy oil and the sap of wild lettuce and apply it to the forehead and temples of the child. The Victorians went one step further. They gave the child laudanum, which is opium suspended in wine. If the baby did not die from the effects of opium and alcohol it became placid and very quiet. Laudanum was used for almost every childhood illness and children often became addicted to opium for the rest of their lives.

The Victorians were very good at creative advertising. No parents would want to give their baby opium but dress it up as "Mother's Blessing," "Mrs. Wilkinson's Soothing Syrup" or "Godfrey's Cordial" and it became acceptable. Even the children in the royal nursery at Windsor were given their own mixture and one company cashed in on this knowledge by producing "Adkinson's Royal Infant Preservative" with the implication that it was approved by Queen Victoria. Victorians were caring parents and it is probable that the majority were unaware of any negative side effects of laudanum since opium was the basis of most medications prescribed for adults by doctors.

HOUSEHOLD FRESHENERS AND FUMIGANTS

Herbs played a significant role in making the home comfortable and clean. They sweetened the smell of the room, and repelled or killed vermin and insects. Houses and castles in Europe, especially in northern Europe, tended to be damp while the poorer farmers shared space in their homes with pigs, sheep and poultry. Sanitation was rudimentary and cleanliness was not a major consideration. If food fell on the floor it was not swept away; instead another layer of rushes was placed over it. Rotting food, the mouldy smell of dampness, and innumerable species of vermin were common household conditions.

The Greeks burned dill as a room freshener. Flowers, saffron and strewing herbs covered the floors in ancient Rome. Chamomile and hyssop were popular strewing herbs as they released their scent when stepped upon. During the Middle Ages rushes and strewing herbs covered the floors of castles and houses. According to folk legend, the Normans planted wallflowers near the windows of castle walls, supposedly to allow their scent to reach the rooms through the open slit windows and counteract the musty smell of dampness. This legend probably arose from the habit of wallflowers of growing wild in the crevices of the rocks which made up the castle walls.

Herbs and flowers were used to sweeten the smell of beds and linen. Wealthy Romans stuffed their mattresses and cushions with plants, preferably rose petals and saffron, and the Emperor Nero slept on a mattress of rose petals. He supposedly was said to complain if one of the petals was bent as he could feel the crease.

Valerian flowers were used in the Middle Ages throughout Europe to sweeten linen and by the 14th century, herbs and roses were placed in the best beds while bunches of freshly gathered herbs and flowers were set in bed-chambers, sitting-rooms and galleries.

Numerous recipes for these sweet-bags and herb bundles have survived. John Parkinson, in his *Paradisi in Sole*, recommended tying up costmary flower sprays with small bundles of lavender and placing them on top of beds and in the linen cupboards. Perfumed bags for linen or clothes drawers and wardrobes were still being made by the woman of the house into the 19th century. A pleasant-scented perfume bag from the American book, *Mackenzie's 5,000 Receipts*, of 1829, consisted of coriander seeds, cinnamon bark, dried rose leaves, lavender flowers and oak shavings. *The Family Receipt Book*, published in the United States in 1819, recommended the combination of rose leaves, powdered cloves and scraped mace as a linen and wardrobe freshener.

Many herbs were used as insect repellents. Their anti-insect and anti-vermin qualities were discovered in ancient Greek and Roman times and the herbs continued to be used into the 20th century. Herbs with distinctive scents such as mint, rosemary, rue, southernwood, thyme, tansy and feverfew were popular repellents and they were hung in the larder and kitchen to ward off flies. Pennyroyal, also known as fleabane, was effective at keeping fleas at bay.

Moths were repelled by using lavender, rosemary, wormwood or southernwood, all of which have strong scents. An 1860 American publication, *Practical Housewife*, recommended as a preventative against moths the combining of one ounce each of cloves, caraway seeds, nutmeg, mace, cinnamon and Tonguin beans and six ounces of Florentine orris-root. The ingredients were to be ground into a powder, put into little bags and placed among the clothes.

Mice appear to have been a major household problem, given the number of solutions for their removal. Mint was used throughout Europe in the Middle Ages to repel rats and mice which supposedly disliked its scent. However, mice were attracted to the scent of anise which was smeared on traps to act as a lure. Valerian was also used to keep rats and mice away and popular belief held that the Pied Piper used valerian to lure the rats from Hamelin.

European women, especially from the 16th century onward, made serious efforts to perfume the rooms in which they lived. This was a reasonable necessity, given the lack of cleanliness when it came to housekeeping. In most countries, with the exception of Holland, people preferred to mask odours with perfumes rather than wash the rooms to remove the dirt and its attendant odour. This was done with little incense burners. The incense contained storax, a fixative to retain scent; calamint, a mint with a peppermint scent; benjamin, a gum used as a preservative; aloes-wood; and the ashes of willow; these were all bound together in alcohol and pressed into little cakes. These cakes were laid on hot coals and they burned slowly, perfuming the air.

In the 17th and 18th centuries in France a popular means of scenting a room was *oiselets de* Chypre. These were little birds made from gum paste, filled with perfumed powder and covered with feathers. They were placed in ornate cages where their scent would hover in the general area. They were also placed in a censer and as the coals of the censer burned down and melted the *oiselet*, the perfume scented the room.

BATHING, COSMETICS, PERFUMES AND TOILETRIES

To bathe or not to bathe has been a subject of much discussion over the centuries. Some cultures considered bathing an important part of personal hygiene while others considered a bath the first step towards a chill and death. In ancient Greece public baths used herb-scented steam, and herbs, according to their significance, were rubbed onto specific body parts of the bathers. Mint, the scent of strength, was rubbed onto the arms while thyme, the symbol of courage and virtue, was rubbed onto a man's breast. In Athens, to say a man smelled of thyme was popular praise.

The Romans continued the practice of bathing in scented water. Lavender was the choice of those who could afford its high prices, and to smell of lavender was a mark of wealth and elegance. Lavender was also a popular scent because it was thought to relieve fatigue and stiff joints. The Emperor Heliogabalus was said to have bathed in saffron-scented water to display his wealth.

Bathing and perfumes had a mixed relationship in ancient cultures. Whereas the Egyptians and the Romans bathed and used perfumes, Middle Eastern peoples such as the Babylonians rarely bathed but instead covered their body odour with perfumes. The Greeks were somewhere in the middle. They did not bathe as often as the Romans but they did so more frequently than the Babylonians.

Perfumes with an oil, fat or wax base were important in hot countries, especially in the Middle East, where they not only masked body odour but were used as early forms of sunscreen to prevent the skin from blistering and to keep it soft after exposure to the sun. Egypt was one of the largest consumers of perfumes, with the possible exception of Rome. Everyone from the pharaoh to the slaves used perfumes and they had a wide choice of scents. The climate of Egypt was ideal for the continual growing of flowers and the Egyptians were also major importers of spices. Among the more popular scents for Egyptian perfumes were almond, cassia, cedar, cinnamon, citron, ginger, gingergrass, heliotrope, mimosa, mint, myrtle, rose, rosemary, sandalwood and myrrh.

The Greeks and the Romans admired the Egyptian skill in perfumery. The Greek writer Theophrastus in his book, *Concerning Odours*, which included an in-depth study on perfumes, recorded three methods of making perfumes. These were combining scented powders, mixing different scented waters, and mixing scented powders in a scented liquid. Theophrastus considered spices important in the business of perfumes which was a departure from the norm since the Greeks had traditionally made perfumes from flowers.

The Greeks did not have the same variety of scents as the Egyptians and the Romans. They preferred gillyflowers, lilies, marjoram, mint, myrtle, roses, saffron, spikenard and thyme. The Greeks also had different perfumes for men and women. Light-scented rose or lily perfume was considered best for men while women could wear the heavier scents such as myrrh and marjoram. Women also used different scents on different parts of their bodies. This is similar in concept to the use of scents by men after bathing. However, for women there appears to be no symbolic significance to the scents. Their favourite combinations were marjoram on the head, palm oil on the face and nipples, mint on the arms and thyme on the knees and neck.

The widespread use of perfumes in Rome began under the Caesars. By the first and second centuries A.D. Roman consumption of perfumes and spices had surpassed reasonable and rational bounds; the use of scent was so great that it began to bring discomfort to the people, causing headaches and respiratory problems both indoors and outdoors. The Romans perfumed everything. Not only did they perfume their bodies and their clothes but they washed the walls of their houses with floral-scented waters and sprinkled their floors with flower petals. This excessive use of perfumes also occurred in public buildings, including theatres, where saffron was sprinkled on the floors. The Romans seemed determined that there should be no bad smells on themselves or on anything they owned.

Roman women wore pomanders made of fresh roses which were crushed, shaped into balls and left to dry. These were worn around the neck as a form of necklace so that the passing of a Roman woman often left a strong scent of roses in her wake. Roman women continued the Greek practice of applying different scents to different parts of the body.

As Europe slid into the Middle Ages the use of perfumes, especially spiced perfumes, went into a decline. Women and men used a mixture of herbs and spices to create pleasing facial washes. Lavender water was reinvented after the collapse of Roman culture, in 12th-century Germany, by the multi-talented Abbess Hildegarde of Bingen. Rosemary was a major ingredient in Hungary water which was much in demand by women in the 14th and 15th centuries. According to legend, the recipe was given to Queen Elizabeth of Hungary by a hermit who said that washing in the water would preserve her beauty until death. Carmelite water was first made by the nuns at the Abbey of St. Juste in the 14th century. Its main ingredient was balm which became an important part of toilette preparations of both men and women in medieval Europe.

The use of perfumes in England and Europe was born out of necessity. With their dislike of bathing and their habit of not washing their clothes, people literally stank of body odour and dirt. The English distrust of bathing is illustrated in a gardening calendar called *Little Dodoen*, which was written by William Ram in 1606. According to him, nobody should wash their head in January and it was definitely not advisable to wash any part of the body in November. February and April were safe months for bathing and June was good if the individual did not "tarry" in the water. In May it was acceptable for a person to wash their face if there was clean, running water available. Clearly, washing was not considered safe or good for a person's health.

Elizabeth I of England was a consummate user of perfumes. She loved syrup of musk, rose water and damask water (a variety of rose water made from damask roses) and had each sprinkled on all her clothes and in every room. The queen's rose water was sprinkled from special bottles called "casting bottles" and Elizabeth's favourite was made of carved agate.

Elizabeth also had a passion for perfumed leatherware, a popular fashion in Europe. When the Earl of Oxford returned from Italy, which was the source of the best perfumed leatherware, he brought the queen a pair of perfumed gloves. She was so pleased that she had her portrait painted wearing them. Elizabeth continued to acquire perfumed gloves and among her other perfumed leatherware were a cloak and a number of pairs of shoes.

The rose pomander necklace, as worn by Roman women, made a comeback although it is unlikely that the Tudor women knew they were using a Roman invention. Little pomanders made of scented flowers and spices were made into necklaces or strung on the ladies' girdles which were their outer belts. English women preferred strong scents such as a combination of musk, civet and rose water which was probably an indication of the extent of the unpleasant odours of the people and their living quarters.

In England the use of perfumes was forbidden during the Commonwealth period from 1653 to 1660. The Puritans encouraged a revival in bathing which is summed up in the 18th-century adage "cleanliness is next to Godliness." Cleanliness was considered a virtue and in order to be clean a person must bathe. For the Puritans, the taking of baths was not a pleasure but was considered part of their Christian duty. With the Restoration and the return of Charles II to England in 1660, French perfumes along with French manners and culture were in vogue.

France has become famous for its perfumes and the two most important events to affect the French perfume industry were the bubonic plague and the Napoleonic wars. In the 14th century Charles V ordered gardens of lavender, hyssop, sage, roses, lilies and violets to be planted at his palace, the Louvre, in Paris and he encouraged the planting of herb gardens in other cities as a means of combating the bubonic plague. The increase in herbs allowed the women to make flower-scented waters which were considered a luxury, since herbs and some flowers were essentials as food and medicine. Napoleon's contribution to the French perfume industry was the capture of new territories in Europe. These areas provided an increased tax base and created additional revenue which provided the money to purchase the more expensive spices needed by the perfume industry.

The French, like other Europeans, turned to perfumes and scented waters as a means of disguising body odours. The French, however, took perfume-making very seriously. Whereas in most countries part of the women's household duties was to make their own perfumes from available ingredients, the French turned the production of perfumes into an art form perfected by professionals.

Of all the kings of France, Louis XIV, who lived from 1638 to 1715, reputedly used the most perfumes, and the preferences of the king immediately became those of his courtiers. Louis had a liking for Florentine iris, an orris-powder perfume, and used it to scent not only himself but objects in his palaces. As a result the Florentine iris became the most popular perfume in France; it was commonly used in sachets which were worn amongst layers of clothes to combat body odour.

Louis was fascinated with the production of perfumes and he even had his perfumer, an artisan named Martial, mix his perfumes in Louis' private chambers where the king could watch. Martial became famous for his perfumes and received many royal favours, including being made valet to the king's brother.

It is hard to imagine the smell of these people, unwashed and filthy, dressed in silks and satins and drenched in heavy perfumes. A popular anecdote emphasizes the state of smell created by years of non-bathing. According to the story, Louis XIV had an argument in public with his mistress, Madame de Montespan. It ended with Madame having the final word: that for all her faults at least she did not smell as bad as he did.

In the end Louis XIV, who had loved perfumes so much, came to hate them. As he aged, he suffered through many illnesses, and perfumes, especially those with heavy scents, made him ill and gave him violent headaches. The only scent that he could tolerate was that of orange water. The courtiers, especially those who came in contact with the aging king, had to refrain from using their more exotic scents, and the perfume industry at the court languished until the king's death.

Lavender water was one of the favourite toilet waters in France in the 16th and 17th centuries. One of the surviving recipes recommended using lavender from Montpellier, which was considered to produce the best lavender, and allowing the perfume to mature for three years until it was at its best. The ingredients to produce three pints of lavender water consisted of a half pound of lavender flowers, two ounces of rosemary flowers, two ounces of wild thyme, three ounces of orange flowers, four ounces of mint or balm and six pints of *eau-de-vie* or spirit of wines.

Napoleon's second wife, the Austrian archduchess Marie Louise, had a lasting effect on the perfume industry. With the defeat of Napoleon at the Battle of Waterloo and his subsequent exile on the island of St. Helena, Marie Louise went to live in Parma, Italy. She noted the flourishing growth of violets in the area and established a small pharmacy at the monastery of San Giovanni Evangelista where the monks, through experimentation, developed the formula for Parma violet water. The business is still flourishing in Parma today.

Napoleon III, the nephew of Napoleon, who lived from 1808 to 1873, was ahead of his time when he decreed that the manufacturers of any floral waters which were to be taken internally or applied to the skin had to list their ingredients on the label on the bottle. The manufacturers of Eau de Cologne and many other floral waters refused to comply as they considered their recipes to be trade secrets. In the end Napoleon III changed the law and made the labelling a requirement only for those floral waters which were to be taken internally as a tonic. With this one move, floral waters became perfumes only and their supposedly medicinal qualities rapidly declined in the mind of the French public.

Unlike their French counterparts, the ladies of Victorian England continued to believe that different scents from floral bathing waters would cure a variety of ailments, especially "nervous illness," a term used to describe a large number of health problems. The most popular floral bathing waters were chamomile, hyssop and lavender, each of which was considered to be a cure for nervous illnesses.

Floral waters could be purchased in perfume shops throughout Europe. In England stores had signs with symbols to indicate what was sold within and the perfume shops tended towards signs with a civet cat. Still, many women made their own floral waters as it was cheaper and provided them with a pleasurable pastime. Recipes for floral waters can be found in household books right to the end of the 19th century.

Parkinson, in his *Paradisi in Sole,* provided a recipe using basil combined with other unspecified sweet-scented herbs for perfumed waters for washing. The British public must have felt that scented water was healthier than ordinary water, and given the state of contamination of water in both the city and the country, especially from sewage, the public was probably correct. To make floral waters, alcohol or boiled water was used as the base. In either method the floral water would have been comparatively free of bacterial contaminants.

The Family Receipt Book offered the following recipe for lavender water which used the distillation method.

Put two pounds of lavender pips into two quarts of water, put them into a cold still, and make a slow fire under it; distil it off very slowly, and put it into a pot till you have distilled all your water; then clean your still well out, put your lavender water into it, and distil it off slowly again; put it into bottles, and cork it well.

The *American Economical Housekeeper* of 1850 provided a more complex household recipe for lavender water. It required a quart of highly rectified spirits of wine, two ounces of the essential oil of lavender, and five drachms of the essence of ambergris (one drachm equalled four grams). These ingredients were put in a bottle and shaken until perfectly blended. Another method of making lavender water, taken from the same book, consisted of putting two pounds of lavender blossoms into a half gallon of water and setting them over a slow fire until the water was boiled off. Another half gallon of water was added and the process repeated. The remaining lavender mixture was then bottled and corked.

Rose water was created in much the same way. The *American Economical Housekeeper* recommended picking the roses when they were in full bloom and removing the leaves. For every quart of water a peck of rose blossoms was added. The combination was put in a still over a slow fire and the water distilled gradually. The water was bottled and left to stand for three days and then corked.

Other recipes relied heavily on spices rather than flowers. The recipe for Eau De Melisse De Carmes, which appeared in *Mackenzie's 5,000 Receipts*, required four ounces of dried balm leaves, the dried peel from two dozen lemons, one ounce each of nutmeg and coriander seeds, four drachms each of cloves, cinnamon and dried angelica roots, and two pounds each of spirit of wine and brandy.

While the majority of people in Europe used perfumes to disguise body odours, and floral waters for washing and as a perfume, there was a soap industry, albeit not a large one. Soap-making began to assert itself as a potential business in the seventh century in Italy, France and Spain, countries which had a regular supply of high quality olive oil and large quantities of plants of the Salsola genus, the ashes of which produced lye. The soap industry did not become established in England, however, until the 12th century. Perfumed soap, which had a lye base, was considered to be a luxury and it was heavily taxed in England and continental Europe. The average person used the leaves of soapwort, a wild species of carnation, which, when crushed and mixed with water, formed a green lather. This soap was used not just for washing the body but also for household linens and clothes. When the English repealed the soap tax in 1853, soap fell within the financial means of the majority of people and there was an increased interest in personal hygiene.

Perfumes and cosmetics are associated in the mind of the general public. Perfumes give a woman an alluring scent and cosmetics make her more beautiful and both were a means of attracting a man, especially a husband. Cosmetics which improved the complexion have always been in demand. The desire for perfect, flawless, wrinkle-free skin is not a modern concept. Cleopatra was said to wash only in asses' milk to achieve her perfect complexion. Other women had to resort to less expensive methods.

White skin was a sign of wealth and social status in most European cultures from the ancient Greeks to the 20th century. To have sunburned skin meant that a woman had to work outdoors whereas women in wealthy families could remain indoors, away from the sun. An ointment to cure sunburns and remove wrinkles appeared in the 1657 English publication, *Adam in Eden*, consisting of the leaves of cowslips combined with hog's grease. The author also recommended the distilled water of cowslips to achieve the same results. Cowslips were believed to be under the influence of Venus and this would give the blossoms the ability to increase or restore beauty. Parkinson in his *Paradisi in Sole* recommended cowslip juice to clear up blemishes, remove wrinkles and make the skin "smooth and faire." Parkinson also prescribed sweet marjoram distilled in water as a facial wash.

Even if a woman managed to prevent a sunburn she often developed rough skin from exposure to the weather, especially wind, while a lack of washing did nothing to help encourage healthy skin. To achieve the appearance of a smooth, white complexion many women resorted to the use of a white paint with a lead base.

This was in common use from the times of the ancient Greeks and even then women were being warned of its poisonous effects, although to no avail. Women also traditionally painted their cheeks with ceruse, a red colour with a lead base. White lead paint and ceruse cheek colouring were common into the 19th century.

The use of lead in cosmetics had disastrous results. The white lead leaked poison into the body which caused receding gums, and most women who used lead-based cosmetics lost their teeth. The lead in ceruse pocked the skin, caused baldness, and was often the cause of premature death. Lead paint exacerbated problems of the skin and resulted in a never-ending cycle of applying paint and trying to cure its effects with a variety of remedies.

A fashionable remedy for poor skin in the 16th century was Soliman's Water which was supposed to cure all skin problems. However, its main ingredient was sublimate of mercury which acted as a chemical peel, removing the outer layer of skin and corroding the skin below.

In England cosmetics came into common usage during the reign of Elizabeth I who painted her face to conceal less than beautiful features. Women followed the fashion dictated by the queen and herbals are filled with recipes for skin fresheners, toners and blemish removers.

Freckles are commonly listed under blemishes and they were considered a serious skin disfigurement. One well-known individual to suffer from this skin "deformity" was Lady Jane Grey, who was Queen of England for nine days before being overthrown and beheaded by the supporters of Mary I. Freckles were also used as a generic term for any form of skin blemish.

A wide variety of cures for skin problems was available. One rather unpleasant medication used in 15th-century France to heal deep pitted spots consisted of asparagus roots, wild anise and white lily bulbs, all soaked in milk of asses and goats. The concoction was then aged in warm horse manure and filtered through felt before being spread on the face with pieces of bread.

Violets were thought to possess cosmetic qualities because of their cold and moist properties. An infusion of violets in goats' milk applied to the face was supposed to increase an individual's beauty by curing inflamed and infected acne. An infusion of marigold petals made a good astringent and disinfectant for oily skin. It was also used to lighten the colour of a woman's hair; the idea that men prefer blondes can be be traced back to the ancient Romans.

In the Middle Ages vervain was a popular remedy for acne. Vervain was wrapped in a cloth and the unlucky individual with acne pimples stood outside at night waiting for a shooting star to pass. Once this occurred the cloth would be rubbed over the pimples and the acne was supposed to disappear. A later variation was developed by Nicholas Culpeper in his 1653 *Herbal*. His treatment is easier, requiring the individual to mix the bruised leaves or juice of vervain with vinegar and apply it to the face. It also had the added attraction of removing dandruff if used as a shampoo.

Smallpox was a common illness and many people who survived the disease had to deal with the problem of a pitted complexion. Parkinson, in his herbal the *Theatrum Botanicum* of 1640, suggested an ointment made from lupins mixed with the gall of a goat and lemon juice. It would supposedly make the person "look more amiable."

Culpeper's 1653 herbal shows the concern that women had for their complexions. Among his numerous cures for freckles, blemishes and other skin disfigurements there were infusions or ointments made from broom flowers, centaury, cowslips, elecampane, feverfew and lovage.

The general attitude towards cosmetics, in England, changed during the Victorian period when Christian morality became a strong social force. The Christian church had always maintained that the use of cosmetics was morally wrong but it was not until the 19th century that fashion followed the dictates of the church and cosmetics were seen as a sign of self-indulgence and vanity.

The complexions of Victorian women were just as bad as their predecessors although the absence of lead-based paint was an improvement in one area of their health. Women wore no make-up and left their faces exposed to the elements which resulted in red, rough, virtuous cheeks. This rejection of cosmetics, even as a screen against sun, wind and cold, combined with a stodgy diet, left women with spotted and sallow complexions and they resorted to floral waters such as lemon verbena, sweet basil or yarrow leaves to help improve the condition of their skin. There was little change in the attitude towards cosmetics during the Edwardian period although women were using crushed geranium or poppy petals to colour their lips.

Italian women were highly conscious of their appearance. During the Renaissance Venetian women formed clubs or societies in which they would test new forms of cosmetics. Belladonna or the deadly nightshade was used by Italian women in the 16th century as an ointment to whiten the skin and, in a distilled form, to dilate the pupils of their eyes. *Bella donna* in Italian means beautiful woman but the plant's botanical name, *Atropa belladonna*, refers to the plant's poisonous properties if ingested. Atropos was one of the three Fates who determined the length of a person's life and her role was to cut the thread of life, resulting in death.

Just as a beautiful face was important, people began to appreciate the benefits of clean teeth and fresh breath. Mint was used in the Middle Ages to whiten teeth although it was more effective as a breath freshener while the distilled water of rosemary was used as a mouthwash to sweeten the breath. An Italian scientist of the Renaissance, Giambattista della Porta, developed a toothpaste which included among its ingredients leaves of sage, nettles, rosemary, mallow, and plantain plus brambles, myrtle seeds, rosebuds, sandalwood, coriander and cinnamon. This was boiled in black wine and distilled to form a mouthwash which acted as a toothpaste. Individuals would fill their mouths with the liquid and rub their teeth with linen wrapped around a finger.

There were, however, simpler remedies. *Dr. Salmon's Family Dictionary*, published in the United States in 1710, advised keeping teeth clean by washing the mouth every morning with lemon juice mixed with a little brandy and afterwards rubbing the teeth with a sage leaf. Sage is still listed today as an ingredient in homemade herbal toothpastes. Dr. Salmon also recommended rinsing the mouth, after eating meat, with water mixed with brandy.

While women worried about their complexions, men were concerned over greying hair and receding hairlines. The Romans used the juice of elderberries as a hair dye and it was still being recommended by Culpeper in the 17th century for the same purpose. During the Middle Ages fenugreek juice applied to the head was a popular cure for baldness, although by the 16th century, Gerard recommended rubbing onion juice into the scalp on a sunny day to encourage hair growth. A century later

Culpeper advised the use of either mustard seeds or southern-wood. He believed that mustard seeds, prepared as a poultice and placed on the head, acted to prevent hair loss and the heat generated by the mustard would stimulate hair growth. An infusion of southernwood leaves was supposed to revitalize dull hair, cure dandruff and stop hair loss.

Olive oil and oil of rosemary were popular ingredients in 19th-century American hair restorers. *The Family Receipt Book* promoted hair growth by mixing equal parts of olive oil and spirits of rosemary with a few drops of nutmeg oil. The mixture was to be rubbed into the hair every night and the amount gradually increased until the desired amount of hair growth was achieved. The *Practical Housewife* contained a recipe which used one pound of olive oil, one drachm of oil of origanum, and one and one quarter drachm of oil of rosemary.

MEDICINAL THEORIES

Plants were among the earliest forms of medicine. Archaeologists have found plants in the graves of Neanderthals, which date back to over 60,000 years ago, and they surmise that the plants were placed in the graves to be taken as medicine into the afterlife. Early humans discovered the effects of flowers, herbs and berries through trial and error but although they knew the effects, they could offer no explanation as to how the plants worked.

The healing process was attributed to the gods working through the plants and most of the early healers were also priests or priestesses. This connection between the healing plants and religion or magic is one of the major themes in herbal medicine. It goes back to the beginnings of herbal medicine and was still a belief in the late 19th century when the author of an American book of medicinal remedies stated that all medicinal knowledge came from God and referred to him as the "Great Healer."

The Egyptians prayed to the goddess Isis for relief from illness as she was the supreme goddess of healing and the provider of all of man's knowledge of medicine. Egyptian herbal remedies have survived on papyrus scrolls but they were only a small part of the healing process. Magic and religious ritual were also extremely important and the Egyptian healers, when visiting a patient, carried with them a casket of medicines and a magic rod. As in most ancient cultures they believed that disease and illness were caused by evil spirits or demons. The rod was used to call upon the gods to cast the evil spirits out of the body and the herbal medicines were then used to heal the body.

The same ideas occurred in the Mesopotamian region, home to a number of great civilizations including Sumeria, Babylonia and Assyria. Like the Egyptians they believed that sickness was caused by evil spirits within the body and that many of their gods were physicians who passed on their knowledge to man. Magic and astrology were combined to determine which were the most effective medicinal plants. Numbers, which formed an important part of ancient Mesopotamian astrological beliefs, influenced the choice of plants for medicinal purposes. Seven and nine were very powerful numbers, and plants that incorporated either of these numbers in the form of seven or nine petals or lobes on the leaves were considered to be potent medicine.

Herbals are books which list plants, and often minerals and animals, which have medicinal properties. They describe the plant and what parts are to be used and how. In the early cultures of the Near East, they were not always illustrated but by the time of the Greeks and the Romans, most herbals were illustrated to allow the reader to identify the plants needed for medicinal preparations.

The earliest surviving herbal comes from Assyrian Mesopotamia. This herbal is dated around 600 B.C. and lists over 250 vegetable drugs and 120 mineral drugs. Because of the large number of vegetable drugs it is assumed that herbal medicine among the Assyrians had risen to a high art, and archaeologists speculate that special gardens were planted to grow these plants.

The Greeks took many of their medicinal beliefs from the Egyptians and Mesopotamians. They believed that the first herbalists and physicians were the gods who passed their knowledge on to mankind and the Greeks had their own god of medicine, Aesculapius, the son of Apollo, while Apollo was the patron of medicine. Both these gods also appear in the Roman pantheon.

Important members in the Greek chain of medicine were the rhizotomists or root-gatherers. These men wandered about the countryside gathering herbs and roots which they sold to pharmacists, who prepared them into medicines. The root-gatherers followed complex rituals using prayers and chants as they removed the plants or picked the blossoms.

The Romans further developed the Greek ideas. The most famous of all herbals is the *De Materia Medica* of Dioscorides. He was a Greek physician with the Roman army whose herbal was written in the first century A.D. His book contains first-hand observations supplemented with material from Hippocrates and other Greek physicians. The *De Materia Medica* mentions some 600 plants and it remained the standard reference book for 1,500 years.

Dioscorides recommended that violet leaves, with their cooling quality, be placed on the eyes or the stomach to heal inflammations while a mixture of the violet blossom and water would help control epileptic seizures. However, Dioscorides says almost the same for the aster, prescribing its leaves as a cure for inflammations of the stomach and eyes while the flowers mixed with water would ease the problems of epilepsy. He had some improbable cures such as drinking delphinium seeds in wine to cure scorpion bites, based on the idea that scorpions became faint if they came near a delphinium. Dioscorides also recommended alkanet, a herb whose root produces a red dye, as a cure for venomous snake bites. If a person was eating alkanet leaves at the time of the snake bite and could spit some masticated leaves into the mouth of the snake, the snake would die. Dioscorides did, however, fail to mention that the plant could be poisonous if ingested.

The Romans developed the Doctrine of Signatures which was a theory that plants were placed on Earth for a specific medicinal purpose, and to help man identify the use of the plant it was marked or shaped to resemble the part of the anatomy or the disease it was to cure. This became an important idea in the 16th and 17th centuries in Europe and has had a strong influence on herbal medicine.

While the Greeks and Romans had medicinal cures based on non-scientific evidence, there was a growing interest in how the body worked and what was the cause of disease. The Greeks were the first to establish a scientific approach to medicine and Hippocrates, whose life spanned the fourth and fifth centuries B.C., is considered to be the father of modern medicine for his belief that diseases were caused by natural phenomena rather than evil spirits. Roman physicians carried on Hippocrates' work and

Galen, who lived from 131 to 201 A.D., was interested in how the
body worked. In an attempt to acquire a better understanding of
human anatomy, he even dissected a sheep, in the belief that its
anatomy was the same as a person's.

During the Middle Ages herbal medicine was kept alive in
monasteries, where the monks were the physicians, and by
women, who were the traditional family dispensers of medicine.
Folklore, which had begun to decline with the work of Galen and
his followers, returned as an important component of medicine
and many remedies were steeped in legend and magic.

Some herbs required special charms or spells to allow them to
be picked or to increase their potency. Vervain, during the Middle
Ages, was known as the Holy Herb and the Simpler's Joy. Herbs
were known as simples and a simpler was a person who gathered
or worked with herbs. Vervain was held in great esteem as a healer
of wounds and when it was gathered in England it was important
that the person repeat this verse:

> All heal, thou holy herb, Vervain,
> Growing on the ground;
> In the Mount of Calvary
> There wast thou found;
> Thou helpest many a grief,
> And stanchest many a wound.
> In the name of sweet Jesus,
> I take thee from the ground;
> O Lord, effect the same
> That I do now go about.[4]

In another version of the charm for vervain the gatherer
repeated:

> In the name of God, on Mount Olivet
> First I thee found;
> In the name of Jesus
> I pull thee from the ground.[5]

Some herbs were considered more potent than others. Angelica,
which was named after a European monk's dream encounter with

the archangel Raphael, was considered a heal-all because of its divine associations. There is, however, no consensus as to which monk, country or year. Instead, it appears to be a generalized folkloric story found in most European countries.

Sage was another herb with supposedly incredible medicinal powers. The Latin name for sage is *salvia* which means to heal. Sage was first used by the Greeks and Romans as a meat preservative but its reputation grew as a medicinal herb. Around the 10th century, Arab physicians believed that sage extended life to the point of immortality. European contact with physicians in Muslim Spain brought this idea into Christian Europe and the Crusaders, on their return, reinforced the idea that sage was a miraculous healing herb.

Sage leaves and oil had a wide variety of uses although they were most useful in reducing excessive sweating, and lactation in mothers who wished to wean their children. There is some basis for its use as a mild antiseptic and it was used with success as a gargle for sore throats.

At the medical school in Salerno, Italy, which was one of the great schools of medicine in medieval Europe, students were taught to recite: "Why should a man die who grows sage in his garden?" This thought later evolved into the medieval English proverb, "He that would live forever must eat sage in May."

Plants often were considered to have special qualities which would protect them from the root-gatherers and these had to be approached with magical rituals or appropriate precautions. Peonies were one of the plants which were considered dangerous. They were thought to be protected by woodpeckers who would come and peck out the eyes of anyone who tried to dig up the roots. As a precaution the root-gatherers would only dig up peony roots at night.

The mandrake was considered extremely dangerous to unearth because of its resemblance to the human form. However, the root was believed to confer wisdom, luck, fertility and success in love on its possessor and its acquisition was therefore worth the challenge. The root was also used as a narcotic for surgery. The mandrake is the most famous of plants surrounded in magical ritual and it has spawned a series of bizarre legends which date back to the time of the ancient Greeks. According to one ritual, a person had to draw three circles around the mandrake with a sword, and cut it while facing west. If a second cut was needed the person had to dance around the plant first.

The most famous attribute of the mandrake was its ability to shriek so frightfully when pulled from the earth that those who heard the sound went insane and died immediately. Shakespeare alluded to this belief when, in *Romeo and Juliet*, Juliet says,

> And shrieks like mandrakes torn out of the earth,
> That living mortals, hearing them, run mad.[6]

In order to remove a mandrake root and not hear the deadly shriek, a man would plug his ears with pitch and make use of an unfortunate dog. He would tie its tail, though some say its neck, to the plant, walk some distance away, and then entice the dog with food. The dog would tug to get to the food and uproot the mandrake in the process, although the dying screams of the mandrake would kill the dog. Grimm, in his *Teutonic Folklore*, compiled in the 19th century, recorded that this superstition demanded that a black dog without a single white hair in its body be used and that the deed be performed before sunrise on a Friday.

An ancient Anglo-Saxon manuscript declared that it was also necessary to draw a circle round the plant with some form of iron instrument and loosen the soil with an ivory tool. Pliny, the Roman, reported that a person about to gather the mandrake must take every precaution not to have the wind blowing in his or her face. Three circles were traced around the plant with a sword, then the person would turn to face the west and dig up the plant.

It was believed that witches could pull up the plant without danger. In Ben Jonson's *Masque of Queens*, presented in London in 1609, the third witch says,

> I last night lay all alone,
> O' the ground to hear the mandrak grone;
> And pluckt him up, though he grew full low:
> And, as I had done, the cock did crow.[7]

Albertus Magnus, a 13th-century herbalist, believed that the mandrake root increased its power when grown under a gibbet, as the plant was fertilized by the rotting flesh which fell from the criminal's dangling corpse. By the 19th century in Germany, the creation of a more potent mandrake had become even more specific. According to Grimm, only the semen or urine of a thief who had preserved his chastity could produce exceptionally potent mandrakes.

Since the roots of the mandrake roughly resembled men or women, quacks fed on the credulity of people and developed these characteristics by carving the roots to have a greater resemblance to a person and planting grass seeds on the tops of the plants for hair. Even as late as the 19th century in North America these doctored mandrake roots were being sold, although more for magical purposes than medicinal. It was common at this time in the United States for a farming family to have a mandrake which they kept wrapped in a silk cloth in a special box. The mandrake would be brought out before the crops were planted and carried around the field: a continuation of the belief in the plant's strong fertility qualities.

A plant's medicinal potency was determined in a number of ways besides that of observed effectiveness of treatment. Sacredness was an important quality. During the Roman period, plants sacred to a deity were used to cure illnesses related to the area of the body under the control of that deity. Jupiter was the supreme god, and the head was the supreme part of the body. Therefore, pansies, his sacred flowers, were used as a cure for headaches and memory loss. This relates to the idea of remembrance and Ophelia, in *Hamlet*, refers to pansies in her last speech — "and there is pansies, that's for thoughts."[8]

The rose and myrtle, sacred to Venus, were used to cure what the herbals called "female complaints," which was anything relating to female sex organs or childbirth. The black hellebore or Christmas rose was sacred to Pluto and Hecate, the deities of the underworld. It was believed that these deities could inflict enormous suffering on man through disease and madness, so the black hellebore root was used to cure epilepsy, depression, insanity or any illness or condition related to the brain or the nervous system.

Dreams were also responsible for a plant's perceived medicinal value. People believed that the gods spoke to mankind through dreams. According to Roman tradition the rose was used to cure rabies because a mother dreamed that her son, who was a soldier, would be bitten by a rabid dog. In her dream she applied a poultice of rose leaves and rose oil and her son recovered. The next morning she immediately sent a message to her son and coincidentally he had just been bitten by a rabid dog. The army doctor tried the mother's remedy and her son was cured. The story is most likely apocryphal but the Romans, nonetheless, believed that roses could cure rabies.

Charlemagne, Emperor of the Holy Roman Empire, once had a fever which refused to go away and the best doctors in the kingdom could not find a cure. One night Charlemagne had a dream in which God sent an angel to him; the angel told him to go to a field, shoot an arrow into the sky and where the arrow landed Charlemagne would find his cure. The next day he went out to a field and his arrow fell next to a carline thistle, the *Carlina acaulia*. A broth was made from the thistle and Charlemagne's fever disappeared. As a result of this cure people accepted the carline thistle as a cure for fevers. Today, the carline thistle is used by veterinarians to stimulate the appetite of cows.

Sarsaparilla (*Smilax ornata*) is a woody vine whose roots were used to make a tonic. It acquired its credentials as a healing plant because it was an import from North America which made it unusual and therefore potent. Today, sarsaparilla is best known from movies set in the Wild West, in which the cowboy walks into the bar and asks for sarsaparilla. All the "real" men at the bar, who are drinking whisky, laugh at the poor man who supposedly does not believe in drink. This is Hollywood's version of how the West was won. In reality sarsaparilla was considered to be a cure for syphilis and when the cowboy walked into the bar and ordered sarsaparilla he was literally announcing to all in hearing range that he had just been to the local brothel.

In 1665, as the bubonic plague raged through London, a cure was "discovered" by a monk who dreamed of an angel, and people interpreted it to mean that the herb angelica was the cure. Angelica water was developed by the Royal College of Physicians and sold under the name of "The King's Excellent Plague

Recipe." This was a fleeting reminder of the time when people believed that the touch of a king would cure disease.

The bubonic plague, which first appeared in Europe in the 14th century, was the result of increased trade. It was merely a matter of time before contamination from the East, where the bubonic plague originated, arrived in Europe. Rats covered with infected fleas left the ships and ran through the ports, and the disease began its unchecked spread throughout Europe. It is ironic that the European demand for luxury goods was responsible for so much misery.

Flea bites were not associated with the outbreak of the plague. People thought the plague was caused by evil forces in the air and, therefore, pleasant scents would provide some degree of protection. In London in 1664 and 1665, fires were lit in the streets and strong-smelling tars and resins were burned. Hand-held pomanders were highly regarded as protective devices, the most popular being an orange stuck with cloves. A more complex version consisted of an orange with its insides scooped out, and filled with vinegar and a combination of herbs and spices.

Rooms were perfumed to prevent the plague from entering the house. A common perfume was a mixture of dried rosemary, juniper, bay leaves and/or frankincense burned in a chafing dish. Rose water and vinegar were frequently sprinkled over the floor as additional protection.

If a person became ill with the plague a physician would make a house call but he wore a special costume as a form of protection against contamination. It consisted of a leather gown, gloves and a mask. The mask had glass eye holes and a long beak covering the nose which was filled with spices or aromatic herbs to mask the odours and filter out the "evil" air.

Sponges soaked with extracts of cinnamon and cloves were placed beneath the nose of the patient, and saffron, juniper wine, and garlic soup were the prescribed medicines. The rooms in the house which contained an infected person were fumigated with the smoke of burning sage leaves. Should anyone want to visit the sick they were advised, in addition to carrying their orange pomander, to suck on cinnamon, a clove or a piece of mastic (which is a tree resin).

The idea that evil in the air was the cause of disease carried over into the courthouses of Britain. From the Middles Ages into the

19th century it was a common practice for judges to carry a small nosegay of herbs, particularly rosemary and rue, when they entered the courtroom. Prisoners regularly contracted a form of jailhouse fever which was contagious. The nosegay was held by the judge, underneath his nose, to prevent the evil airs which carried the fever from causing infection.

One of the more extraordinary theories of herbal medicine was developed by Paracelsus, a Swiss physician who lived from 1493 to 1541, and whose full name was Philippus Aureolus Theophrastus Bombastus Paracelsus von Hohenheim. He combined a high level of knowledge with skill in scientific areas but he managed to lose the respect of the scientific and medical community through his beliefs in superstitious practices which had fallen out of favour with the majority of physicians.

Some scholars have tried to explain Paracelsus' eccentricities by suggesting that the 16th century was a time when medicine and magic were still intermingled and that there was no clear dividing line between the two. This may have been true to a certain degree but Paracelsus seems to have departed from the acceptable form of medicine.

He became deeply interested in theology and philosophy which he tried to apply to medicine by divining the secret virtues of each herb. His medicinal approach was along the lines of the Doctrine of Signatures of the Romans although it has been referred to as the Doctrine of Sympathetic Resemblances.

Paracelsus believed that God had provided mankind with all the plants necessary to cure illness but it was up to man to discover each plant's healing qualities. The medicinal properties of a plant would be revealed through its shape, colour or scent. He exhorted physicians to look within themselves to find the spiritual insight necessary to recognize the energies given off by these medicinal plants and to discover for themselves the healing nature of each plant. In order to achieve this spiritual state the physician should sit, quiet and relaxed, in a meadow and, in a state of meditative prayer, wait for divine guidance to lead him to the plants he required.

In spite of Paracelsus' emphasis on spiritual guidance to discover the healing properties of plants, the concept of the Doctrine of Signatures was very simple. The leaves of the cyclamen were considered a cure for earaches as they resembled the shape of a human ear. Canterbury bells were used to treat bronchitis because the corolla of the blossom looked like the throat, while wood sorrel was used for heart ailments due to its heart-shaped leaves.

Colour was an important indicator. Yellow flowers were thought to represent the yellow bile in the liver. Yellow broom was considered a cure for jaundice while dandelions and saffron were a cure for any liver disorder. Hepatica was also used to treat liver ailments since its leaves take on a liver-like colour when they are dried at the end of the growing season. Following the same reasoning, red flowers were considered a cure for bleeding cuts and wounds.

According to the Doctrine of Signatures, hollow-stemmed plants were beneficial for respiratory problems and angelica was a popular treatment in this category. Tarragon was used to cure snake bites because its winding roots resembled a slithering snake. Later, tarragon was used in the Doctrine of Signatures as a treatment for rabies although no obvious reason was given. It is possible that believers in the doctrine felt that if tarragon could cure a poisonous snake bite then it could also cure a poisonous dog bite.

Lily-of-the-valley was used to cure heart attacks and this was one of those strange coincidences in which the plant was actually effective due to a natural chemical which affected the heart. According to Paracelsus and those who followed his Doctrine of Signatures, heart attacks were caused when the humours in the brain dropped downward. Since the blossoms of the lily-of-the-valley drooped downward they saw this as a sign that the blossoms could effectively cure a heart attack. However, the lily-of-the-valley did have medicinal value in the chemical digitalis, which is found in the blossoms and is effective in increasing the heart rate.

Apart from the few exceptions like the lily-of-the-valley, which contain chemicals which could actually alleviate the health problem, the majority of plants used by Paracelsus were quackery at best. The Doctrine of Signatures did not die out with Paracelsus. It had its popular adherents and even into the next century William Coles, a British physician who lived from 1626 to 1662, still prescribed medications on the basis of the doctrine.

Another aspect of magic in medicine is found in *The Book of Secrets* attributed to Albert Magnus who died in 1279. Books of secrets dealt with the marvellous and magical properties of animals, herbs, stones and even the human body. Reputable scholars scorned these books but their opinions did not stop people from buying them.

The Book of Secrets, however, was not written by Albert Magnus but is a compilation of writings probably put together by one of his followers. *The Book of Secrets* first appeared in England in 1550 and its last printing was in 1637. By this time it was not intended to be taken seriously and in the 1617 edition the preface suggests that the book be read for entertainment and enjoyment. However, this does not mean that many of its readers were not serious about its recipes for miracles.

The section on herbs appears to be written by two different authors. The first section deals with the magical properties of 16 herbs and the second discusses the magical and medicinal properties of seven herbs. The herbs from the first section are the marigold, nettle, wild teasel, celandine, periwinkle, penny-royal, hound's-tongue, henbane, lily, mistletoe, centaury, sage, vervain, smallage, rose and snake's-grass. In the second section the plants are the daffodil, *Polygonum aviculare*, (a herb of the knotweed genus), chickweed, plantain, cinquefoil, henbane and vervain.

Of all the herbs listed in the first section only the celandine served any supposed medicinal purpose. The plant was placed on the head of the patient and if the individual began to sing in a loud voice then he or she would die. However, if the patient began to cry the outcome would be restored health.

Charms created with other herbs were used to recover stolen property, stop dogs from barking, kill unwanted rabbits in vegetable gardens, open locks, and, at their most lethal, cause a person to die. Marigold had marvellous virtues if it was gathered when the sun was in the sign of Leo. If this flower was wrapped in a bay or laurel leaf with the tooth of a wolf added, no one would be able to speak badly of the person who carried the charm. More importantly, if anything was stolen from owners of the charm, all they had to do was lay it under their pillow and they would see the thief and how the theft was committed.

Nettles were part of a charm to catch fish. If a man mixed nettles with the juice of leeks and then poured it over his hand he would be able to reach into the water and pull out fish. Hound's-tongue, when mixed with the heart of a young frog, would cause all the dogs in the village or town to gather together in one place. As a bonus, if a person put the herb under his or her big toe, all the dogs would be unable to bark.

The real damage caused by *The Book of Secrets* comes from the second section on herbs. These herbs were presented as medicinal cures but astrology played an important role in the healing process. This connection between astrology and herbal treatments reduced herbal medicine to the realm of quackery and was in part responsible for the denigration of any legitimate claim herbs might have had as effective cures for illnesses.

The seven herbs in *The Book of Secrets* were associated with the seven known planets plus the sun and moon. Daffodils came under the influence of the planet Saturn and would cure pains in the bladder or return sanity to the mentally ill. The *Polygonum aviculare* was under the influence of the sun and apart from being an aphrodisiac, it also healed problems with the eyes and lungs. Chickweed, which was known as moonwort or moonflower, was good for easing pains in the stomach and spleen, and improving eyesight. Plantain, under the sign of Aries the ram, was good for headaches as Aries is in the house of the planet Mars and this was considered to be the head of the whole world. It was also used as a cure for hemorrhoids.

Cinquefoil was under the influence of Mercury and healed toothaches, sores in the mouth and swine pox. Henbane came under the sign of Jupiter and was used to treat gout. The juice of henbane was also considered good for diseases of the liver because the liver was under the jurisdiction of Jupiter. Vervain was the herb of the planet Venus and was used to heal a wide variety of illnesses ranging from swine pox to genital swellings to hemor-rhoids. All the herbs which were under the influence of the planets had to be gathered from the 23rd day to the 30th day after the full moon in order to be in their most potent state.

Followers of astrological herbalism also believed that each plant was not only governed by, but derived its healing attributes from, the classical gods and goddesses for whom the planets were named. Jupiter and Venus had a good influence on the body while Saturn and Mars were considered evil. The sun and the moon were in the middle and Mercury was good or evil depending upon the circumstances.

Each planet also had control over specific parts of the body. Jupiter was considered a warm and moist planet and the god was a friend to mankind. Plants under the influence of Jupiter healed the liver, lungs and blood, and controlled lung infections, headaches, heartburn and blood diseases. These plants were also under the control of Sagittarius or Pisces and included dandelions and oaks.

The goddess Venus was born from the sea and therefore was cold and moist. Plants under the influence of the planet Venus controlled the sex organs, kidneys and stomach, and determined the course of colds. The astrological signs of Taurus and Libra were under the domain of Venus. Columbines, which were considered to speed childbirth, came under the control of Venus, as did cowslips which were believed to increase or improve beauty.

The sun had a hot and dry influence over the body. It governed the brain, the right eye of men, the left eye of women, the mouth and the ears, and was responsible for curing hot and dry diseases such as fevers. Leo was the astrological sign under the influence of the sun, and plants, especially yellow plants like marigolds, if picked during the astrological period of Leo, had increased medicinal potency, due to the life-giving force of the sun.

The moon was considered cold and moist. It was the opposite of the sun and therefore governed the left eye of men and the right eye of women. Plants under the influence of the moon would cure rheumatism and other similar ailments. Cancer was a moon sign. Poppies, wallflowers and white lilies were under the control of the moon and could be used to heal any illness affected by the moon such as erysipelas, a contagious skin disease, and epilepsy.

In spite of the various dubious practices involving herbal medicine, many plants did provide relief and sometimes a cure. Some herbal remedies worked because people, through trial and error, had actually managed to find a plant which contained a chemical substance that would cure the illness. One treatment which met this criterion was the use of rose oil by the Romans for earaches and sore throats caused by bacterial infection. The medicinal property was not the rose but salt. In the process of making rose oil, large amounts of salt were placed between the layers of rose petals. Rose oil was salty and it was the salt which acted as the anti-bacterial agent and healed the earache or the sore throat.

The most famous accidental herbal cure was the use of the juice from foxgloves and lily-of-the-valley for heart conditions. Both plants contain digitalis, the chemical component of heart medications, which is used to increase the heart beat. The flowers were distilled in wine and drunk as a tonic. Today, large fields of foxgloves are grown in Mexico for the manufacture of digoxin or digitalis for pharmaceutical companies. The other major herbal discovery was the poppy, *Papaver somniferum,* which provides opium and morphine, both very important pain-killers.

Thyme oil was being sold in apothecary shops in the 17th century as an antiseptic under the name oil of origanum. In 1719 a German chemist named Caspar Neuman managed to extract the basic ingredient of oil of thyme which he called "camphor of thyme." In 1853, the French chemist, Lalemand, gave this oil the name "thymol" by which it is still known today. Up until the end of World War I thymol was highly regarded as a disinfectant. There was a major shortage of thymol in Europe and North America during World War I as most of the oil was made in Germany. Chemists scrambled to find other disinfectants, and in hospitals and other areas which require strong disinfectants, thymol has been replaced by more effective synthetic products. However, thymol is still used today in antiseptic mouthwashes such as Listerine.

Meadowsweet is one of those herbs which became important in modern medical history, although traditionally it was used as a strewing herb for floors and as a sweet-scented herb in bridal bouquets. It gained prominence in 1839 when a German chemist discovered the chemical salicin in meadowsweet. Salicin is a powerful pain-killer and anti-inflammatory element and is effective in reducing fevers although in the wrong quantities it has potentially lethal side effects.

Chemists continued to work with salicin and in 1853 German chemists developed an extract from meadowsweet which they called "acetysalicylic acid." The new drug's name was a combination of the "a" from acetyl, the chemical that was added to salicin and "*spirin,*" the Latin name for meadowsweet. Today, meadowsweet is best known as aspirin rather than as a bridal flower.

113

Part Three: MYTHOLOGY, RELIGION AND SUPERSTITION

Early Mythology and Religion

Religion and mythology are entwined in the mind of the average person when he or she thinks of the gods and goddesses of ancient Greece and Rome. Ancient Greece developed religious beliefs which were a radical departure from earlier religions. The Greeks placed mankind in the centre of their universe and created the gods in their own image. They worshipped their gods with offerings of flowers, herbs and spices and with animal sacrifices. The Greek myths were a means of explaining natural phenomena. They were, in essence, an early form of science explained through the lives of the gods.

In both religion and mythology, flowers and spices played an important role. Scent was a means of honouring the gods. The burning of incense and spices sent a sweet-smelling smoke into the air where it would disperse towards the abode of the gods on

Mount Olympus and please them. It was also believed that prayers were carried to the gods on smoke from the burning of special herbs, flowers and spices.

All flowers held a special place in Greek thought. Greece is not blessed with rich, fertile soil and when the wild flowers are in bloom their colourful blossoms stand out on the rocky landscape. The Greeks believed that everything on Earth was linked to the gods in heaven and a beautiful flower was considered to be the direct creation of a god for his own purpose.

Individual flowers and herbs were sacred to specific gods. These plants were often grown at the temples and the worshipper would place wreaths or bouquets of the herb or flower on the temple altar. Temples were also purified and cleansed with herbs and flowers, thyme being most commonly used to purify and perfume the temples in Greece.

The Greek and Roman pantheons of gods were very similar. The Romans by and large took over the Greek gods and Latinized their names. The gods, for the most part retained their same roles and the plants sacred to the Greek gods continued to be sacred to their Roman counterparts.

The aster was sacred to all the gods, and wreaths of the flower were placed on the altars of temples on all festive days. The name aster comes from the Greek word for star and according to mythology the aster was created out of star dust which fell from the heavens as the tears of Virgo.

Zeus/Jupiter as the supreme ruler of the gods had a number of plants sacred to him which reflected his many different roles. The pansy, which seems almost too insignificant for the supreme god, was given as an offering. This is confirmed by the Roman poet Juvenal, in the first century A.D., who wrote: "Here I will entreat my own Jupiter: here will I offer incense to my paternal Lares and scatter pansies of every hue."[1]

Sage was also dedicated to Zeus/Jupiter. The herb symbolized domestic virtue or marital fidelity. It was thought to cure sterility and was considered a preserver as well as a giver of life. These are fitting attributes for the senior god although Zeus/Jupiter as an example of domestic virtue is rather hard to understand, Greek and Roman mythology being filled with stories of his extramarital affairs with beautiful women.

Vervain was a herb sacred to numerous gods. It was dedicated to Zeus and used to clean the altar in his temples before any solemn occasion. Vervain was also sacred to Aphrodite. Priests in early Rome believed vervain was formed from the tears of Juno and called the plant *"Herba sacra."* It was used to decorate the altars and sacrificial animals of these three deities.

The lily was sacred to Juno, the goddess of women and marriage, and it was sometimes called "Juno's rose." According to legend the lily was created through a trick played by Jupiter. Having fathered a son, Hercules, by a mortal, Jupiter wished to confer immortality upon him. While Juno was sleeping, Jupiter placed the child Hercules on her breast to nurse. When he had finished and was being removed from Juno's breast, some of her milk was split. It fell through the sky, forming the Milky Way, while a few of the drops reached Earth to become white lilies. The lily, through its association with Juno, became the symbol of marriage and motherhood.

A cornfield dotted with scarlet poppies was thought to be the creation of the Roman earth goddess Ceres. To allow her crops to grow safely she always planted poppies in the field so that they could be given as gifts to the gods. The poppy was known as the Red Rose of Ceres and during the rites of Ceres her statue was decorated with garlands of barley and poppies.

The poppy had many connotations to the Greeks. Because of its many seeds it was the symbol of fertility and therefore sacred to the Greek earth goddess Demeter, who gave fertility to the earth. The Romans also made the poppy, with its fertility symbolism, sacred to Venus in her role as goddess of the gardens. The narcotic properties from the opium in the poppy made it the symbol of deep sleep. Ovid in the *Fasti* describes night with "her placid brow crowned with poppy." As the symbol of deep sleep it was not difficult to see how the poppy also became the symbol of death. Poison was used for capital punishment in Greece and was administered in the form of hemlock and opium. The most famous Greek to die from this death sentence was Socrates, the fifth-century B.C. philosopher.

Aphrodite/Venus, as the goddess of love, had many sacred herbs and flowers. The rose was sacred to Aphrodite from the time she was worshipped as an Asian fertility goddess right through to her transformation into Venus by the Romans. White roses, symbolic of pure love, were planted around her temples. The pathways to the temple were covered with rose petals and her priestesses wore roses in their hair. The white-blossomed myrtle and the violet were also sacred to Aphrodite. According to the Greeks, when Aphrodite was born from the sea foam she was preceded by nereids carrying garlands of myrtle. Ovid, the Roman poet, contended that myrtle grew on the seashore and when Venus rose from the sea, she used myrtle branches to cover her nakedness. The Greeks also believed that marjoram was created by Aphrodite, whose touch gave the herb its sweet scent.

Apollo, as one of the major gods of Mount Olympus, had a number of sacred plants, which, as in the case of Jupiter, reflected his various duties to mankind. Apollo was the principal god of prophecy and divination, the god of the arts, especially music, and the god of archery. He was the patron of medicine and later became known as the sun god.

The laurel or bay tree was regarded as the emblem of Apollo's powers of protection against evil and his ability to guard mankind's well-being, and crowns of bay leaves were worn by the winners of the Pythian games which were held in his honour. Initially they were a musical contest but later, athletics were added to the competition.

Bay leaves played an important role in the functioning of the Delphic oracle. To utilize Apollo's powers as the god of prophecy and divination, believers travelled to Delphi, where a priestess of Apollo would, through a trance, reveal the words of the god. Her predictions were uttered through teeth clenched on bay leaves. The priestess of Delphi was considered a very powerful oracle and it is thought that she gave her prophecies while in a state of drugged frenzy brought on by the fumes of the datura or thorn apple and other plants inhaled from a burning pit. The datura plant contains stamonium, which is a strong hallucinogen and would be the main source of the prophecies.

Hecate, as the goddess of the underworld and of magic, needed to be propitiated by mankind. The Greeks considered garlic a fitting food for a goddess and it was placed on piles of stones at crossroads as a meal for Hecate. Crossroads were chosen as they played an important role in magical rites and were often the place where robberies took place. Murderers and suicides were often buried at crossroads, giving the places an even more sinister feeling.

The aconite or monkshood, which is a very poisonous plant, was sacred to Hecate. The existence of aconite was the result of the last of the 12 labours of Hercules, in which Hercules had to bring Cerberus, the watchdog of the underworld, to Earth. Cerberus was no ordinary dog. He had three heads and a snake's tail and he could spit poisonous venom.

Hercules was successful in kidnapping Cerberus from Hades and carrying him to Earth. Cerberus, in his anger, was spitting venom and wherever a drop fell an aconite plant sprang up. After performing this task, Hercules returned the dog to Hades. The Roman Emperor Trajan, who reigned from 98 to 117 A.D., banned the growing of aconite, making it an offence punishable by death.

Cinnamon was dedicated to Mercury, the god of thieves and merchants, and Persephone, queen of the underworld, was honoured with parsley. Artemis, goddess of hunting and archery, and the twin sister of Apollo, had the laurel as a sacred plant, plus the herb dittany, which is also known as dictamnus. It is a perennial plant native to the Mediterranean region and has fragrant white or rose-coloured flowers. It is still grown in gardens. Iris, goddess of the rainbow, appropriately had the iris as her sacred flower while violets were dedicated to Orpheus, the son of Apollo. Orpheus was a beautiful musician and it was said that wherever he laid down his lyre, violets would spring up. The chrysanthemum was sacred to Pallas Athena, the Greek goddess who was the patron of war, and of crafts and manual skills. Through its association with Athena, the chrysanthemum supposedly acquired divine qualities and was worn as a crown during magical rituals.

The Greeks and the Romans had many festivals dedicated to the gods and their flowers. The most important floral festival in Greece was the Hyacinthia, a religious festival observed in the state of Sparta to honour the death of Hyacinthus, a Spartan prince. The rituals took place over a three-day period and it was a time of mourning and of restraint. During Hyacinthia people did not wear wreaths of flowers in their hair at meals and they abstained from wheat bread, cakes and singing songs to Apollo who was indirectly responsible for the death of Hyacinthus.

However, in the middle of the festival there was a spectacle with boys and girls marching, playing flutes and lyres, and singing. National songs were sung and ancient dances performed while men rode gaily decorated horses and women paraded in highly ornamented wicker carts. Human sacrifices were also made. The day ended with people entertaining their friends to dinner. Then they returned the next day to the solemn manner in which the festival began.

Floralia was a Roman festival to honour the goddess Flora. Initially, she was the goddess of grains, vines and fruit trees but later, flowers were added to her jurisdiction. She was originally called Chloris but became known in Latin as Flora. She was married to Zephyrus, the god of the west wind, and upon their marriage Zephyrus gave her a garden full of fruit trees. He filled it with beautiful flowers and proclaimed her queen or goddess of flowers. Every day the Hours came to her garden to pick flowers and the three Graces came to make flower garlands and wreaths for their hair.

Flora's cult was initially concerned with good harvests but in recognition of her role as goddess of flowers, the Floralia games were instituted in 173 B.C. and were held annually. The festival took place over six days, from April 28th to May 3rd. The participants covered themselves in garlands of flowers and the tables used in feasting were covered with roses. Floralia was a time of wining, dining, and singing, and no serious business took place during the festival.

Rosalia was another Roman festival revolving around a flower. During its celebration a race was held in which the participants held in their hands a rose which signified the passing of youth and beauty.

In Roman culture, spices were under the sign of Sirius, the Dog Star, whose appearance in the sky marks the moment when the Earth and the sun are in closest proximity. It was considered to be a period when people would exhibit bizarre behaviour resulting from the heat of the sun. The Romans believed that at this time the Earth gave off all its perfumes, and spices that had reached maturity must be gathered. Women were considered to be in danger of abandoning themselves to lasciviousness which was believed to totally overwhelm them at this time and model wives were supposedly changed into shameless whores.

The Adonia, a festival in honour of Adonis, was celebrated at this time. It was a fertility festival related to the life-cycle of vegetation. Women planted miniature gardens in little earthenware pots and placed them on the rooftops where they would be exposed to the extreme heat of the summer sun. In these pots were lettuce, fennel, wheat and barley seeds which would quickly germinate, wither and die. At the end of the eight-day festival the women threw the pots into springs or into the sea.

Greek and Roman mythology attributed the creation of many plants, especially those with exceptional beauty, to the actions of the gods. Plants were often considered to have been semi-divine creatures or mortals who, through contact with the gods, were changed into flowers or herbs. Conflict, unrequited love or death were often the catalysts which resulted in the metamorphosis.

On another level metamorphosis legends were part of the fertility rituals of death and rebirth. These myths emulated the growth and harvesting of crops and reflected the concept of one individual upon death being replaced by the birth of another. Like the individuals who were transformed upon death into another living object, the human race would continue its procreation and crops would follow the annual seasonal cycle.

The rose had two myths to explain its creation, one Greek and the other Roman. In the Greek version Chloris, the goddess of flowers, was walking in the woods one morning when she stumbled across the body of a dead nymph. She decided to give the nymph new life and changed her into a flower which surpassed all others in beauty. Chloris wanted to do something special for the flower so she called on the gods of Mount Olympus to help her. Aphrodite gave the flower beauty while the Three Graces added brilliance, joy and charm. Zephyrus, the west wind and husband of Chloris, blew away the clouds which allowed Apollo to bless the flower with his sun rays and Dionysus, the god of wine, added nectar. When the gods had finished, Chloris gathered dewdrops and crowned the flower, naming it the rose.

The second version of the creation of the rose involved the birth of Aphrodite/Venus. The goddess was born from the foam of the sea and when she walked from the water onto the land a rose bush sprang up where her feet first touched the ground. The gods came and sprinkled the rose bush with nectar and it burst into white flowers.

With the passage of time new stories were created to explain the different attributes of the rose. The first roses were white but red roses were created when the white blossoms were stained with blood. The legends differ, however, on whose blood created the red rose. One version involves the love affair of Venus and the mortal Adonis. Adonis was a handsome youth who loved to hunt and Venus was afraid that one day his love of hunting would lead to his death. Inevitably Venus' fears came true when Adonis was gored by a stag. As he lay dying Venus rushed to his side and in her haste she stepped on a rose bush. Its thorns cut her foot and the blood that fell from the wound turned the white blossoms red.

In a later story Cupid, the son of Venus, annoyed his mother and she beat him with a rose branch. The thorns pricked his skin and his blood created the red roses. As a result of the various myths regarding the creation of white and red roses, each colour took on its own meaning. White roses symbolized innocence and purity while red roses were associated with love and desire.

During the later centuries of the Roman Empire Cupid and the rose became a popular subject with poets. In one poem Cupid was dancing with the gods and upset a cup of nectar. This drink of the gods fell on some roses, which accounted for the beautiful scent of the flowers. In another poem Cupid was smelling a rose and a bee stung him on the lip. To soothe him Venus removed the stingers from a handful of bees. She strung the bees along Cupid's bow and placed the stingers on the stem of a rose where they remained to become thorns.

The best known of flower myths is probably that of the creation of the narcissus. Narcissus, the son of the river god Chephisus and a water nymph, was an extremely handsome young man. Narcissus was loved by many young women but he was too proud to love any of them in return. His excessive pride attracted the attention of Nemesis, the goddess of retribution, and she answered the prayer of one of Narcissus' rejected lovers who had asked that Narcissus fall in love but not gain what he loved.

When he was out hunting Narcissus saw a reflection of himself in a pool of water and immediately fell in love with the face, not realizing that it was his own. The face was always beyond his grasp and finally when he realized that he had fallen in love with himself he died of grief. A flower which was then named narcissus appeared where his body lay.

In ancient Greece people avoided looking at their reflections in water as it was considered an omen of death brought on by water-spirits who lived in the pools and ponds and would capture a person's soul. Without a soul the person would quickly perish. Sir James George Frazier suggested in *The Golden Bough* that this was the probable source of the Narcissus myth.

The Furies, who were female spirits of justice and vengeance, supposedly wore wreaths of narcissus blossoms around their heads. They drove their victims to madness and it was the painfully sweet scent of the narcissus which helped to cause the madness, a reminder that narcissism, a combination of egotism and conceit, would be punished in the end.

The hyacinth became sacred to Apollo, and since Apollo was the god of wisdom, the hyacinth became a symbol of prudence and wisdom. Hyacinthus was the son of the king of Sparta, and Clio, the muse of history. As a handsome young man he was loved by Apollo. One day they agreed to a discus-throwing contest. There are two versions of what happened during the contest. In one, Apollo's discus rebounded off the earth and hit Hyacinthus in the forehead while in the other, Zephyrus, the west wind, through his jealous love of Hyacinthus, blew Apollo's discus off course and it hit Hyacinthus in the head. The result, however, was the same: Hyacinthus died. Apollo, unable to restore him to life, decreed that a flower should be created as a sign of his grief and from Hyacinthus' blood the purple hyacinth flower emerged.

In the ancient world the blood-red anemone became a symbol of sorrow and death, and the Greeks believed that the anemone blossom never opened except when the wind was blowing. The anemone, also, has two myths to explain its creation. In one version Zephyrus, the husband of Chloris, fell in love with a nymph who was an attendant on Chloris and when Chloris realized what had happened she had the nymph banished. As a result of her treatment by Chloris, the nymph pined and died. Zephyrus persuaded Venus to change the dead nymph into a flower which always comes to life in the spring. However, Zephyrus soon lost interest in the nymph-*cum*-flower and abandoned her to his brother Boreas, the north wind. Unable to gain her love Boreas pulled her blossoms open and caused her to fade immediately. This gave the anemone its name "wind flower." The second myth goes back to the story of Venus and Adonis. After the death of Adonis, Venus sprinkled his blood with nectar and the anemone appeared.

Crocus was a young man who loved the nymph Smilax but she rejected him and he died of a broken heart. At the place of his death appeared a flower which was named after him. As a result of this association with love the Romans used the crocus as a tonic for the heart and in a love potion.

The marigold came into existence as the result of jealousy. Four nymphs who were attendants on Artemis/Diana, the virgin goddess of the hunt, fell in love with Apollo, the twin brother of Diana. The nymphs became jealous of each other in their efforts to attract the attention of Apollo and they quarrelled incessantly. This displeased Diana who turned them into gold-coloured flowers. It is from this myth that yellow became associated with jealousy.

> *How Marigolds Came Yellow*
> Jealous girles these sometimes were,
> While they liv'd, or lasted here:
> Turn'd to flowers, still they be
> Yellow, markt for jealousie.[2]

In the ancient world the orchid symbolized lust and fertility and its roots were considered a potent aphrodisiac. Orchis was a satyr, a man with goat legs, whose duty was to preside at feasts held in honour of Priapus, the god of fertility and of the gardens. During one feast night Orchis became drunk and tried to rape one of the priestesses of Bacchus, the god of wine. This incensed the Bacchanals, the frenzied female followers of Bacchus, and they tore Orchis to pieces. The father of Orchis pleaded with the gods to bring his son back to life and they transformed his corpse into an orchid.

Mint is an aromatic herb which releases its scent the more it is crushed. Menthe or Minthe was a naiad or water nymph who became the mistress of the god Hades. Persephone, his wife, discovered their liaison and in her anger she trampled Menthe into the ground, turning her into mint.

The laurel tree was created as a result of Apollo's love for a virgin nymph named Daphne. After Apollo had mocked the hunting skills of Eros, the god of love, Eros sought to punish him and he fired two shafts from his bow. The arrow with the gold tip pierced the heart of Apollo who became enamoured with Daphne. The arrow with the lead tip, however, pierced the heart of Daphne and she was impervious to any feelings of love. She fled from Apollo and when he was about to catch her, at the bank of a river, she prayed to the river god to save her; she was promptly rooted to the spot and changed into a laurel tree.

In Pharaonic Egypt the most sacred plants were onions, saffron and the lotus. Onions were a favourite food in ancient Egypt and one variety was worshipped as a deity. According to the Roman, Pliny, onions were addressed by the Egyptians as deities when oaths were taken, and in parts of Lower Egypt onions were considered too divine to be eaten.

Saffron was dedicated to the sun and the Egyptians called it "The Blood of Thoth." Thoth was the god of wisdom and magic and was worshipped by the burning of saffron during religious ceremonies. When the Egyptians wanted to make a special sacrifice, they would blend saffron with frankincense and myrrh to produce an incense which they hoped the gods would find exceptionally pleasing.

The lotus, to the Egyptians, was a symbol of rebirth and fertility. According to one legend the lotus rose from the primeval waters and when its blossom opened the sun god, Ra, was seen inside. As a consequence the lotus was used to decorate the columns of his temple in Thebes. In another legend, however, it was Thoth, the god of wisdom and the inventor of speech, who was inside the first lotus to blossom.

The lotus was associated with the sun god because its blossoms opened when the sun rose and closed when it set. It symbolized rebirth because the closed blossom sank to the bottom of the water at night and rose to the top at daylight. The lotus was also associated with the gods Nefertum and Osiris. Nefertum, whose name means lotus, was the god of rebirth. Osiris was the god of the underworld and of vegetation. In the *Book of the Dead of Ani*, Ani and his wife, Tutu, offer lotuses to Osiris.

The lotus was a popular sacred flower in India, China, Tibet and Japan in Hinduism and Buddhism. It is in this context that most people in the West are familiar with the lotus. It brings to mind multi-armed gods and goddesses seated on lotus blossoms or the Buddha seated or standing on the blossom.

In Hinduism the lotus plays a significant role in the birth of the god Brahma, one of the triad of important gods which includes Vishnu and Siva. When the universe is destroyed by the god Siva, Vishnu sleeps on a coiled serpent on the cosmic ocean. During one of these periods of sleep a lotus emerged from the navel of Vishnu and seated on the lotus was Brahma. The lotus is considered to be a manifestation of the goddess Padma, whose name means lotus, the wife of Vishnu. She is also known as Sri or Laksmi, the goddess of prosperity and fortune.

The lotus in Hinduism and Buddhism is a symbol of purity, eternity and prosperity. It represents purity because at night the flower sinks down into the mud of the pond but in the day it rises to the surface and is clean. In some schools of Buddhism, if a believer prays to the Amida Buddha, upon death the person is instantly whisked away on a golden lotus to the Amida Heaven or Paradise. However, the lotus, in religious iconography, has become the seat of almost every god or goddess in the Hindu and Buddhist pantheon and is a common decorative motif in religious and secular buildings in Asia.

THE BIBLE

The Biblical version of the creation of plant life is succinct. On the third day God said: "Let the earth put forth vegetation, plants yielding to seed, and fruit trees bearing fruit in which is their seed, each according to its kind upon the earth."[3]

The first plants that flourished in the Garden of Eden were tended by Adam and Eve. None of the plants growing in Eden are referred to by name in the Book of Genesis except for the tree of life and the tree of knowledge of good and evil. However, with the passage of time, details were added. The forget-me-not is an example of how flowers in Eden were personalized through folk tales. There are at least three legends which explain how the forget-me-not received its name.

According to one story, after God had created the plants He went to each one and gave it a name. One flowering plant, being very small, was overlooked by God and as He was leaving the plant called out, "What about me?" Looking down, God saw the tiny blue blossoms and with a smile said, "I shall call you forget-me-not so that I will always remember you." In another story God had given all the plants their names and admonished them not to forget. One plant, however, had already forgotten its name, and as a permanent reminder God renamed the flower forget-me-not.

A third folk tale involving the forget-me-not took place when Adam and Eve were expelled from the Garden of Eden. All the plants and animals turned away in disapproval except for the forget-me-not which showed them kindness by asking them not to forget the little blue flower. As they left, it called out, "Forget-me-not."

The rose was also personalized in Christianity. According to legend the first roses were white. However, Eve was so taken by the beauty of the roses that she kissed the blossoms and they blushed out of modesty. With these blushing roses, the first red roses came into existence. It was also believed by Hebrew and early Christian scholars that the rose was without thorns before the fall of man. Basil, one of the early Christian fathers, wrote that the rose acquired more thorns as mankind grew more corrupt.

When Adam and Eve were expelled from Eden, God placed angels and a flaming sword at its entrance. As Eve sat crying outside the gates of Eden, it began to snow and an angel tried to comfort her by turning the snowflakes into snowdrops. According to Hebrew legend the lily sprang from the tears of Eve when she was expelled from Eden.

Herbs and spices were cited in the Old and New Testaments primarily as utilitarian plants while flowers were presented in a symbolic context. One of the earliest references to herbs and spices comes when Joseph was sold by his brothers to spice traders on their way to Egypt. Balm (*Melissa officinalis*), along with gum and myrrh, was among their trade goods. Later, during the famine, Jacob sent his sons to Egypt to buy food and they took presents which included balm, honey, gum, myrrh, pistachio nuts and almonds.

During the time of the ten plagues which the Lord sent to Egypt, the last plague resulted in the feast of Passover. The Israelites in captivity were instructed by Moses and his brother Aaron, on the word of the Lord, to kill and roast a lamb which they were to eat with unleavened bread and bitter herbs. This feast was to be kept throughout the generations. The Seder meal of Passover has followed the original dictates and the Seder plate contains symbolic foods related to the original meal. Parsley is dipped in salt water as a reminder of the tears shed by the Jewish slaves in Egyptian captivity. The Haroseth or Charoset is a mixture of walnuts, cinnamon, apples and wine and represents the mortar used to build the brick buildings for the pharaoh. The Book of Exodus is not specific regarding the bitter herbs which the Jews were required to eat. During the Middle Ages and the Renaissance, dandelion leaves were eaten but horseradish, lettuce and radishes are used in contemporary Seder meals.

The hyssop (*Origanum syriacum*), which is native to the Middle East, not the European hyssop (*Hyssopus officinalis*), was used in purification rituals including the cleansing ceremonies for lepers. If the priest pronounced a man cured of leprosy the man was to bring to the priest two living, clean birds, cedarwood, scarlet cloth and hyssop. One of the birds was killed and the living bird, along with the cedarwood, scarlet cloth and hyssop, was dipped in the dead bird's blood and the blood sprinkled over the healed leper seven times.

Hyssop was also used in the ashes of the burnt sin offering. In this cleansing or purification rite a heifer was slaughtered and burned. The priest took cedarwood, hyssop and scarlet cloth and cast them into the flames. The resulting ashes were used in rituals to purify a person who had become unclean by touching a dead body or a grave. If someone died in a tent then a clean person would take hyssop, dip it in water and sprinkle it on the tent and all its furnishings.

Spices were a valuable commodity. They were important in religious ceremonies and as a sign of wealth and honour. Moses was commanded by God to make an anointing oil of the "finest spices" — liquid myrrh, cinnamon, sugar cane, cassia and olive oil — which was to be used to anoint the tent of meeting, where the Ten Commandments were kept.

Spices were offered to King Solomon as a form of tribute. When the Queen of Sheba came to visit Solomon in Jerusalem around 950 B.C., she came with "a very great retinue, with camels bearing spices, and very much gold, and precious stones." The spices were the greatest gift, for it is recorded that "never again came such an abundance of spices as these which the queen of Sheba gave to King Solomon."[4] Solomon was also sent yearly gifts, including spices, as tribute from the local rulers.

Spices were used as a means of beautification. Esther was taken into the harem of King Ahesu-erus, who reigned over an area from India to Ethiopia. She pleased him and he arranged that she be provided with the appropriate beautification treatment which involved anointing her body with oil of myrrh for six months, and spices and other perfumed ointments for a following six months.[5]

The book of Proverbs shows that spices had erotic sexual overtones. Solomon warned his son of prostitutes who had beds perfumed with spices.

> I have perfumed my bed with myrrh, aloes, and cinnamon.
> Come, let us take our fill of love till morning; let us delight
> ourselves with love.[6]

There are few specific references to flowers in the Bible and when they are mentioned it is often in the context of a metaphor. Job warns that "Man that is born of a woman is of few days, and full of trouble. He comes forth like a flower, and withers; he flees like a shadow and continues not."[7] In the New Testament Jesus preaches to his followers not to be anxious about life and uses the lilies of the field as an example, noting that "they neither toil nor spin" yet "even Solomon in all his glory was not arrayed like one of these."[8]

One of the most contentious verses in the Bible regarding flowers comes from the Song of Songs:

> I am a rose of Sharon,
> a lily of the valleys.[9]

The identification of the two flowers is the subject of heated academic and religious debates between Biblical scholars and botanists. The flowers in the opening verse of chapter two of the Song of Songs have been subject to numerous discussions and their identification varies according to translation.

Roland Murphy in his commentary on the Song of Songs translated the verse as:

I am a flower of Sharon
a lily of the valleys.[10]

while in the most recent translation of the Song of Songs, by
Ariel and Chana Bloch, it is interpreted to be:

I am the rose of Sharon,
the wild lily of the valleys.[11]

Neither botanists nor religious scholars can agree on the two
flowers. H. and A. Moldenke, in their *Plants of the Bible*,
commented that "anyone delving even superficially into the literature of Bible plants, will be impressed at once by the striking
discrepancies, contraindications, palpable misidentifications, erro-
neous statements and general confusion which exist there."[12]

The "rose of Sharon" is read as the Hebrew word *habasselet* and
it has been translated as rose, tulip, lily, crocus, narcissus,
asphodel or wild flower. The "lily of the valleys" or *sosannah* has
been translated as lily, lotus, hyacinth and narcissus.

Michael Zohary, professor of botany at the Hebrew University in
Jerusalem, in his study *Plants in the Bible* is certain that the Hebrew
shoshan (*shushan*) or *sosannah* is the white madonna lily which
grows in Galilee and on Mount Carmel and was once very
common in the Holy Land. The rose of Sharon presents its
problems and Roland Murphy suggests that it may be an
asphodel, a narcissus or neither. Murphy is more certain about the
identification of the lilies of the valley. He thinks they are water-
lilies, as the word seems to be derived ultimately from the
Egyptian word for the blue lotus or water-lily. The sonorous
phrasing of the "rose of Sharon" and the "lily of the valleys" from
the King James Version, however, remains the usually accepted
Biblical translation while scholars argue the finer points of linguis-
tics and botany.

There is also disagreement among scholars as to the meaning of
the two flowers. Murphy insists that when the woman describes
herself as a flower she is "not laying claim to any extraordinary
beauty."[13] According to him there were so many flowers on the
plain of Sharon that the woman is describing herself as one of
many, which also means she is nothing special. Other scholars also

see the comparison as an admission of modesty. Francis Landry, in his *Paradoxes of Paradise*, however, takes a different point of view. To him the lily is a solitary and fragile flower whose funnel-shaped appearance has female sexual connotations. He considers the lily a metaphor for "the simple and sublime feminine principle, untouched and unguarded."[14]

The Blochs believe that the botanical identity is less important than the symbolic value of the flowers. Both the *habasselet* and the *sosannah* are used in prophetic visions about the restoration and blossoming of Zion to her former glory and they quote as examples Isaiah 35:1-2: "The arid desert shall be glad, the wilderness shall rejoice and blossom like the habasselet" and Hosea 14:5: "I [God] will be as the dew to Israel, he shall blossom as the sosannah." The Blochs contend that the woman, by identifying herself with the blossoming *habasselet* and the *sosannah* of the fertile plain of Sharon, is making a statement on her blossoming beauty and sexuality.

The Song of Songs uses fruit, flowers and spices to suggest sexual awareness. The man describes the woman in botanical terms.

> Your shoots are an orchard of pomegranates
> with all choicest fruits,
> henna with nard,
> nard and saffron, calamus and cinnamon,
> with all trees of frankincense,
> myrrh and aloes,
> with all chief spices . . .

The woman also uses the same metaphors to describe her beloved.

> His cheeks are like beds of spices,
> yielding fragrance.
> His lips are lilies,
> distilling liquid myrrh.

When the man comes to the woman's home at night, she goes to open the door and her hands "dripped with myrrh."

The spices associated with love and sex are nard (spikenard), saffron, cinnamon, frankincense and myrrh which were extremely expensive commodities. The spices convey in the song-poem a sensuous quality, with the connection between exotic fragrance, wealth and sexual attraction.

FLORAL SYMBOLISM

Flowers were used symbolically in religious art and literature of the Middle Ages and the Renaissance. Floral symbolism was derived from many sources although Greek and Roman mythology provided the basis. Flowers that were sacred to the ancient gods became symbolic of Christ while flowers sacred to the goddesses were assigned to the Virgin Mary.

The medicinal properties of plants were another source of symbolism. The geranium was used to cure bouts of melancholy and in religious art it signifies a sad event, often illustrated in connection with the Passion of Christ and the Crucifixion.

The rose and the lily are the two most commonly used flowers in Christianity. The rose is the principal symbol of the Virgin Mary and it was borrowed from the Roman worship of Venus. The Virgin Mary was referred to as a "rose without thorns," a reference to the idea that the thorns on the rose represented the wickedness of mankind whereas Mary was the only human to be exempt from original sin and its consequences.

The Madonna with the white rose symbolized Mary's love for her child while the Madonna with the red rose signified her sorrow at the Crucifixion. A common artistic motif was the "Virgin of the Rose Garden" in which the Virgin Mary, holding the Christ child, was represented seated in a garden surrounded by trellises covered with white and red roses. The red rose was also used as a symbol for Christian martyrs. Red was symbolic of blood, and St. Ambrose, in the fourth century A.D., stated that the thorns of the rose represented the torments of the martyrs.

The second major flower is the white lily or the Madonna lily. It was the sacred flower of motherhood throughout the ancient world and appears in the religious practices of Babylon, Assyria, Greece and Rome. As the sacred flower of Juno, the Roman goddess of motherhood, the lily was an obvious symbol for Mary in her role as the mother of Christ.

In Christianity the while lily was a symbol of purity, chastity and innocence, the attributes of the Virgin Mary. This association made the lily ideal as a symbol of the Annunciation. In art the archangel Gabriel holds a white lily in his hand as he appears to Mary to announce that she is to be the mother of God's son. The lily also became a symbol of Gabriel through this artistic association.

The lily, like many of the flowers in Christian art, has many meanings. As a flower that blooms in the spring it became a symbol of the Resurrection, the event that is celebrated at Easter. The lily is also a symbol of the confessor saints who died a natural death and it represents their purity of spirit.

Almost every known flower and herb had some symbolic meaning to European Christians. There were often many levels of meaning, while the symbolism could also vary from country to country. The iris is a good example of the complexity of religious symbolism. The flower was named after Iris, the divine messenger of Greek and Roman religion. She was also the goddess of the rainbow, and the large bearded irises of Europe were considered to show the colours of the rainbow.

The iris in northern European art was interchangeable with the Madonna lily as a symbol of the Annunciation. Whereas in southern European art only the lily was used, northern European artists were not so restricted and would place either the Madonna lily or the iris in the hand of the archangel Gabriel.

The iris flower, through its association with the goddess Iris, took on deeper theological ideas. In Christianity, the rainbow is a symbol of peace, and as Iris was the goddess of the rainbow, the iris flower symbolized Christ's role as the messenger of God, who would bring peace to Earth.

Irises were shown in different colours to indicate different ideas. A purple iris was used in Annunciation scenes as part of the imagery of Christ the divine messenger and peace-maker. Yellow was equated with gold, a royal colour, and the yellow iris stands as an allusion to Christ being the King of Heaven.

Flowers could be generalized. Massed flowers indicated Paradise or Heaven, for it was believed that all flowers bloomed continually, without regard to seasons, in Heaven. Spring flowers were representative of the Resurrection and Easter, while blue flowers were a generalized symbol of Heaven. This was a reflection of the concept that Heaven was skyward.

The choice of flowers as religious symbols in art was rarely left to the discretion of the artist. Paintings were commissioned either for a church or as a devotional work for an individual, and the religious ideas within the painting would be developed by a member of the clergy who was well versed in the complexities of floral symbolism. Flowers were rarely random background additions to a painting; they were part of a cohesive religious statement.

This conscious choice of flowers can be seen in the Portinari Altarpiece, painted by Hugo van der Goes in 1475 and now in the Uffizi Gallery, Florence. It is a nativity scene and in the foreground of the painting, in front of the Virgin and Child, are two vases and a sheaf of wheat. The vases contain white and purple irises, an amaryllis or day lily, carnations, violets and columbines. The combination of flowers is a statement on the life of Christ; he was born to be crucified for mankind.

The irises are symbolic of the Annunciation of Christ's birth, the white iris commenting on the virginity of Mary and the purple iris alluding to Christ's role as divine messenger. The day lily is another flower used in northern European painting as a symbol of the Annunciation. Carnations are a floral metaphor for motherhood and reflect the event which has just taken place. Violets are symbolic of the humility of both Mary and Jesus. The Holy Ghost is represented in art by a dove, and the columbine, which was thought to resemble four doves, became the symbol of the Holy Ghost. The wheat sheaf represents the bread used in the Eucharist and symbolizes the Last Supper and the Crucifixion. In this combination of flowers the viewer is told of the special announcement of Christ's birth, the role of Mary as a mother, and Christ as a messenger of God and saviour of mankind through his death by crucifixion.

The major attributes of Christ and the events in his life were symbolized through flowers. The lily-of-the-valley, which is one of the first flowers to bloom in the spring, is symbolic of the Incarnation or the conception of Christ. The anemone, buttercup and dandelion are symbolic of his Crucifixion. The anemone acquired its association with death through the Roman legend of Venus and Adonis. Buttercups are known for their poisonous properties while the dandelion was one of the bitter herbs used in Seder during the Feast of Passover which occurred prior to the Crucifixion.

The pansy, which was originally sacred to Jupiter, was transferred to Christ. It is known in France and Italy as the Trinity Herb for the three colours of its blossoms. The pansy also represents the Passion of Christ, the events which led to his Crucifixion. The colour purple represents his blood and the five petals his five wounds.

The Virgin Mary had many flowers associated with her life and her character. The carnation, which symbolized pure love, was often used in paintings of the Madonna and child. Chrysanthemums, which were sacred to Athena, the virgin goddess of Athens, were used as a reference to Mary's virginity, and the white lotus was also adopted by Christianity as a symbol of purity and dedicated to Mary. All white flowers were symbolic of Mary because the colour white symbolized virginity and purity. Marigolds were also a symbol of Mary. The word marigold comes from "Mary's Gold," which was the name the country people in the Middle Ages gave to the yellow flower.

Flowers which represented character could be used for Christ, the Virgin Mary or various saints. Violets were a symbol of humility because they grew close to the earth, while crocuses represented divine wisdom and Christian charity. There is no specific reason for crocuses being associated with wisdom except for the crocus being sacred to the Roman god Jupiter. The yellow colour of the crocus connected the flower with money, and good Christians were expected to be charitable.

Some flowers also had a symbolic meaning for more than one religious figure or concept. Daisies are a spring flower and the majority of flowers which bloom in the spring came to symbolize the Annunciation and the Incarnation of Christ. The daisy was also used as a metaphor for the innocence of Christ, and the blessed souls in Heaven. Periwinkles, due to their blue colouring, became a symbol of Heaven and they were also the flower of Christ, Mary and the angels who reside in Heaven. In European folklore, the cornflower was considered an enemy of snakes and as the devil or Satan was associated with the snake, the cornflower symbolized

Christ who overcame Satan. The cornflower's blue colour also made it a symbol of Heaven and the Ascension of Christ.

Flowers which were dedicated to or associated with specific saints were generally in bloom at or near the time of the celebration of the saint's day. The hypericum or St. John's Wort symbolized St. John the Baptist as the plant is usually in bloom on St. John's Day, June 24th. It was believed that the red sap in its stem and leaves was the blood of the martyred saint. St. John's Day is close to Midsummer's Day, the traditional pre-Christian celebration of the summer solstice. The pagan Norse god, Baldur, represented the sun, and the hypericum was originally dedicated to Baldur. When the Viking tribes were Christianized it was easy to switch the hypericum from Baldur to St. John.

Parsley became the herb of St. Peter. It was first dedicated to Persephone, wife of the god of the underworld and transferred to St. Peter when he became the Christian guide to the souls of the dead.

Flowers were associated with saints through specific events in their lives. St. Dorothy was a Roman woman who was martyred in the fourth century for refusing to marry a non-Christian. On her way to her death a young man mockingly asked her to send him some fruit and roses from the Garden of Paradise. She agreed and as she knelt down and was beheaded, an angel appeared carrying a basket containing three apples and three roses. The young man tasted the apples and was immediately converted to Christianity. St. Dorothy's Day is celebrated on February 6th and her flower is the rose.

St. Elizabeth of Hungary, who lived in the 13th century, was a pious queen who spent large amounts of money on almsgiving, and hospitals for foundlings. When her husband died in the Crusades the throne passed to her brother-in-law who had her banished from the court. She joined a Franciscan convent as a lay person and lived out the remaining few years of her life in extreme austerity. Before her banishment, Elizabeth always gave money and food to the poor. Her hated brother-in-law objected to her acts of charity and one day he intercepted her and asked what was in her basket. She replied, "Roses." Since it was in the middle of winter he did not believe her and insisted she show him the contents. Instead of finding bread, as he expected, the basket was miraculously filled with roses.

Many flowers acquired special characteristics through contact with the Virgin Mary or Christ or through the flower's presence at an important event in the life of Christ. According to one legend lilies were originally yellow until they were touched by the Virgin Mary, whose purity turned them white. Thyme was in the hay and straw bed of Mary and the Christ child when they stayed in the stable in Bethlehem and through this encounter thyme acquired its sweet scent.

Rosemary and lavender both came in contact with the Virgin Mary and Christ during the flight into Egypt. According to legend rosemary will never grow higher than the number of years in Christ's life and once the plant has lived 33 years, it will spread outward rather than up. Its flowers were originally white but they were changed to blue when Mary threw her blue cloak over a rosemary bush during the flight. Rosemary was known as the Rose of Mary and in the Middle Ages it was thought to grow only in the gardens of the righteous.

Lavender is also part of the legends that grew up around the flight into Egypt. People believed that lavender acquired its fresh smell when Mary hung Jesus' clothes on a lavender bush to dry.

The Crucifixion was held responsible for changes in many flowers. Orchids were believed to have grown at the foot of the cross and the spots on the individual orchids were formed by the drops of blood which fell onto the flower from Christ's body. The white jasmine is known as the Star of Divine Hope and was associated with the purity of the Virgin Mary. When Christ was crucified the most beautiful flowers in the world curled up and died. The jasmine, which was at the time a pink flower, closed its petals and quietly bore the pain of the world. The morning after the Crucifixion, the plant was still alive. Its flowers opened but the pink had left forever.

The persicaria (*Polygonum maculatum*) has a dark spot in the centre of every leaf. According to folklore, the spotted persicaria grew beneath the cross and, like the orchid, received its spots from the drops of blood which fell on its leaves from Christ's wounds. Another legend says that the Virgin Mary used its leaves to manufacture a valuable ointment but that on one occasion she sought for it in vain. Finding it afterwards, when the need had passed, she condemned it and gave it the rank of an ordinary weed. This is expressed in an English rhyme:

> She could not find in time of need,
> And so she cursed it for a weed.[15]

In Reverend Hilderic Friend's book, *Flowers and Flowerlore*, published in 1884, he comments that the persicaria is now the only weed that is not useful for something.

Violets were another flower changed by the Crucifixion. It was thought that they were strong and upright until the shadow of the cross fell on some violets on Mount Calvary and ever since then the flowers have bowed their heads in shame.

The crown imperial, which did not become familiar to Europeans until the 17th century, was nonetheless given a religious explanation for the way its flowers hang down below its leaves. According to Renaissance folk legend all the flowers were told to bow their heads when Christ walked by carrying the cross to Calvary. The crown imperial was the only flower to keep its head erect. After the Crucifixion the crown imperial was filled with sorrow and since that day has always held its head down.

Vervain was believed to have been used to dress Christ's wounds when he was removed from the cross. As a result the plant is called "the Herb of the Cross" and it was popularly believed in Europe during the Middle Ages and Renaissance that it would cure many ailments because it had grown on Mount Calvary.

The passion flower refers to the Passion of Christ, the last events in Christ's life which began with his entry into Jerusalem and ended with his Crucifixion. The passion flower is said have all the attributes of the Passion of Christ. It has ten petals which correspond to the ten faithful disciples; exempt are Peter who denied him and Judas who betrayed him. The corona resembles the crown of thorns, the five stamens represent the five wounds Christ received on the cross and the three styles are the three nails which held Christ to the cross.

In some parts of England cowslips are called "the keys to heaven." According to tradition St. Peter heard that some wicked souls were attempting to get into Heaven through the back door and as he hurried to stop them, he dropped the keys to Heaven which fell to Earth. Where they landed cowslips sprang up.

By the 12th century, the Virgin Mary was strongly associated with the rose. Initially the Christian church rejected the rose as it had a long history of being associated with sensuality and for a period of time in the early history of Christian Europe, prostitutes wore the rose as a sign of disgrace. However, it was impossible for the

Christian church to entirely ignore the rose so it underwent a change and became the most important flower in the Garden of Paradise. It was the floral symbol of the Mother of God, and the Virgin Mary lay on a bed of roses upon her death. Although the rose was also the floral symbol of the Crucifixion of Christ it came to be more strongly identified with the Virgin Mary. Instead of being a pagan flower associated with sensual pleasures it was transformed into a flower of spiritual values: purity, chastity and sorrow.

Dante's *Divine Comedy* develops the concept of the spiritual rose to its fullest, presenting in graduated steps the unfolding of all the mystical attributes of the rose in relationship to the Virgin Mary. The rose becomes a symbol of spiritual perfection and everything that Christianity perceives in its spiritual concepts of God, Christ and the Virgin Mary.

The rosary developed out of the prominence given to Mary in popular Catholic faith during the Middle Ages. Although Mary did not have a large role in the New Testament she suddenly was elevated in the eyes of the devout as an intercessor between them and God. The word rosary comes from the Latin *rosarium* or rose garden. Taken to a symbolic level, it is the heavenly rose garden of the Virgin Mary.

The rosary was used in a sequence of prayers to the Virgin Mary and was given official papal sanction by Pope Innocent III in 1216. The first rosaries were made of rose petals crushed into little balls and strung together. These were later replaced by rose hips and finally the "roses" were made of wood or any number of expensive products such as ivory, or crystal.

WITCHES, FAIRIES, LIGHTNING AND OTHER EVILS

Throughout the history of the world people have perceived their environment as inhabited by creatures and forces beyond their control and intent on doing them evil. They believed that witches would cause harm by casting spells or through access to the devil. Europe, from the Middle Ages into the 18th century, was an agricultural society and one of the greatest damages that witches could inflict on a community was the destruction of their crops. Witches were believed to be able to blight grain, cause destructive rains and bring diseases on domestic animals. Within the household the witch's harm was equally great. She, since witches were usually women, could cause impotence in men, failure to conceive in women, miscarriages, stillbirths and the death of young children. A witch was a serious, evil force in everyday life who had to be destroyed for the safety of the community.

Witches were the ideal scapegoat in a society which had little understanding of the workings of nature. Women accused of witchcraft were often on the margins of society. They rarely had a male to support them, being either unmarried or widowed, and they were also usually poor and uneducated.

During the mid-16th century society believed that witches had joined forces with the devil. The Catholic church, rocked by the Reformation, viewed this religious division as a sign of God's displeasure and witches were considered part of a vast army of devil worshippers who had yielded their souls and bodies to Satan. Both Catholics and Protestants feared witches and saw them as part of a large underground movement to destroy Christianity and place the devil in control of the Earth.

Fairies were another problem, especially during the Middle Ages. They were powerful spirits and people felt they had good reason to fear them. Fairies would steal a human baby and leave a fairy changeling in its place. They carried away humans, bewitched them with diseases, and killed their crops and cattle. On a less serious level fairies would clean the house and do other chores at night in return for food and drink left out for them. However, if the food and drink were forgotten the fairies would pinch the person black and blue. There were also stories of fairies living in houses and if the housemaid was slovenly she would be pinched as punishment.

Fairies were associated with witches and in the 16th and 17th centuries many witches confessed to having spent time with the fairies as well as the devil. Popular belief held that fairies were under the control of the devil and in Scotland there was even a law which pronounced them "spretis [sprites] of the devill," which was a serious offence. Fairies were believed responsible for initiating women into witchcraft.

Between the witches and the fairies, medieval people found themselves living in an unsafe world and they required protection from the evil of these creatures. Protection came in many forms, including plants.

Some plants were general in their abilities. Holly, hung over the door of the house, was believed to ward off evil, and in the process, attract good fortune. Gardeners often left a wild holly bush unpruned in the garden to provide protection for the house. The holly had special religious powers as it symbolically represented the crown of thorns worn by Christ at the Crucifixion. Peony seeds and roots were worn as protection against evil spirits. This idea came from the ancient Greeks who believed that the peony flower glowed at night and would drive away evil spirits. It would also protect those who grew it. Agrimony would ward off the devil and it formed part of a potion which, when drunk, would allow a person to recognize witches. Rosemary sprigs were worn to avert the evil eye and they were also placed under the bed to ward off nightmares. Angelica was considered an infallible guard against witches as the plant and any person carrying it were under the protection of the archangels.

Garlic was also considered to be a potent charm against evil. It was found in the tomb of King Tutankhamun with the probable purpose of keeping away evil spirits, but obviously not archaeologists. In European folklore garlic provided powerful protection against vampires and was hung in rooms throughout the house to ward off the evil eye. The smell of garlic was considered the source of its power.

Hyssop, which was used to cleanse churches and holy buildings as far back as the first tent erected by Moses to house the Ten Commandments, was hung inside the house or rubbed on the frames of doors and windows to keep out witches and evil spirits. In Germany the hypericum, or St. John's Wort as it was known in England, was called "*hexenkraut*" or "witches' herb." It was also called "*sol terristris*," in other parts of Europe, for it was believed that the spirits of darkness, such as witches and devils, would disappear in its presence just as they would disappear with the rising of the sun. In England people put it under their pillows to keep away witches.

Dill was called the "magician's herb" and it was used in spells against witches and also hung on doors and windows to prevent the entrance of evil. The couplet of Michael Drayton, the 17th-century English poet,

> There with her Vervain and her Dill,
> That hinderth Witches of their will

reflects the beliefs of the average person in England of the period.

Pimpernel was also good for the prevention of witchcraft. For it to be effective the following verses had to be recited while it was being gathered:

> Herb pimpernel I have thee found
> Growing upon Christ Jesus' ground:
> The same gift the Lord Jesus gave unto thee,
> When He shed his blood upon the tree:
> Arise up, pimpernel, and go with me,
> And God bless me,
> And all that shall wear thee. Amen.[16]

After the pimpernel had been successfully picked, the root would be worn as an amulet around a person's neck or carried in a pocket.

Many of the plants which were used to ward off the evil of witches had one thing in common: they were used in medicine as antidotes to venomous snake bites. Agrimony, St. John's Wort, rosemary, and pimpernel were standard herbal remedies against snake bites. With agrimony, St. John's Wort and pimpernel, tonics were made from their flowers, leaves or seeds steeped in wine while oil made from rosemary was applied externally. They were generally ineffective against poisonous snake bites but agrimony has some degree of antibiotic qualities which may have soothed the inflammation of a non-poisonous bite. The association between snake bites and plants which provided protection from witches goes back to the religious association of the devil or Satan with snakes. As witches were considered to be under the influence of the devil, any plant which would cure a snake bite would, by association, also protect against witchcraft.

Flowers associated with fairies were often different from the flowers which affected witches. Fairy flowers fell into two categories: those that provided protection against fairies and those that belonged to or were used by the fairies. Throughout Europe St. John's Wort was the chief flower for protection against fairies, as people believed that it could heal any illnesses caused by fairies. Together with verbena and ground ivy, it could also protect crops from fairy blight.

In England people believed in seven herbs which, if used correctly, could protect them from being injured by anything natural or unnatural: St. John's Wort, vervain, speedwell, eyebright, mallow, yarrow and self-help. These herbs had to be gathered at noon on a bright sunny day, near the time of the full moon. A four-leaf clover could break fairy spells and give a person the power to see through all the glamour of fairy life. People believed that fairies created spells which caused them to see the fairy world as bright, beautiful and wealthy whereas in reality fairies lived in a world that was dark, filthy and poverty-stricken. Unlike the plants used against witchcraft, there is no common link established among in the plants used for protection against fairies.

Certain flowers had to be avoided because they were believed to be under the power of fairies. Yellow flowers were often associated with the devil and there are many folk tales of children and adults picking primroses and being taken away by the fairies, never to be seen again. Red campion and devil's-bit scabious were also fairy flowers to be avoided and periwinkles were called "sorcerers' violets" in Somerset where the word sorcerer meant fairy. Wild thyme was under the control of fairies and it was considered dangerous to bring it into the house as it would allow evil to enter with it.

Foxgloves were fairy flowers and if they were picked, bad luck would follow the person. In Ireland, however, they believed that the juice of ten foxglove leaves would cure a child of any illness caused by fairies. Since the causes of illness were unknown, any illness could be attributed to fairies. Fairies used broom in their spells and they felt that garden tulips were special. People believed that if they cut tulips in the garden they would suffer bad luck and should they sell the tulips their bad luck would be even worse.

The house was very important in medieval culture. It was the centre of the family, the place where they were protected from the outside elements and dangerous people. The house, therefore, had to be protected against the entry of witches, fairies and evil spirits. Throughout Europe fennel was hung over doors to ward off evil spirits. Fennel paste was also smeared on the udders of cows to prevent their milk from being bewitched and curdled by witches and fairies. Sprays of marjoram and wild thyme were laid by the milk stored in the dairy to prevent it being curdled by thunder.

Thunder and lightning were believed to be caused by the forces of evil. The houseleek (*Sempervivum tectorum*) was planted on the thatched roof of a house or grown in pots beside the house to provide protection against lightning, fire and evil spells. Culpeper, in the 17th century, recommended bay as protection against witches, devils and lightning. This idea was not new as bay was used in ancient Rome to protect against thunder and lightning. The Emperor Tiberius, who reigned from 14 to 37 A.D., was reported to be afraid of thunder and during storms he would put a bay wreath on his head and hide under his bed.

Plants could bestow good or bad luck depending on the circumstances. Parsley was associated with evil and black magic because it was believed to visit the devil in Hell before germinating. In a black-magic ritual parsley was plucked and the victim's name spoken in the belief that the person named would die within 48 hours. A daffodil with its head hanging towards a person meant that they could expect one year of back luck. However, in Wales the person who found the first daffodil bloom of the year would be lucky in acquiring gold and silver in the future. It was also considered good luck in England to tread on the first daisy of the year but if it was uprooted then bad luck would follow instead.

Some flowers could be brought into the house while others would create evil or bad luck if they were inside. Marigolds, because they were thought to be flowers of the sun, could be safely brought into the house while daffodils, because they were once used in Britain as a substitute for sacrifices, were to be left outdoors. Primroses sent mixed messages. To bring a single primrose into the house was bad luck but a bouquet of primroses was acceptable because it caused neither good nor bad luck. Bouquets in general with fewer than 13 flowers had to be protected by adding violets or else it was unlucky to take them into a church or a house.

Snowdrops were considered flowers of death in England. This may have been due to their tendency to grow on the grounds of village churches and in graveyards. In England any flower which grew in a churchyard was considered unlucky. There was a country tradition that snowdrops must not be touched, as the whiteness of their petals resembled a shroud and people did not want to tempt fate. Understandably, snowdrops were unwelcome in hospitals.

Red and white flowers should not be brought together into a home and never to a hospital. The ancient Romans associated red and white flowers with deceased lovers and, though the finer details may have changed, a bouquet of red and white flowers is even today thought to symbolize death. In more modern terms they have been called "blood and bandages" and it is considered very bad luck to bring a bouquet of red and white flowers to a hospital patient.

Part Four: TRADE AND POLITICS

The Quest and the Adventure

Spices have always exuded a sense of the exotic. Today, spices are bought, prepackaged and less than fresh, in supermarkets, but their smell, the "Sabean odours from the spicie shoare of Arabie," still serves as a reminder that they are not from this part of the world. This unique quality of spices is conveyed in the very word "spice," which is derived from the Latin *species*, meaning an item of special value.

Unlike herbs, which grew plentifully in Europe, spices came from overseas. Since their places of origin were initially unknown to Europeans, spices were considered luxuries shrouded in mystery. The first spices that made their way into Europe were from China, southeast Asia and India. Native to China were cassia, ginger, pepper, saffron and turmeric. Southeast Asia, which included Indo-China and the islands of today's Indonesia and Malaysia, produced cassia, cloves, mace, nutmeg, and pepper.

India was the natural home to cinnamon, ginger, pepper, saffron and cardamon while cinnamon was also widely grown in Sri Lanka.

The use of spices predates recorded history. Archaeologists have found caraway and sesame seeds in prehistoric sites in the Near East. The Chinese used cassia, a bark similar in taste to cinnamon, as early as 3000 B.C. One thousand years later there are Pharaonic Egyptian records of cassia and cinnamon, two spices essential to the Egyptian embalming process, being imported from China and southeast Asia. The Ebers Papyrus, which dates from around 1550 B.C., lists over 800 medicines used in Egypt, including cassia, saffron, sesame and cardamom.

Mesopotamia was an important area for the trade in spices during the first millennium B.C. The Babylonian King Merodack-Baladan II, who reigned from 721 to 710 B.C., took a serious interest in horticulture. Records indicate that 64 different species of plants were grown in his royal gardens in the city of Babylon and he wrote a treatise on vegetables in which he discussed the spices cardamon, saffron and turmeric.

Assyria, a formidable and powerful Mesopotamia-based empire which survived from 2000 to 600 B.C., developed a well-organized spice-trading system. The Assyrian kings controlled the operation of the spice trade in their empire and used the profits to purchase luxury goods for the royal court. The exact kinds of spices traded by the Assyrians are not known but they are most likely those listed in a scroll from the royal library in the capital city of Nineveh. The scroll, dated to the seventh century B.C., records sesame, cardamon, turmeric, saffron and myrrh.

Kings quickly realized the phenomenal wealth spices could bring into any royal treasury through both the imposition of taxes on spices moving through their kingdoms and the collection of revenue on the sale of spices within their kingdoms. The Mycenaean kings of the Greek Aegean, like the Assyrians, developed their own trading system. By the 13th century B.C., when King Agamemnon was busy fighting the Trojan War, merchants were importing ginger grass from Syria, cumin from Egypt, sesame from Mesopotamia and Cyperus seed (plant unknown) from Cyprus.

Ancient Greece, after the Mycenaean Age, continued to import spices, although the greatest contribution to the

European spice trade came from Alexander the Great. Alexander began his conquest of Asia in 334 B.C. He took his armies from Greece through Egypt, Syria, Iraq, Iran and across the Hindu Kush Mountains into the Punjab of India. He opened up large areas of the Middle East and part of India by developing trade routes and establishing colonies of Greek merchants throughout his empire. Alexander also founded the city of Alexandria in Egypt which became an important port for international trade. After his death in Babylon in 323 B.C., Alexander's empire broke up into numerous kingdoms and principalities but the trade ties remained.

Following Alexander the Great, Rome emerged as the most powerful military state in southern Europe. The Romans became the greatest importers of spices in the ancient world. Seasonings were enormously important to Roman cooking, especially in the time of the Caesars, and the Roman demand for spices was insatiable. The market of Trajan in Rome, built under the auspices of Emperor Trajan between 109 and 113 A.D., was a vast emporium for spices and other luxury goods. South Indian pepper was the number one spice by volume imported by the Romans, with ginger a close second. Other spices which no well-stocked Roman kitchen would be without included cumin, saffron, Indian spikenard, cinnamon, cardamon, nutmeg and cloves.

The Romans either purchased their spices directly from Egypt, which after 30 B.C. was a Roman province, or traded with the Arab merchants doing business out of North Africa. The majority of these Arab merchants had their home base in the Arabian peninsula. They had a monopoly on the sale of spices and for a long time Europeans thought that all spices grew in Arabia. The only spices to grow in Arabia, however, were myrrh and frankincense which were and still are found in the present-day areas of Yemen and Oman. The Arabs developed a complex system of spice trading which included numerous land and sea routes to bring the spices to Arabia from China and India.

Trade further improved for the Arab merchants with the introduction of the single-humped camel, which occurred around 1000 B.C. Prior to the camel, merchants used donkeys but camels could carry larger loads and required little food and water. The use of camels cut down costs and increased the profit margin.

147

One of the most famous Arab spice traders was the Prophet Muhammad, who lived from 570 to 632 A.D. As a young man he began working for his uncle who was a spice merchant in Mecca. Muhammad's abilities and reputation for honesty brought him to the attention of the widow Khadija, who owned a spice-trading business. They were married and he led camel caravans between Syria and Mecca.

The spice trade was so lucrative for the Arab traders that they went to great lengths to protect their knowledge of the sources of the spices. To prevent the Greek and Roman importers from doing direct business with the spice producers in India and China, the Arabs claimed that all spices came from Africa. As a further deterrent the merchants spread incredible tales of the dangers that awaited anyone who attempted to harvest spices.

These tales were first told by the fifth-century B.C. Greek historian Herodotus in *The Histories*. To harvest cassia, the Arabs would cover themselves in leather, with only their eyes visible. According to them the cassia grew in shallow ponds and on the banks lived "winged creatures, very like bats, with a dreadful squeak and very ready to fight."[1]

Harvesting cinnamon was even more difficult. The Arabs would not say where the cinnamon was grown but huge birds carried the sticks to their nests, situated on sheer cliffs which could not be climbed by men. The Arabs solved the problem by cutting "out the limbs of dead oxen and asses, taking as much of the limbs as possible," and carrying them to where the nests were located. "The birds swoop down and carry off the limbs of the beasts to their nests, and the nests, being unable to bear the weight, break and fall down, and the Arabians approach and collect what they want."[2]

Theophrastus, the third-century B.C. Greek writer, described another version of the problems faced in collecting cinnamon. The cinnamon grew in valleys and was guarded by poisonous snakes. The Arabs would protect their hands and feet to collect the cinnamon and when they had gathered enough they would "divide it into three parts and draw lots for it with the sun; and whatever portion falls to the lot of the sun they leave behind; and they say that, as soon as they leave the spot, they see this take fire."[3] Theophrastus was not taken in by these Arab merchants' tales and informed his readers that they were fables.

These stories were also noted by Pliny in his *Natural History*. His version of the cinnamon harvest closely followed that of Herodotus but Pliny added that if the spice-gatherers' patience wore thin or if there was an immediate need for cinnamon then they would assist the nests to fall by shooting lead-loaded arrows into them. Pliny also reported that cinnamon could only be cut with the permission of the god Jove or Jupiter. The cinnamon-gatherers would sacrifice 44 oxen, goats and rams to obtain the god's permission, which was only good between sunrise and sunset.

The Arab merchants in the cities of Alexandria, Antioch and Tyre also surrounded their spices with frightening tales of sea travel involving monsters which would destroy ships and devour sailors. Since the spices were not native to Arabia or the Middle East the question arises: how did the spices reach these markets before being sent to Europe?

The answer involves a complex variety of overland and sea routes. The oldest overland route is the famous Silk Road to China. This consisted of two main routes with many side routes leading to the great trading cities of Asia, India and the Middle East. Within China goods were transported to Tun-huang in the northwest on the edge of the Takla Makan Desert. According to the second-century B.C. Chinese traveller Zhang Quan, the name Takla Makan in the local dialect literally meant enter and die. At the Takla Makan Desert the route split. One route followed the northern rim of the desert and passed through the cities of Tashkent and Samarkand. The other route passed along the southern rim of the desert and followed the Oxus, now the Amu Darya, River. Both routes had to cross the treacherous, snow-covered Hindu Kush Mountains, the arid plateau of Iran and the Syrian Desert before reaching the ports on the Mediterranean.

Depending on the route and the hazards the merchants had to face (hazards which ran the gamut of robbers, sandstorms and snowstorms, treacherous mountains, deep, fast-flowing rivers and illness) the trip could take years and cover as much as 7,000 kilometres. It is hardly surprising that many lives were lost and the hardships that had to be endured pushed the cost of the spices into the luxury bracket.

The sea route was called the "Spice Route." Merchants purchased spices in China, Malaysia, Thailand, Sri Lanka, the

Spice Islands, and Java. The Spice Islands, now called the Molucca Islands, are a group of small islands to the south of the Philippines and east of Sarawak. The Spice Islands were the only source of nutmeg, which gave them importance far out of proportion to their size until the 18th century when the French and English managed to grow smuggled seeds on the islands of the West Indies and produced an alternative source.

Spices such as cassia, ginger, turmeric, cloves, mace and nutmeg were transported by sea to the ports of Calicut, Broach and Barbaricon on the coast of the Indian subcontinent. At these ports merchants picked up additional spices from India such as cinnamon, ginger, pepper and saffron, and added them to their consignment of Chinese and south Asian spices. The spices were then reloaded onto Indian ships for their journey to the ports in the Middle East.

Marco Polo on his trip to India in the late 13th century described these Indian spice boats. They had a single deck and a space below divided into approximately 60 small cabins which were reserved for the merchants. There were four masts on each boat and the majority were double-planked as a prevention against leaks. The boats were caulked with oakum and the bottom smeared with a preparation of quick-lime and finely cut hemp. The crew varied from 150 to 300 men depending on the size of the boat; the largest could carry up to 6,000 bags of pepper.

The Indian spice boats would travel westward across the Arabian Sea and stop at ports such as Hormuz and Apologos in the Persian Gulf, Salalah, Cana and Muza on the southern coast of the Arabian Peninsula and Jeddah, Leuce Come, and Myos Hormus along the Red Sea. From these ports the spices were loaded onto camel caravans and carried overland to Syria and Egypt.

The extreme length of the trip from China or India to Rome meant that a consignment of goods was never entirely in the hands of one merchant. The merchants traded or sold their goods to others along the routes and the spices, along with other luxury goods such as silk, slowly made their way from the East to Europe.

The first great period in the spice trade between Europe and the Middle East was during the Greek and Roman periods, from the fourth century B.C. to the fifth century A.D. The Romans paid for their spices primarily with gold and silver. During the reign of

Augustus, 27 B.C. to 14 A.D., at least 120 Roman ships sailed from the Red Sea ports to India each year with trade goods, gold and silver. Tiberius, who reigned from 14 to 37 A.D., began to worry that the gold being used to pay for luxury items, including spices, was draining away the riches of the Roman empire.

Pliny the Elder, writing in the following century, recorded an annual drain of 55,000,000 sesterces to India and a further 45,000,000 sesterces to China and Arabia. A rough estimate of the value today is 1,000,000 sesterces equals £50,000. The Roman emperors realized that at that rate of depletion the Roman economy, which was based on gold and silver, would not be able to keep up with the demand for spices and other luxury items. Trajan, in the third century A.D., tried to redress the balance by invading Iran which had major spice-trading cities and controlled overland routes to China. The idea was to remove both the middleman, and the need to pay taxes to a hostile empire.

The Romans introduced pepper, ginger, cumin, saffron, cinnamon, cardamon and cloves into Europe through their system of colonization and the development of extensive overland trading routes with safe, efficient roads. However, most spices were lost to Europe in the early Middle Ages as a result of the collapse of the trading routes and the disintegration of the roads following the fall of the Roman Empire. It was not until the Crusades in the 11th century that spices reappeared in Europe in large quantities. The Crusaders developed a taste for spicy foods in the Middle East and soon cinnamon, saffron, cloves, nutmeg and pepper were being imported into Europe.

The Crusades opened a second major period which historians refer to as the Italian spice trade. The emperor of Byzantium gave the city state of Venice the right to trade on behalf of the Byzantine Empire, the eastern portion of the former Roman Empire. Venetian merchants entered into trade agreements with their Muslim counterparts in North Africa, and Venice became the centre of the European spice trade. The city consequently grew rich on its profits.

Venice was the primary supplier of spices to Europe by the 12th century but by the 15th century Venetian control of the trade had begun to falter. The transportation system, with its constant rerouting of spices, could not keep up with the European demand for spices, and also there was a change in international politics. The Mamluk rulers of Egypt and the Turkish rulers in Asia Minor were not particularly happy doing business with the "infidel." They imposed high tariffs on the merchants and there was always the threat that the caravan routes would be cut off by the use of military force. The cost of spices spiralled upwards. In the end the Venetian monopoly was broken when Portuguese sailors discovered the sea routes to southern Africa, India and China, and began to trade directly for spices.

Spices, because of their value, were a driving force in European history whereas common European herbs played a passive role. The demand for spices forced Europeans to expand their horizons, leading to a period of discovery and colonization. Without this demand there would have been less interest in discovering a sea route to India and China; Christopher Columbus might not have discovered America and explorers such as Martin Frobisher and Henry Hudson would probably not have attempted to find the Northwest Passage through northern Canadian waters to China. Perhaps Europeans would have been content for a longer period of time to remain in Europe, with their spice trade centred around the countries of the Mediterranean.

The Portuguese were the first to make a serious attempt to circumvent the Venetian-Arab monopoly of the spice trade. The first major obstacle to finding a European sea route to the spice lands was to pass the Cape of Bojador on the west coast of Africa, in present-day Western Sahara. Up until the 15th century no European sailor would pass this point as it was believed that there was no land beyond, and the sea currents were so strong that all ships with their crew would be destroyed. Prince Henry of Portugal, however, decided that this was nonsense.

The Portuguese sailors were not easy to convince. Finally, in 1444, five years after Prince Henry first proposed the expedition, Portuguese sailors conquered their fears, rounded the cape and found land a few miles to the south. The captain saw rosemary growing on the sands and brought back a sprig. It has been said that with one sprig of rosemary a whole era of superstition was ended.

The rounding of the Cape of Bojador led to other sailing adventures for the Portuguese. The sailors were encouraged by an edict from Pope Eugenius IV which gave their souls a plenary indulgence or early entry into Heaven should they die on any exploration mission.

Bartolomeu Dias continued the Portuguese discovery of the African coast and in 1488 rounded the Cape of Good Hope. In 1497 Vasco da Gama landed on the Malabar coast in India and announced that he had come for Christians and spices. Religion followed hand in hand with the voyagers and for the Portuguese and later the Spanish, the discovery of spice lands also meant heathen souls to convert and save.

When the Portuguese arrived in India the majority of merchants were Arabs who negotiated the sale of spices and also sailed the ships or "dhows" which took the spices up the west coast of India into the Persian Gulf or to the Red Sea ports. The Indian spice trade was one of peaceful coexistence between the local Hindu population and the Arab and Jewish merchants who had settled in the Indian coastal towns and cities.

Vasco da Gama believed that the Portuguese should take total control of the Indian spice trade and presented a gift of six wash-basins to the Raja of Malabar in exchange for a trade monopoly. Unimpressed, the raja decided to leave the spice trade as it was, in the hands of the Arab traders. Annoyed, da Gama attacked and burned a Muslim pilgrim ship returning from Mecca. This was not an auspicious beginning to the Portuguese presence in India and it set the tone for future contacts.

Two years later the Portuguese were back in Malabar. This time Pedro Alvarez Cabral, complete with a letter from the King of Portugal, demanded that the Raja of Malabar expel all Muslims from his territory. This would have removed the majority of spice merchants and conveniently given the Portuguese an almost total monopoly on the Malabar spice trade. The raja reiterated that the spices of Calicut were available to all merchants no matter what their religion, provided they were willing to pay the going price. Cabral, unhappy with this reply, proceeded to sack the city of Calicut.

It was Afonso d'Albuquerque who started a serious quest for control of the Asian spice markets. In 1502 he arrived in India and after establishing a trading fort at Goa on the west coast, he went on to expand the Portuguese trading empire by acquiring Malacca, a trading city on the Malay Peninsula, the Island of Hormuz and the Spice Islands (Moluccas), all by force. The Portuguese realized the financial importance of the Spice Islands and had settlers on the islands as early as 1512. Albuquerque's conquests effectively destroyed the Arab monopoly of the spice trade.

Spain entered the race for spice lands shortly after the Portuguese. When the Portuguese king turned down the request of Christopher Columbus to seek a route to China, it was the Spanish monarchs, Ferdinand and Isabella, who decided to take the risk. Columbus set sail from the port of Cadiz in 1492 and arrived in the Caribbean the same year. Instead of finding another route to China he had discovered a new continent, and given the Spanish access to the West Indian spices of vanilla, allspice and capsicums.

The papacy entered the colonial arena in 1494 when Pope Alexander VI divided the overseas world between Spain and Portugal. By a papal bull which was finalized in the Treaty of Tordesillas, a north-south line was drawn approximately 1,000 miles west of the Azores. All lands to the west belonged to Spain and all lands to the east to Portugal. Spain received the New World of the Americas and Portugal had control of Africa and the islands to the east of that continent, including the Spice Islands.

This arrangement may have made Spain and Portugal happy but it was not acceptable to the other European economic powers. Protestant England and Holland, and even Catholic France refused to accept the pope's decree. All three countries formed their own trading companies and in their search for new spice-producing areas also acquired overseas colonies.

The earliest trading company was the East India Company of England which was founded in 1600. Its first territorial colonization, as a result of a search for spices, was the island of Pulo Run, which they acquired in 1603, and it was followed shortly afterward by Pulo Ai. These islands, which were given to the English by the natives in return for protection from the Dutch traders, are part of the Banda Islands at the eastern end of the Indonesian archipelago. Pulo Run is two miles by half a mile in size and Pulo Ai is even smaller. Their importance lay in their production of nutmeg and mace. In the early 17th century the mark-up on the price for these two spices, from point of purchase to point of sale, was 32,000%. Their financial importance was recognized by King James I of England who styled himself "King of England,

Scotland, Ireland, France, Pulo Ai and Pulo Run."⁴ The British kept the two Banda islands until 1660 when, under the terms of the Treaty of Breda, they ceded them to Holland in return for New Amsterdam, later New York, in America. When the political and military jostling for control of spice areas was finally settled in the 18th century, the British spice trade was confined mainly to India, Sri Lanka and China.

The Dutch East India Company (Vereenigde-oost-indische Companie) was formed in 1602 and by the end of the century had forced the Portuguese out of the Spice Islands. The Dutch became the primary trading and governing power in the Asian islands, establishing themselves as both strong and ruthless.

In 1760 there was a glut of spices on the European market and prices plummeted. In a successful attempt to create an artificial shortage and inflate prices, the Dutch government officially burned a ten-year supply of nutmeg, mace and cloves which had been stored in Amsterdam warehouses. To guarantee the continued shortage of cloves with its attendant inflated price, the Dutch East India Company, in the same year, destroyed all the clove trees on the Spice Islands except those on the island of Amboyna.

This action had serious repercussions for the native people who planted a clove tree at the birth of a child. According to tradition, as long as the tree lived, the child would prosper, so the destruction of the clove trees caused unnecessary fear and terror among the people, who expected to see their children die.

The Dutch East India Company tried similar methods with nutmeg, destroying all the trees on the Spice Islands except for Amboyna and the Banda Islands, in the mid-18th century. According to local folk history the Dutch forgot to take into account the bowel movements of pigeons. Nutmeg trees were replanted on the other islands from the seeds in their droppings. The birds were supposedly attracted to the mace, the covering of the nutmegs, which explains why the pigeons ate the nutmegs but not the cloves.

The last of the major trading companies to be formed was the Compagnie des Indes or the French East India Company, a comparative latecomer in 1719. The French, however, made up for the delay and soon had ousted Spain from her colonies in the West Indies and was a serious contender in India. The French were also a major factor in the collapse of the Dutch East India Company. They managed to smuggle some clove seeds out of the Spice Islands and successfully grew clove trees on the island of Mauritius off the east coast of Africa; their first harvest took place in 1776. The effects of the French competition combined with a British blockade of their Asian ports forced the Dutch East India Company into bankruptcy in 1799.

What had begun in the 17th century as a rush for spices had, by the end of the 18th century, turned into a fight for control of overseas territories. The European trading companies were no longer interested entirely in commerce. Although it remained their primary concern, the companies were also seriously involved in military operations in what was the beginning of imperial colonization. The English East India Company and the French East India Company made extensive colonial gains while the Dutch government consolidated its control over the Asian territories formerly administered by the Dutch East India Company. In the end, it was England and France, who, with the groundwork laid by their trading companies, fought for colonial control in Asia and the New World.

TRADE AND COMMERCE

The spice trade was always a very lucrative adventure and given the large profits to be made, there was always some form of control of the trade, through either the laws of kings or the laws of the guilds. The business of selling flowers also developed into a lucrative profession but not initially with the enormous profits that were generated by spices.

Egypt was the centre of the spice trade from the second millennium B.C. into the first century A.D. The Romans acquired Egypt's spice trade through conquest and as the Roman demand for spices increased, the government saw an easy means of revenue. The Red Sea ports, where the spice ships landed, were under the control of the Romans and the government levied a 25% tax on all goods entering these ports. Cinnamon, pepper, cassia, myrrh, ginger, cardamon and other spices which arrived from India provided a massive increase in the empire's revenue.

The collapse of the Roman Empire in the fifth century A.D. saw the emergence of two political entities. The western empire, renamed the Holy Roman Empire, retained its capital in Rome. The eastern section was called Byzantium. Byzantium was technically a Christian theocracy, a government under the rule of an emperor who viewed himself as a link between the common man and God. Its capital, Constantinople, was a rival to Rome in the trade of spices. Byzantium, because of its close proximity to the Persian empire, had an advantage through direct contact with the Persians who, as the main traders with the East, imported spices from as far away as China.

The demand for spices and their use in perfumes resulted in an increase in the number of perfume-makers and sellers. The Byzantine government felt compelled to issue numerous rules and regulations in an attempt to impose control on a lucrative and unwieldy business. Under these rules and regulations, each craft was defined and graded in status. Perfume-makers were given a high status, being equal to the candle-makers and silk workers.

The merchants who sold spices and perfumes were allowed to have their market between a portion of the royal palace and the great church of Hagia Sophia. This allotment of space indicates the importance of spices and perfumes in Byzantine life. The merchants were placed between the two most important symbols of the empire: the emperor's palace and the highest ranking church in the empire.

The laws which controlled the sale and trade of perfumes were drawn up during the reign of Leo VI, around 895 A.D., and are found in the *Book of the Eparch*, Eparch being the official title of the Governor of Constantinople. According to the laws it was very important that the goods be of the best quality, and perfumers and spice merchants were warned not to keep any inferior goods in their shops. The book provided a list of what goods were permitted to be sold by the merchants. These were pepper, cinnamon, amber, incense, balsam, sweet-smelling herbs, thapsia wood (a source of yellow dye), spikenard, aloes-wood, musk, myrrh, indigo, mint and capers.

The punishments for anyone who broke the law ranged from unpleasant to painful. A merchant, depending on the extent of his crime, could be shaved, flogged or banished. It was unlawful to hoard spices in the hope of selling them at a later time for a greater profit. Spices, however, presented a problem to the

Byzantine officials who wished to keep everything in its place. Spices could be used both as perfumes and as flavourings in food, so the laws prevented a grocer from selling spices which could be made into perfumes and perfumers from selling spices to anyone they suspected of using them for culinary purposes. The records are sketchy on how the authorities managed to enforce these finer points of the law.

Spices were important in Byzantine church rituals as they formed the basis of incense which was burned at the altars and during mass. The Byzantine traders did a lucrative business with the West in the sale of spices for religious consumption and also with the monasteries for flavouring food and preserving meat.

In the eighth century the Abbey of Corbie in Gaul authorized the purchase of 10,000 pounds of oil, 30 hogsheads, each weighing 63 gallons, of garum (a condiment), 30 pounds of pepper, 150 pounds of cumin, two pounds of cloves, one pound of cinnamon, two pounds of nard (spikenard) and 30 pounds of costum. The nard, costum, cinnamon and cloves were most likely used in the incense-burners and in the anointing oil for the church. The remainder of the goods were for the kitchen.

Apart from the merchants there were enterprising monks and pilgrims who travelled to the Middle East and returned with spices which they hoped to sell at a good profit. The lay monks of the Order of St. Anthony regularly brought spices back to England when they returned from pilgrimages to the Holy Land. Lay monks, who were attached to various monastic orders, often wandered through the countryside selling their spices. Although the lay monks were not as numerous as the spice merchants, they did present a threat to the merchants' profits.

The merchants formed a guild to protect their interests. The Guild of Pepperers, which was formed in England in 1179, dealt with the sale of all spices. The Pepperers were founded "to the honour of God, the Virgin Mary, St. Anthony and All Saints." The guild controlled the quality of spices and a regulation from 1316 listed the many things which a guild member was not permitted to do if he wished to remain in good standing. Among the various illegal or unacceptable actions were mixing new and old spices together so that the quality would be adversely affected, and moistening spices to inflate their weight. Spices had to be sold by the 12-ounce measure, and all the weights of the guild members had to agree. The City of London administered the weights and measures act and would rent weights to spicers to guarantee that each spicer had a correct measure.

Strict laws against the adulteration of spices were imposed in all European countries. In early times white pepper, which is the pepper seed with its outer skin and pulp removed, was preferred to black pepper, which could be easily mixed with ground olive stones. The strictest laws and severest penalties were reserved for the adulteration of saffron in the 14th century.

Saffron was, and still is, the world's most expensive spice, requiring 75,000 blossoms to make one pound of powder. It could easily be mixed with ground marigold petals, which, since the time of the Romans, had been used as a substitute for saffron by those who could not afford its price. Saffron was also used as a drug to strengthen the heart, improve memory, cure ailments of the lungs, ease the side effects of smallpox and measles and cure jaundice, and the authorities viewed any debasement of the spice as a debasement of a medicine which could have serious consequences to the sick. It was important that the buyer know that the saffron being bought was what it claimed to be and that it was pure.

In 1444 a European merchant named Findeker was found guilty of debasing saffron and he, with his saffron, was burned alive. One would have thought the severity of that penalty would have acted as a deterrent. However, in 1456, Hans Kolbele, a merchant in Nuremberg, was buried alive with his impure saffron. Later, the penalty in Germany was reduced to a severe fine rather than death.

Kings have always appreciated the value of spices and used it to their benefit. The Romans taxed spices at their point of entry into the empire and they also took spices in lieu of money for payment of personal taxes. In the Bible, Matthew refers to paying tithes with mint, anise and cumin.

Pepper was first mentioned in England in the Statutes of Ethelred, which date from 978 to 1016, when the Easterlings, who regularly came to London to trade, had to pay a tax of cloth, five pairs of gloves, two barrels of vinegar and ten pounds of pepper at Christmas and Easter.

Pepper became so valuable that each peppercorn was counted individually and used to pay taxes, tolls and rents. This use of pepper as a form of currency was in part due to the shortage of gold and silver coins in the Middle Ages. By the end of the 10th century in England, landlords were charging a rent tax of one pound of pepper a year and this later evolved into the peppercorn rent, by which a token rent of peppercorn was paid.

Spices were also used to pay quitrent. This was a form of tax paid to the king in the early Middle Ages, before the development of a national standing army. It was paid by the lords and vassals in lieu of providing men for feudal service to the monarch. Many of the customs regarding quitrent have continued into the present day. In 1937 King George VI of Great Britain made a tour of the Duchy of Cornwall where he was personally presented with one pound of cumin, the traditional quitrent of the duchy to the monarch.

It is difficult to determine the value of spices in the Middle Ages in terms of today's monetary system. However, their value can be worked out in relation to other aspects of medieval life. In 14th-century England one pound of saffron was roughly equivalent to one horse, one pound of ginger equalled one sheep and two pounds of mace would buy one cow. Two pounds of sugar were equal to one pig or as much as a carpenter earned in ten days of work.

Cloves were an extremely expensive spice in the early Middle Ages in Europe. In 1265 one pound of cloves sold for ten to 12 shillings in England. Since mace was at the same time equal to four shillings a pound or three sheep, one pound of cloves would have been worth the equivalent of six to nine sheep. In 1393 nutmeg in Germany soared in price to equal seven fat oxen for one pound of the spice.

A later anecdote, which involves the sale of nutmegs, comes from the 17th century, when the Dutch were in control of their trade. The Yankees of Connecticut supposedly carved nutmegs out of wood, dipped them in lime and sold them as real nutmegs to the Dutch in New Amsterdam. Whether this story is true or not, it gave Connecticut its nickname, the Nutmeg State, by which it is still known today.

FLOWER MARKETS AND FLOWER SALES

Egypt, Greece, and Rome had strong flower-market economies. The Egyptians, due to their climate which allowed for a wide variety of flowers to be cultivated over a long growing season, not only had a thriving domestic business but also a lucrative export business which was almost entirely with Rome.

The demand for flowers in almost every aspect of Roman life led to the growth of market gardening and the importation of flowers. Flowers that were out of season in Rome could be purchased from Egypt. However, even Egyptian imports proved to be insufficient in the later days of the empire and the Romans had to develop their own systems of forcing flowers into bloom in greenhouse-like conditions. Rome also imported flowers for their variety. The flowers which were native to the Italian peninsula were limited in comparison to what was available from Egypt. As the Roman empire grew the Romans demanded a greater variety of flowers in the markets and Egyptian imports fulfilled this need.

In Rome carnations, roses, violets, gladioli and tuberoses were grown for the cut-flower markets. The flower dealers made these flowers into garlands as well as selling them to other merchants such as the perfume-makers. An individual with a garden near the city could make extra money by planting flowers to be sold to the flower dealers and the suburban area outside the city of Rome was well known for its development of market gardening.

Varro, the second-century B.C. Roman scholar, in his *De Re Rustica*, a treatise on farming, briefly addressed the positive aspects of the Roman desire for flowers. According to him it was profitable for a citizen living near a city to have a home with a large garden as violets and roses were much in demand.

During the early centuries of the Middle Ages when people were struggling to provide themselves with the basics of life, the city flower markets died out. Flowers were used as food and medicine; there was no room in daily life for flowers as decoration. However, by the 13th century the flower gardener was back in business. In general, the men did the gardening and the women were responsible for selling the flowers in the towns. There must have been a large number of flower sellers in the markets since France instituted a guild system to regulate the sale of flowers.

The flower-market system developed faster in Holland than in any other European country. The richness of the reclaimed soil combined with Dutch overseas contacts with Asia, South Africa and the Americas for exotic plants set the stage for rapid market growth.

Flower merchants hired pretty girls to sell flowers from baskets on street corners or at stalls in the markets. It was believed that the young gentlemen would be more likely to buy on impulse at the sight of a pair of lovely eyes and a pretty face. This idea was not new. The ancient Greek flower merchants who hired girls to sell their flowers in the markets insisted that the girls be pretty to catch the attention of the young men.

The flower girls developed their own system of rank. The senior girls sold their flowers inside restaurants and on the café terraces. Their flowers were made up into little bunches for the women and as buttonholes or *boutonnières* for the men. These girls carried their flowers in small baskets which allowed them to move easily between the tables. The girls with lower seniority walked the streets or stood on the corners. These girls sold only one type of flower and they used street cries to attract the attention of customers. Two of the popular flower-seller cries in London were: "Will you buy my sweet lavender?/Three bunches for one penny?" and "Buy my sweet violets,/A penny a bunch."

Flower sellers were from the lower classes but it could be a means of moving up the social ladder. Nell Gwyn, who became a mistress of Charles II of England, was selling oranges in the streets of London when she caught his eye. Many flower sellers married their male employers and lived a comfortable life. The flower girl who was transformed into a lady was the basis of George Bernard Shaw's 1913 play *Pygmalion* which was recreated as the musical "My Fair Lady."

The single most important business transaction which has remained part of general public knowledge regarding flowers is the phenomenon known as tulipmania. Tulipmania, which took place in 17th-century Holland, was one of the greatest investment disasters in history. At first glance the idea of wagering enormous fortunes on how a flower bulb will blossom seems ridiculous but that is probably because today tulips are common flowers. In the 17th century, however, when tulipmania was at its peak the tulip was a rarity.

Tulips are native to the Middle East and parts of the Himalayan region. The emperor of Turkey had a passion for tulips and any European visiting the royal court in Istanbul would have seen his wonderful displays of the flowers. The Middle Eastern tulip made its appearance in Europe in 1554 when the Austrian ambassador to Turkey, Ogier Ghiselin de Busbecq, brought back tulip bulbs and gave a large number to Emperor Charles V's imperial garden, which was under the care of the botanist Clusius. When Clusius left for Holland he took the bulbs with him and they aroused enormous interest.

Tulipmania lasted for a very short period of time, from 1634 to 1637. It worked much like today's commodities stock exchange in which people could become wealthy overnight or be reduced to poverty. The tulip was an ideal flower for speculation because its blossom could suddenly change its colouring. The bulbs which were brought into Holland were cultivated species and among these hybrids were tulips which might, in one year, produce flowers which had patches or stripes of colour. However, the Dutch did not know that this effect, called "breaking," was caused by a virus. They were well aware, though, that if they bought a bulb cheap and it broke when it bloomed, they would make a fortune.

The tulip bulb consists of a group of smaller bulbs called "offsets" which sprout from the main bulb, and when the tulip has bloomed the offsets can be broken off and planted to start another plant. If, when the tulip bloomed, its colour had broken into streaks, the offsets would produce a tulip of the same colouring, and it was the sale of these offsets that would make a man wealthy.

Holland in the 17th century was a prosperous country. It had a large wealthy upper class and a solid middle class, both with money to spend. Trading tulip bulbs began slowly as a means of amusement and rapidly began its roller-coaster ride. For many, tulip-bulb trading became a full-time occupation. It was a form of gambling and it was easy to become addicted, especially when there was money to spare. It only lost its pleasure when the market crashed and people's life savings and livelihoods were wiped out. There was a saying which seemed appropriate to tulipmania: "I invest, he speculates, they gamble."

The price of tulip bulbs reached astronomical heights and it would almost be funny if it were not for the number of people who suffered when the bottom fell out of the market. Tulips were exchanged not only for money but for goods such as food, wine, and clothing. Often, bulbs sold for the equivalent of a year's salary for a merchant family.

A single Victory bulb was traded for two loads of wheat, four loads of rye, four fat oxen, eight fat pigs, 12 fat sheep, two hogsheads of wine, four barrels of beer, two barrels of butter, 1,000 pounds of cheese, one bed, one suit of clothes and one silver drinking cup.

The most famous transaction was for the Semper Augustus bulb which was sold for £2,800, the equivalent of feeding, for one year, the entire crew of the ship that brought it to Amsterdam from the Middle East.

Trade in tulip bulbs was regulated through the tulip mart and it was illegal to deal in tulips outside official channels; that was considered gambling, and gambling in Protestant Holland was illegal. By 1636 the demand for rare tulips had climbed so high that regular markets for their sale were established on the stock exchange in Amsterdam, Rotterdam and other major cities. The trading of bulbs quickly turned to pure speculation and people stopped buying bulbs and traded in paper instead. They signed contracts which promised the delivery of bulbs at a future date and at a fixed price. When the date came, if the price was high a profit was made. If it was lower the person took a loss.

Within three years people began to realize that tulips could not command such high prices forever and panic ensued. The Dutch government issued a decree forbidding speculation in the bulbs but it was too late. The government tried to force people to honour their contracts but they failed and lawsuits were filed. Judges, overwhelmed by the number of lawsuits, refused to try the cases on the grounds that they were gambling debts, not debts of law. Hundreds of people suddenly found themselves the owners of bulbs no one wanted. Many families were reduced to poverty and fortunes were slashed. It took the Dutch economy years to recover from this madness over tulips.

However, the speculation in tulips did not in the long term hurt the Dutch. They capitalized on their ability to grow flowers and became the world's leading supplier of bulbs and cut flowers. The most important flower auction in the world is still held at Aalsmeer, 16 kilometres outside Amsterdam. It was established in 1912 and in 1968 it came under the control of a flower-growers' co-operative. Its official name is Verenigde Bleomenveilingen Aalsmeer but it is better known as the V.B.A. Today it accepts flowers from over 8,000 flower producers around the world.

The Aalsmeer auction house is huge, covering 135 hectares, roughly the size of 55 British soccer fields, making it one of the world's largest commercial buildings. The number of cut flowers auctioned at Aalsmeer is enormous. The auction, which takes place five days a week, starts at 6:30 A.M. and is finished by 10:15 A.M. The flowers are auctioned off by means of a clock whose hands start at the top, the highest price; as they move counterclockwise the price drops until a buyer pushes a button to indicate a purchase.

There are 13 clocks at Aalsmeer and roses, the most popular flower, have two clocks for themselves; one for large-blossomed roses and a second for baby roses. Over 900,000,000 roses are sold annually. Other popular flowers are carnations, irises, lilies, chrysanthemums and tulips. There are over 130,000,000 lilies sold each year while during the spring tulip season over 115 different species, adding up to approximately 216,000 blossoms, are sold per day. Overall, four billion flowers are auctioned annually at Aalsmeer, bringing in over two billion Dutch guilders.

CORONATION CEREMONIES

Plants have been used throughout recorded history as emblems of cities, states and countries. They have been the rallying symbols of kings, politicians and political parties, and through religious associations they have bestowed legitimacy on ruling dynasties.

Coronation ceremonies are the focal point of the proclamation of a ruler and in many cultures, both ancient and modern, one of the most important rituals is the anointing of the ruler. The anointing oil has varied among cultures and with individual rulers but at its most basic level it has consisted of an oil, such as olive or palm, to which aromatic herbs and/or spices have been added.

The use of anointing oil to proclaim kingship in Western culture originated in the kingdoms of Mesopotamia and Pharaonic Egypt. The Assyrian, Babylonian, Egyptian and Persian dynasties all anointed their kings as an indication of the acceptance by their gods of the individual's right to rule. Cyrus, who was king of Persia in the sixth century B.C., was often referred to in official documents as the "Lord's anointed."

European use of anointing oil in the coronation ceremony had its origins in the anointing of the kings of Israel, and it bestowed religious legitimacy upon the ruler. Scholars believe that the Israelites acquired the idea during their Egyptian captivity in the second millennium B.C. Prior to their captivity in Egypt the Israelites did not have a system of kingship. After their exodus, the people urged the prophet Samuel to appoint a king. Saul was chosen and Samuel poured a vial of oil over Saul's head, proclaiming:

> Has not the Lord anointed you to be prince over his people of Israel? And you shall reign over the people of the Lord and you will save them from the hand of their enemies round about. And this shall be the sign to you that the Lord has anointed you to be prince over his heritage.[5]

Samuel also anointed David, who succeeded Saul while David's successor, Solomon, was anointed by Zadok, the priest and Nathan, the prophet. The anointing of the kings by prophets and priests was the indication of divine approval of the ruler. Zadok remains of interest today, as the official coronation anthem of Britain is "Zadok the Priest."

The use of holy anointing oil to confer divine approval was not practised during the pagan Greek and Roman periods. The Romans, during the time of the caesars, had a coronation ceremony but it involved invoking the blessing of the people rather than the gods. The Roman emperor would stand on a military shield and be elevated above the people. Following this ritual a coronet was placed upon the emperor's head.

The return to the use of anointing oil corresponded with the acceptance of Christianity as the main religion of Europe. The Byzantine empire, which lasted from 330 to 1453 A.D., in spite of being a Christian kingdom, continued to use the traditional Roman ceremony. The exact date when anointing entered the Byzantine coronation ceremony is controversial but it was known to be in practice after 1204. The use of holy oil in the coronation service emphasized the emperor's role as protector of the church.

Byzantine emperors considered themselves divinely inspired to rule and were viewed as God's vicars on Earth.

The earliest use of anointing oil in Christian coronation services occurred in seventh-century Spain and spread through the rest of Europe. Pepin, who was the first anointed king of France, had the distinction of being anointed twice; first in 750 A.D. by St. Boniface and again in 755 A.D. by Pope Stephen III. Charlemagne, who was crowned the Holy Roman Emperor in 800 A.D., was anointed by Pope Leo III.

Charlemagne was oiled from head to foot but this was extremely unusual. In the Middle Ages it was traditional for the king to be anointed on the head, breast and arms. This was to symbolize glory, sanctity and strength, attributes expected of a good king.

The oil used in Christian European coronations was the chrism or holy oil which was used in the sacraments such as baptisms, confirmations, consecrations and supreme unction. The chrism had an unguent of oil as its base and the herb balm was mixed into it. Balm was probably used in the belief that it was the Biblical Balm of Gilead. The European balm, however, was *Melissa officinalis* while the Biblical balm could have been either a balsam shrub (*Commiphora gileadensis*), or the storax tree (*Liquidambar orientalis*).

The coronation service used for Elizabeth II of Great Britain descended directly from the service used at the coronation of Edgar which took place in 973 A.D. in the city of Bath. The first coronation ceremony to include the anointment ritual, however, was that of Ethelred II in 978 A.D. The consecration prayer at his coronation ended with "God would anoint thee king with the grace of His Holy Spirit," and then Ethelred was anointed with the sacred chrism oil.

The coronation ceremony of a British monarch, which included the use of holy anointing oil, was viewed as a sacramental act which made loyalty to the crown a Christian obligation. The oil varied in degrees of density; some were more liquid than others depending upon how they were mixed for the coronation. The holy oil was considered so sacred that until the 16th century, the piece of linen used to wipe off excess oil was burned in a special ceremony to prevent the oil from being contaminated. The king's hair, in deference to the sanctity of the holy oil, was covered with a thin cap to absorb any excess oil and after eight days the Abbot of Westminster would remove the cap and ceremonially wash it.

The importance of using properly blessed oil was evident in the 1553 coronation of Mary I, the eldest daughter of Henry VIII. There was sufficient chrism oil in a vial which had been used for the coronation of Edward VI, Henry's son. However, Edward was a Protestant and Mary, who had remained a devout Catholic, was afraid that the oil had lost its potency in the hands of Protestant bishops. She insisted on having freshly consecrated holy oil brought in for her coronation and it was supplied by the Catholic Bishop of Arras, in present-day Belgium.

The first recorded complaint regarding the holy oil came from Elizabeth I who objected to its being greasy and having an unpleasant smell. It was Charles I who decided to have a special anointing oil made for his coronation in 1626. This oil included orange flowers, roses, cinnamon, jasmine, sesame, musk, civet and ambergris and a sufficient quantity was made to last for several coronations. As long as the oil was consecrated by a high-ranking member of the clergy, it was considered holy and therefore acceptable for the religious aspect of the anointing ritual.

Charles' mixture was reproduced many times; the first problem was the result of the longevity of Queen Victoria. When it came time to crown her son, Edward VII, the oil had coagulated and a new batch had to be prepared. This oil was also used in the coronation of George V in 1911.

A new supply was made for the coronation of Edward VIII, which never took place due to his abdication, and was used instead for his brother George VI in 1937. There was sufficient oil left for the coronation of Elizabeth II but when the preparations were being made in 1953, it was discovered that the vial, which had been stored in the Deanery of Westminster Abbey, had been shattered during the bombing of London during World War II.

Under normal circumstances this would not have presented a problem but no one had apparently taken into consideration the possibility that the firm that made the anointing oil would go out of business and the formula would be lost. As in a good detective story, government officials tracked down an elderly employee who had worked at the firm and had kept a few ounces of the oil as a souvenir. The oil was analysed by a chemist who reproduced the original formula of Charles I, and Elizabeth II was anointed with the traditional coronation oil.

In France the special ingredient of the anointing oil was called the "Sainte Ampoule" and it occupied an extremely important position in French coronations from the ninth to the 19th centuries. According to legend the vial that contained the special oil was brought from heaven for the coronation of King Clovis by a white dove which signified the Holy Ghost. The dove gave the vial to the Archbishop St. Remi.

The vial was kept at the Abbey of St. Remi, from which it was removed with solemn ceremonies to the Cathedral of Nôtre Dame de Rheims, where the kings of France were crowned. This vial of holy oil was viewed as a sacred relic and great precautions, which included the holding of noblemen as hostages, were taken to guarantee its safety.

The main ingredient of the Sainte Ampoule was balsam. At the coronation, the Archbishop of Rheims would remove a small portion of the oil with a golden pin, as the oil had congealed over the centuries. This balsam was then mixed with the chrism oil.

During the French Revolution the tomb of St. Remi was broken into and the vial removed. It was displayed in the public square at Rheims on October 6, 1793, where a member of the French ruling committee smashed it with a hammer. People standing near the vial picked up the pieces which were covered with the holy balsam. When the monarchy was restored in 1825, Charles X was crowned King of France and anointed with some of the balsam which had been salvaged from the glass fragments.

Part of the coronation ceremony which is common in many countries is the procession to the church. The coronation procession of the English Queen Elizabeth I in 1559 came to a halt on its way to Westminster Abbey. According to legend a ragged woman stepped out of the crowd and moved towards the young queen. The guards were about to push her away when Elizabeth stopped them. The old woman offered a sprig of rosemary to Elizabeth who graciously accepted the gift and carried it to her coronation.

The gift of rosemary was appropriate since rosemary was considered the most potent charm against evil. The story became popular across the kingdom as the people took it to be a sign that their new queen was kind and sympathetic and, they hoped, not willing to continue the bloody religious persecutions which had accompanied the reigns of her father, Henry VIII, and her half-sister, Mary I.

Another feature of the British coronation was the Herb Woman. It was customary for the Herb Woman and her maids to lead the grand procession from Westminster Hall to the Abbey. Their duty was to carpet the raised platform with fragrant flowers. This was a highly prestigious position and its origins can be found in the belief that sweet-scented herbs would act as a deterrent to illness, especially the plague. The last Herb Woman was a Miss Fellowes who attended the coronation of George IV in 1821. She wore a white dress, and a mantle embroidered with flowers.

The coronation of George IV was extremely expensive and he lived an extravagant lifestyle to the point of almost bankrupting the royal treasury. When his brother, William IV, came to the throne in 1830, there was little money available for an elaborate coronation. The services of the Herb Woman were dispensed with due to budgetary restrictions and when Victoria came to the throne in 1837 there was no need to bring back the Herb Woman as the chances of the plague occurring were considered minimal.

Specific floral and plant symbols were used on Elizabeth II's coronation gown. It was a white satin dress embroidered with nine floral emblems of Great Britain and the Commonwealth. Great Britain was represented by the Tudor rose of England, the thistle of Scotland, the shamrock of Ireland and the leek of Wales. It had been suggested that the daffodil be used instead of the leek since it was considered to be prettier but this idea was turned down as inappropriate. The Commonwealth countries were represented by the maple leaf of Canada, the lotus of Ceylon (Sri Lanka), the protea of South Africa, the mimosa of Australia, the fern of New Zealand and wheat, cotton and jute for Pakistan. The queen's dressmaker, Norman Hartnell, added an embroidered lucky four-leaf clover on her skirt where she could easily touch it with her left hand.

These floral emblems were elaborate. The leek was embroidered with white and green silk and decorated with diamonds. The shamrock and the lotus also were decorated with diamonds and the rose and lotus were filled with pearls. The thistle was highlighted with amethysts and the maple leaf sparkled with crystal. The cotton flowers shimmered with silver and gold threads outlining diamonds and crystals.

Flowers, as a symbol of festivity, played an important role in the decoration of Westminster Abbey and the royal processional route. Elizabeth II carried to her coronation a bouquet of white flowers prepared by Martin Longman of the Worshipful Company of Gardeners. The flowers — roses, orchids, carnations, lilies-of-the-valley and stephanotosis — came from all parts of the British Isles. On every anniversary of her coronation, June 2nd, a replica bouquet has been sent to Buckingham Palace by the Worshipful Company of Gardeners.

POLITICAL, ROYAL AND HERALDIC SYMBOLS

Flowers have traditionally been used to identify cities, countries and members of the nobility. Pharaonic Egypt was originally two countries which were united during the First Dynasty in the second millennium B.C. The lotus represented Upper Egypt while the papyrus was the symbol of Lower Egypt. In Egyptian art the stalks of the two plants were usually entwined to signify the unification of the two countries.

There are two lotus species native to Egypt: the blue lotus (*Nymphaeae caerulea*) and the white lotus (*N. lotus*). The blue is the more fragrant of the two water-lilies and is represented in art in bouquets or as a single blossom held in an individual's hand. The sacred lotus of India (*Nelumbo nucifera*), which was introduced into Egypt, is easily distinguished from its Egyptian counterparts by its pink flowers. This lotus, however, does not have any special significance in ancient Egyptian culture.

Many flowers were used in Egyptian life. The rose, however, is associated with Egypt through Cleopatra, who reigned in the first century B.C. According to legend Cleopatra had the floor of her banqueting hall carpeted with roses to the depth of 60 cm., or two feet, when she first entertained Mark Antony of Rome. This may have been an exaggeration but there could be some truth to the story, since Egypt had a thriving rose-growing industry and was the main exporter of roses to Rome.

The ancient Greeks used the rose as the emblem of the city Rhodes, which took its name from the Greek word for rose. The coins of Rhodes, which date back to the sixth century B.C., had roses inscribed on them. The other important Greek civic flower was the violet which was the official emblem of the city of Athens.

In ancient Rome roses played a political role as they were considered to be symbolic of courage and bravery. Roses were made into wreaths which were worn by the victors of military campaigns. It was considered a great honour for a successful general to have a wreath of roses bestowed upon him for his triumphal entry into the city of Rome.

According to legend Julius Caesar, in the first century B.C., instituted the wearing of rose wreaths during victory processions to cover the bald spot on the back of his head. However, Romans had been using rose wreaths long before Julius Caesar. The Roman senator Cato, who lived between 234 and 149 B.C., claimed in his writings that Rome was falling into moral decay as rose wreaths were being awarded for every minor military victory rather than being reserved for major victories. He was concerned that the indiscriminate use of rose wreaths would reduce their importance as a mark of military honour.

Cato's sentiments were being repeated two and a half centuries later by the Roman historian Tacitus. Apparently Emperor Vitellius had visited a battlefield near present-day Cremona in northern Italy. Laurel leaves and roses were scattered at his feet as he reviewed the site, and the presence of these plants implied that he was responsible for the victory. Tacitus was outraged since the emperor had not taken part in the battle and therefore was not due the honour of the roses.

The Romans were responsible for the term *sub rosa* which has often been used in a political context. From Latin it translates as under the rose and means that anything spoken or done was in strict confidence and secrecy. The term was derived from the story of Cupid who gave a rose to Harpocrates, the god of silence, so that he would not betray Venus' infidelities to her husband. The ceilings of Roman dining rooms were decorated with roses to remind guests not to repeat anything they may have heard while under the influence of wine.

The idea of the rose as a symbol of secrecy continued through European history. During the Middle Ages, conversations, including those of political delicacy, were carried out in the privacy of rose gardens. In later centuries, a rose was carved into the ceiling of the political chambers of the monarch to reinforce the idea that discussions of a political nature were to be kept secret, unless otherwise indicated.

Plants were also used as personal emblems of kings and the nobility. As individuals succeeded to the throne their badges or emblems became the symbol of the dynasty and, as with the rose, the symbol of the country. The first royal symbol in England was not the rose but the broom flower. Henry II, who reigned from 1154 to 1189, used the wild, yellow broom as the symbol of his dynasty. Henry's father, Geoffrey of Anjou, constantly wore a sprig of broom in his cap. The Latin term for the broom shrub is *Planta genista* and Henry's dynasty is known as the Plantagenets.

The rose first appears as a royal symbol in England during the reign of Henry III, 1216 to 1272. In 1236 Henry married Eleanor of Provence whose personal emblem was the white rose. Henry and Eleanor had two sons, Edward and Edmund. Edward, who later ruled as Edward I, from 1272 to 1307, took his mother's white rose as his personal badge or emblem. His younger brother Edmund, who became the first Earl of Lancaster, chose the red Damask rose. Edmund's rose was a new one which had been brought first to France after being acquired in Damascus during the Crusades.

The two roses represented two opposing sides of one family in what has become known as the Wars of the Roses. The wars lasted 30 years with fighting occurring in sporadic incidents from 1455 to 1485.

Edward IV won the crown at the battle of Mortimer's Cross, on February 2nd, 1461, and added a circle of sunrays to the white rose, thereby changing the Yorkist symbol to the rose *en soleil*. This device occurs often in heraldic references to the House of York and the County of Yorkshire.

Edward IV died in 1483 leaving an under-age heir, Edward V. In the same year Richard of York, who was to become Richard III, usurped the throne from his nephew Edward. The Lancastrian side of the family decided to contest Richard's claim to the throne and fighting broke out again. The Wars of the Roses ended when Richard III was defeated by Henry Tudor, at the battle of Bosworth Field.

This period of political upheaval did not become known as the Wars of the Roses until 1486 when the idea of the roses representing the two opposing sides first appeared in the *Crowland Chronicle*. The Yorkists used the white rose continuously throughout the wars but the red rose was not used by the Lancastrians until the time of Henry

Tudor. According to tradition, the adoption of the two roses as badges of the rival sides occurred in the Temple gardens in London with the plucking of red and white roses by John Beaufort, the Duke of Somerset, and Richard, Duke of York, in 1483.

Henry Tudor ruled as Henry VII from 1485 to 1509. To help heal the political wounds Henry married Elizabeth of York, the niece of Richard III, and amalgamated the two roses to create the heraldic Tudor rose. This combination of a red and a white rose was a symbol of the peace which Henry hoped to bring to England. The Tudor rose is not to be confused with the York-and-Lancaster rose which is a member of the Damask species. The York-and-Lancaster rose, whose existence has been recorded since 1550, can have pink, white or variegated petals. It is the variegated blossoms which have been mistaken for the Tudor rose. The Tudor rose, however, is a distinct symbol with white central petals overlying larger red outer petals and it is definitely not a real rose that can be grown in a garden.

The red and white roses have retained their significance and are in common usage today. They represent three of the six heralds who grant arms at the College of Arms in England. The Lancaster Herald is represented by the red rose, the York Herald by the white rose *en soleil* and the Richmond Herald by a split red-and-white rose which is red on the left and white on the right. The use of the split-coloured rose for the Richmond Herald stems from Henry Tudor who was the Earl of Richmond before he became Henry VII.

The Lancastrian rose has also continued as a military insignia. It was adopted by the South Lancashire Regiment as their emblem during World War II and they chose as their motto, "They win or die who wear the rose of Lancaster." The red rose still remains the emblem of the Queen's Lancashire Regiment.

The Tudor rose was used as the emblem of the dynasty not only by the Tudor monarchs but also by some of their spouses. It appeared on the emblems of three of Henry VIII's wives. Catherine of Aragon combined it with a pomegranate, the symbol of Aragon, and a sheaf of arrows, Jane Seymour had a phoenix rising from a castle with the Tudor rose on either side and Katherine Parr had a crowned maiden's head rising from a Tudor rose.

When it came to floral symbolism Elizabeth I out-did all the Tudors and probably every other monarch who reigned in Great

Britain. She had a whole cornucopia of flowers to symbolize her and her reign. These flowers developed into symbols of popular mythology which emphasized the Golden Age which had come to England under her reign.

Elizabeth continued to use the Tudor rose as a symbol of peace but she also associated herself with the white eglantine rose, and the two roses often appear together in her portraits. The eglantine, or wild brier rose, was symbolic not only of England but of Elizabethan power to vanquish Spain, England's strong Catholic enemy. This political achievement was realized with the English defeat of the Spanish Armada in 1588.

Elizabeth was known as the Virgin Queen and purposely acquired for herself the floral symbolism of the Virgin Mary. One of these flowers was the white rose, a symbol of virginity, and the reign of Elizabeth was referred to as the age of the white rose. Elizabeth used as her motto *Rosa sine spina* which translates as a rose without a thorn. This motto is linked with the Virgin Mary who was called "a rose without thorns."

Another aspect of the cult of Elizabeth was the association of the queen with spring and its flowers. Spring was important symbolically because in mythological Golden Ages it is eternally springtime. Portraits show Elizabeth's dresses covered with embroidered spring flowers such as roses, lilies, pansies, primroses, violets, daffodils, carnations and honeysuckle while the same flowers are used as metaphors for the queen in poetry.

Edmund Spenser in his poem, "The Shepheards Calender" of 1579, used Elizabeth as the model for the "fayre Elisa" who was queen of all shepherds. In the April Eclogue he writes:

> See, where she sits upon the grassie greene,
> (O seemely sight!)
> Yclad in Scarlot, like a mayden Queene,
> And ermines white.
> Upon her head a Cremosin coronet,
> With Damaske roses and Daffadillies set:
> Bay leaves betweene,
> And primroses greene,
> Embellish the sweete Violet . . .[6]

There were special "Elizabeth" gardens which were planted with flowers that were symbolic of the queen. Lord Burghley, upon being informed that the queen would be visiting his home, Theobalds, promptly had his garden torn up and replanted with "Elizabeth" flowers in her honour. His younger son, Sir Robert Cecil, designed the garden as an emblem of Elizabeth and had it planted with "flowers fairest and sweet."[7] The garden was divided into quarters. One of the quarters contained a maze which was laid out entirely with spring flowers. The gardener, who made a speech to the queen upon her arrival, pointed out that the maze was unique as it was planted without the customary herbs of hyssop and thyme. Sir Robert even included an arbour which was covered entirely in eglantine, a most appropriate Elizabethan symbol.

The Tudor rose was replaced by the white rose as the emblem of the Stuarts. James I, who reigned from 1603 to 1625, claimed the throne through descent from his great-grandmother who was the sister of Henry VIII. James I used the white rose because his mother, Mary, Queen of Scots, had been married to the king of France. As a queen of France Mary was entitled to wear the white rose and to pass it on to her son.

The Glorious Revolution of 1688 put William and Mary on the throne of England and the Stuart king, James II, with his wife Mary and their son James, fled to France. Prince James was known as the Pretender and the white rose became the symbol for his supporters. June 19th was his birthday and for a long time it was known as White Rose Day. The white rose was the obvious choice for the supporters of the Stuart Pretender but it also was a symbol of their meetings which were held *sub rosa*.

Elton John continued the tradition of associating English royalty with the rose with the words "Goodbye, England's Rose" in his song "Candle in the Wind 1997" for the funeral of Diana, Princess of Wales.

The connection of the leek and Wales comes from St. David, the patron saint of Wales. There are two explanations. The most historically plausible theory is St. David's diet. The saint ate only bread and vegetables, his favourite vegetable being the leek which he found to be particularly sustaining. According to another legend St. David helped the Welsh in battle by ordering the men to put leeks on their heads to distinguish them from their Saxon enemies. It makes a good story but there appears to be no historical truth to it.

The daffodil acquired its association with Wales also from St. David. His festive day is March 1st and according to tradition the daffodil, which grew wild in Wales, opened its blossoms on March 1st. The daffodil is also called "St. David's leek" and it is customary in Wales, even in the present day, for people to wear daffodils to celebrate St. David's Day.

The national flower of Scotland is the thistle. It came to prominence in the 10th century A.D. during the reign of Malcolm I, a dangerous time due to raiding parties of Norsemen from Scandinavia. During one of these raids a group of Norsemen attempted a surprise night raid on the Scottish forces camped on the hill of present-day Edinburgh. Unable to see the ground, one of the attackers stepped on a thistle with his bare feet. The strong thorns pierced his skin and he let out a yell which woke the guards and alerted the Scottish soldiers to the danger around them. The Norsemen retreated rather than fight at a disadvantage.

The first record of the thistle as a national emblem appears on the coins of James VI of Scotland. During his reign as James I of England, he had coins issued on which half a thistle was combined with half a rose. This motif was also carved on the tomb of his mother, Mary, Queen of Scots, in Westminster Abbey.

The shamrock, which is a form of clover, became the symbol of Ireland also through a saint. It is associated with St. Patrick and his attempts to convert the pagan Irish to Christianity. To explain the trinity, in which three entities are represented in one God, St. Patrick chose the shamrock because its three small leaves make up one larger leaf. This explanation apparently worked and St. Patrick was successful in his conversions. St. Patrick may have been particularly astute in his choice of the shamrock, for the clover was sacred to the Celts of Ireland who considered it a sign of both good and evil.

The *fleur de lis*, which is an iris, is considered the emblematic flower of France but it also has had a long history in England due to England's political and military claims to French territory after the Norman conquest. The *fleur de lis* was on the arms of the United Kingdom until 1801 when King George II had it replaced with the shamrock.

The *fleur de lis* was first used as a symbol of Gaul during the Roman period. According to legend, Clovis I, King of the Franks, was trapped with his army between the Goth army and the Rhine River. Clovis noticed that the water iris grew far out into the river at one place and this suggested the possibility that the river was sufficiently shallow at that point to be crossed. Clovis led his army across the river and they were saved. The appearance of the water iris was viewed as auspicious and Clovis took it as his personal emblem.

A later French king, Louis VII, who reigned from 1131 to 1180, dreamed one night of the iris and it made such a lasting impression that he used it as his emblem during the Crusades. It is said that the *fleur de lis* is named after Louis VII. It was known as the *fleur de Louis* (flower of Louis) which with time changed to the *fleur de lis*. Its three petals were symbolic of the attributes of a Crusader: valour, wisdom and faith.

The *fleur de lis* has been used as a personal emblem of the rulers of France since the time of Clovis but it was not until the reign of Charles IV, 1294 to 1328, that it appeared on the banner or flag of the kingdom of France. Edward III of England claimed France on the death of Charles IV in 1328 and added the *fleur de lis* to his Great Seal and his arms. Edward was not the first English king to use the *fleur de lis*. King Stephen, who reigned from 1135 to 1154, used it on his crown and it was also used on the arms of English nobility who came from France. Given that England often controlled larger parts of France than the King of France during the Middle Ages, it was not unreasonable for English monarchs to feel they had the right to use the *fleur de lis* on the arms of their kingdom.

Botanical emblems, known as charges, are rare in heraldry compared with animals or mythical beasts although they have gained greater popularity in non-European countries in the 20th century. Heraldic flowers are used as the charges of armorial bearings of countries, cities, orders of knighthood, institutions and individuals.

The rose is the principal heraldic floral symbol and appears initially in what is now termed the "conventional" form which is five displayed petals. The conventional heraldic rose is a depiction of the wild rose rather than the multi-petalled roses that made their way into northern Europe from the Mediterranean and North African regions. This rose appears on innumerable English arms. However, heraldic roses have one advantage over living roses: they do not have to follow the colours of nature. Among the unusual roses on English family crests are the blue rose of the Rocheforts, the black rose of the Berendons and the green rose of the Smallshaws.

The lily is usually represented by the *fleur de lis* but natural lilies are found on the arms of such diverse institutions in Britain as the University of Aberdeen, the city of Dundee, and the College of St. Mary the Virgin at Eton.

Other flowers which are used in heraldry include the columbine, gillyflower, narcissus, primrose, marigold, tulip, corn-flower, saffron-flower and lotus. The latter was used on arms for British individuals who distinguished themselves, or made a fortune, in India.

In Great Britain plants are used as emblems on the armorial insignias of knighthood. The oldest and most distinguished is the Most Noble Order of the Garter which was established in 1348. The orders of knighthood have chains or collars which the individual wears around his neck, and the collar of the Order of the Garter consists of 26 buckled garters, each with a rose in the centre. The Order of the Thistle, which was revived in 1687, has a collar of sprigs of thistle and rue. The use of rue is probably a pun on the name of St. Andrew, the patron saint of Scotland. Rue has no national significance to Scotland nor religious meaning for the saint. However, the description of the insignia would read as "thistle and rue." The Order of the Bath, formed in 1725, has a collar of nine imperial crowns alternating with eight devices of the rose, thistle and shamrock all rising from a sceptre.

Plants appear on only two national flags in the western world. Canada has the maple leaf and Lebanon the famous cedar of Lebanon. The maple leaf of Canada is considered, by heraldry experts, to be one of the more spectacular successes in the use of leaves in heraldry. The maple leaf was first referred to as an emblem of Canada in the *Quebec Gazette* in 1805 and shortly after-wards it was incorporated into the regimental banner of the Prince of Wales' Royal Canadian Regiment. The maple leaf was proclaimed the official national flag of Canada, by Queen

Elizabeth II, on February 15th, 1965, and it is featured in the Royal Arms of Canada along with the lily, thistle, shamrock and English rose.

Carnations appeared as political symbols during the French Revolution. The nobles wore carnations on their way to the guillotine and the carnation was used in a plot to free Marie Antoinette from prison. A note with instructions was placed inside a carnation blossom but the guards found it and her would-be rescuers were captured.

An unusual event occurred in Holland where the Dutch showed their support for the French Revolutionaries by banning the sale or growing of orange flowers, fruits and vegetables such as day lilies, marigolds, oranges and carrots. The reason for the ban on orange produce had nothing to do with the reigning House of Orange, in Holland. Instead, the significance lay with the French Royal House of Bourbon which used the orange lily as its symbol.

This politically inspired boycott of plants was not restricted to the Dutch. In 19th-century England, whenever there was an outburst of anti-French feeling, people would stop growing garlic in their kitchen gardens. This occurred at least three times during the Second Empire when France was ruled by Louis Napoleon, followed by Napoleon III.

Napoleon used carnation red for his Légion d'Honneur medal. Carnation red later became the colour of the international communist banner, and red carnations were worn by socialist workers in both France and England in protest marches against their respective governments.

Red roses were used in France to signify a person's socialist political beliefs at the time of the Dreyfus Affair. Captain Alfred Dreyfus of the French army had been found guilty of treason as a result of documents forged by the government and military authorities: an injustice which was compounded by anti-Semitic feelings towards Dreyfus. The country was divided over his innocence or guilt and when he was retried in 1899, after serving five years of a life sentence on Devil's Island, his socialist supporters wore red roses as they lined the streets along the route to the courthouse.

Violets became a revolutionary flower through their association with Napoleon, who ruled France from 1804 to 1814. Napoleon's connection with violets began when he first met Josephine de Beauharnais at a ball. She was wearing violets in her hair and carried a bouquet of the same flowers. As she was leaving the ball she tossed the bouquet to Napoleon. When they were married in 1796, her wedding dress was embroidered with violets, the only flower that she wore. Napoleon always personally sent her violets on their anniversary and he arranged to have violets sent to her every day of their marriage.

Josephine's garden at Malmaison in Paris was famous for its roses. During the Napoleonic wars between France and England the British blockaded the channel. Josephine, however, received many of her rosebushes from the nursery of Lee and Kennedy in London, and John Kennedy was provided with a *laissez-passer*, which allowed him to travel freely between England and France, in order to bring new rose bushes and information on their care to Josephine.

Josephine died in 1814. She was buried in her garden at Malmaison and violets were planted on her grave. When Napoleon died in exile on the island of St. Helena, in 1820, he was found to be wearing a gold locket which contained two violets picked from Josephine's grave.

The violet became the symbol of Napoleon after he was defeated by the Austrians and the British in 1814. He was sent to the island of Elba and the French Bourbon monarchy was restored under Louis XVIII. Napoleon's parting words when he was leaving for Elba were, "I shall return in the spring with the violets." His nickname became Le Corporal Violet.

The English poet Lord Byron wrote "Napoleon on His Departure for Elba" which includes the following verse:

> Farewell to thee, France! but when liberty rallies
> Once more in thy regions, remember me then,
> The Violet grows in the depths of thy valleys
> Though withered, thy tears will unfold it again.

Napoleon did return from Elba in March of the following year when the violets were in bloom; however, he was defeated at the battle of Waterloo and began his final exile on St. Helena.

The departure of Napoleon and the return of the monarchy turned into a battle of flowers. Napoleon's supporters wore violets and sent cards with violets containing the pictures of Napoleon and his wife Marie Louise. The Bourbon monarchy supporters wore orange lilies. Fights constantly broke out between individuals over their respective flowers.

The Bonaparte dynasty was kept alive by Napoleon III, nephew of Napoleon, who became the contender for the Bonaparte throne when Napoleon's son died in 1832. Napoleon III was elected by the working people of France to the Constituent Assembly in 1848. He then resigned and ran for president, an office which he won. Finally, in 1851 he dissolved the constitution and the following year assumed the title of emperor. He married Eugénie de Montijo, a Spanish countess, and in keeping with the family tradition her wedding dress was embroidered with violets and she carried a wedding bouquet of the same family. Napoleon III was overthrown in 1871 and went into exile in England where he was warmly welcomed by Queen Victoria. On his death, two years later, his coffin was covered with violets.

Violets were also associated with Queen Victoria and Prince Albert. Victoria set the fashion for wearing a posy of violets on her dress and it was said that Prince Albert would never walk through the gardens at Windsor without picking a bunch of violets.

The Sweet William, a dianthus, is believed to have been named after the Duke of Cumberland, William Augustus, who brutally defeated the Scottish Jacobite supporters at the battle of Culloden in 1746. To the English he was Sweet William but to his enemies he was "Stinking Billy," which is the name that is still used for the flowers in Scotland.

The primrose became synonymous with the British Prime Minister Benjamin Disraeli, Lord Beaconsfield. Upon his death in 1881 a group of Conservative supporters wished to form a club in his memory and a representative asked Queen Victoria, who had been fond of Disraeli as prime minister, what had been his favourite flower. The queen misunderstood and thought they were asking about Prince Albert's favourite flower. She replied that it was the primrose. Disraeli's supporters, unaware of the mistake, called their club the "Primrose League."

The purpose of the Primrose League was the maintenance "of religion, of the estate of the realm and of the imperial ascendancy of the British Empire."[8] Primrose Day was held on April 19th, the anniversary of Disraeli's death, and individuals who supported the Conservative Party and the ideals of the Primrose League wore primroses as a sign of their allegiance and respect.

Queen Alexandra, the wife of Edward VII, is commemorated by Alexandra Rose Day when money is collected for charity. Alexandra decided upon the idea after a visit to her home country of Denmark where she met a priest who sold roses from his garden to raise money for the poor. The first Alexandra Rose Day took place on June 26th, 1912, and raised over £20,000. Men and women took to the streets selling artificial white roses which were based on the native English wild rose, roses being a favourite flower of Queen Alexandra. The tradition is still carried on today under the patronage of Princess Alexandra of Kent. Roses are sold on the streets by volunteers and a Rose Ball is held, with all the proceeds going to over 35 charities.

PLANTS AND WAR

Plants played their roles in wars in many different ways. They were objects of superstition, procurers of victory, symbols of celebrations and means of initiations. Parsley was considered a bad omen by the ancient Greeks and once, when a Greek army was proceeding to meet with the Persians during the Graeco-Persian wars, the men came across a caravan of donkeys carrying parsley. The soldiers refused to continue, arguing that this was a sure sign that they would die in battle and the generals were forced to find an alternative route to the battle site.

Legend has it that in 333 B.C. the Persian Emperor Darius III sent a sack of sesame seeds, which were representative of the number of his troops, as a challenge to Alexander the Great. Alexander replied by sending a sack of mustard seeds with the message that his troops were more fiery though less weighty. Alexander and his soldiers won the battle easily.

Bay leaves were used by Roman soldiers to wipe the blood off their swords and lances. The bay leaves were considered a gesture of atonement for taking a life and are connected with the role of Apollo leading the souls of men to the Underworld.

During the Crusades borage was added to wine which the ladies gave to their knights before their departure for the Holy Land.

Borage was a symbol of courage and it was thought that the drink would reinforce courage should it waver. An oddity from the Crusades was the inclusion of caraway seeds somewhere on the knight's clothing. It was thought that caraway seeds would keep a man from straying and the wives would sew seeds into their clothes in an attempt to keep their husbands faithful during their absence from home.

The Minden Rose Celebration is both a commemoration and an initiation. It commemorates the British defeat of the French forces at the Battle of Minden in Germany in 1759, during the Seven Years War. The victorious British soldiers passed through a rose garden and picked blossoms which they stuck in their helmets. Every year the Lancashire Fusiliers celebrate the event which includes a dinner at a table decorated with roses. The ceremony includes an initiation of the officers who have joined the regiment within the past year. Placed before each new member is a bowl of champagne with a rose floating in the middle. Each new officer is expected to drink the champagne and eat the rose.

The American Revolution or War of Independence, 1775 to 1783, saw drastic changes in the colonists' drinking habits. Bergamot leaves replaced tea leaves which were heavily taxed. The leaves of the purple bergamot (*Monarda fistulosa*) were used by Indians to make a tea and they were put to good use in 1773 after the Boston Tea Party. The *Ceanothus azureus*, another North American plant, was known as liberty tea because its leaves were widely used also as a substitute for imported tea after the Boston Tea Party and throughout the war.

One of the more unusual floral tributes to come out of a war is the song "The Yellow Rose of Texas." It was written by Charles Rogers in the early 19th century to commemorate an event which occurred during the Texas Revolution. The American settlers in Texas declared their independence from Mexico in 1836 and the Mexican government sent an expedition under the command of General Lopez de Santa Anna. He won the historic battles of the Alamo and Goliad and was poised to defeat the Texan rebels. Santa Anna, however, had not taken into account a beautiful mulatto servant named Emily Morgan, whom he claimed as booty. Emily was loyal to her Texan employer and managed to convey a message regarding the general's movements to Sam Houston who was leading the main Texas force.

Santa Anna is reported to have fallen under the spell of this beautiful woman and he set up camp along the banks of the San Jacinto River in order to spend time with Emily. As the Mexican army waited, its general absorbed in matters other than war, the Texas army attacked. The decisiveness of its victory at San Jacinto resulted in the establishment of the Republic of Texas.

The term yellow rose was a common reference to mulatto women and in the ballad it refers to Emily Morgan, "the sweetest little rosebud that Texas ever knew." Written references to the song appeared shortly after the battle of San Jacinto. The popularity of the song and its obvious strong associations with Texas might lead one to expect the yellow rose to be the state flower of Texas; however, the official state flower is the bluebonnet.

There was an early European belief that red heather was originally white until it was coloured by the blood of heathens killed in battle with Christians. The red field poppy, however, has become the ultimate symbol of the futility of war. There has been a long-held European belief, going back to Roman times, that red poppies sprang up in battlefields as a result of the blood of the dead and the wounded.

It is unlikely that this legend was in the mind of Canadian Colonel John McCrae, who wrote the poem "In Flanders Fields" which, although it refers to the death and carnage of World War I, has gone on to symbolize all wars which have followed.

> In Flanders fields the poppies blow
> Between the crosses, row on row,
> That mark our place: and in the sky
> The larks, still bravely singing, fly
> Scarce heard amid the guns below.[9]

The poem has come to symbolize the sadness of war and the need to remember the dead who gave their lives for a cause in which they believed. The red poppy was adopted as a symbol of remembrance for all wars and the first Poppy Day was held in Britain on November 11th, 1921. The poppy has come full circle from its Graeco/Roman roots as a symbol of fertility, deep sleep and death to remembrance of the dead.

ENDNOTES

Introduction

1.*The Oxford English Dictionary*, 2nd ed., (1989), s.v. "Flowers."
2. Walafrid Strabo, *The Hortulus of Walafrid Strabo*, trans. Raef Payne (Pittsburgh: Carnegie Mellon Press, 1966), p. 45.
3. *Ibid*, p. 47.
4. *Ibid*, p.61.
5. Theophrastus, *The Enquiry Into Plants* I.III.4.
6. Robert Herrick, *The Poems of Herrick*, ed. Henry Newbolt (London: Thomas Nelson and Sons Ltd., undated), p. 3.

Part One: Spells and Rituals

1. Herrick, *The Poems of Herrick*, p. 80.
2. John Keats, *Selected Poems*, ed. John Barnard (London: Penquin Books, 1988), p. 108.
3. Margaret Baker, *Wedding Customs and Folklore* (London: David & Charles, 1977), p. 81.
4. John Gerard, *The Herball or General History of Plantes* (London: Thomas Johnson, 1636) 1st ed. 1597. reprint ed., ed. and abridged Marcus Woodward, (London: Bracken Books, 1985), p, 133.
5. Translation by the author.
6. G.F. Northall, *English Folk-Rhymes* (London: Kegan Paul, Trench, Trubner and Co., Ltd., 1892), p. 429.
7. Gloria T. Delamar, *Mother Goose From Nursery to Literature* (Jefferson, N. Carolina: McFarland & C., Inc., 1987), p. 39.
8. Herrick, *The Poems of Herrick*, p. 125.
9. Other books published during Cecily Mary Barker's liftetime are: *Flower Fairies of the Summer* (1925), *Flower Fairies of the Autumn* (1926), *A Flower Fairy Alphabet* (1934) and *Flower Fairies of the Wayside* (1948).
10. Lewis Carrol, *Through the Looking-Glass and What Alice Found There* (1st ed., 1871, reprint ed., N.Y.: Smithmark Publ, 1995), p. 170.
11. Leigh Hunt, *The Poetical Works of Leigh Hunt* (London: Routledge, Warne & Routledge, 1860), p. 288.
12. Omar Khayyam, *Rubaiyat of Omar Khayyam*, trans. Edward Fitzgerald., p. 19.
13. *Ibid* p. 40.

14. Letter of Lady Mary Wortley Montagu, dated March 10, 1718.

15. Robert Tyas, *The Sentiment of Flowers or Language of Flora* (London: R. Ryas, 1842, 9th ed.), p. vi.

16. Thomas Miller, *The Poetrical Language of Flowers or the Pilgrimage of Love* (London: David Boque, 1847), p. V.

17. Captain Marryatt, *The Floral Telegraph or Affection's Signals* (London: Saunders & Otley, c.1850), p.3.

18. *Ibid*, p. 3.

19. Sara Hale, *Flora's Interpreter and Fortuna Flora* (Boston: Benjamin B. Mussey & Co., 1850), p.1.

20. *Ibid*, p. 254.

21. Louisa Anne Twamley, *The Romance of Nature*, (London: Charles Tilt,1839), p. 174.

22. Hunt, *The Poetical Works of Leigh Hunt*, p. 288.

23. *The Oxford Dictionary of Quotations*, 3rd ed., (1980) s.v. Sir Walter Scott, p. 417.

24. J.M.C. Toynbee, *Death and Burial in the Roman World*, (London: Thames & Hudson, 1971), p. 37.

25. *Ibid*, p. 63.

26. Shakespeare, *Richard II*, act 2, sc. 4, line 8.

27. Herrick, *The Poems of Herrick*, p. 269.

28. *Hamlet*, act 4, sc. 5, line 184.

29. *Hamlet*, act 5, sc. 1, lines 62-64.

30. Nicholas Culpeper, *The English Physician or Herball*, 1653. reprint 1985, p. 34.

31. J.S. Howard, "15 Old English Garden Rhymes," *This England*, (Winter 1969/70), p. 65.

32. *Ibid.*

Part Two: Traditional Foods, Hygiene and Medicines
1. Gerard, *The Herball*, p. 14.

2. John Evelyn, *The Acetaria, The Grand Salad*, 1st edition. 1699, compiled and ed., Madeleine Masson. (Bonchurch, Isle of Wight: Peacock Vane Publishing, 1984), p. 30.

3. *Ibid*, p. 32.

4. Northall, *English Folk-Rhymes*, p. 126.

5. *Ibid*, p. 127.

6. *Romeo and Juliet*, act 4, sc 3, line 47-48.

7. Northall, *English Folk-Rhymes,* p. 169.

8. *Hamlet,* act 4, sc. 5, line 176.

Part Three: Mythology, Religion and Superstition

1. Juvenal, *Satires.*

2. Herrick, *The Poems of Herrick,* p. 215.

3. King James Standard Version, Gen. 1:11.

4. I Kings 10:2.

5. Esther 2:12.

6. Prov. 7.17.

7. Job 14:1-2.

8. Matt. 6:28.

9. Song of Songs 2:1.

10. Roland E Murphy, *The Song of Songs: A Commentary on the Book of Canticles or The Song of Songs,* (Minneapolis: Augsburg Fortress, 1990), p. 132.

11. Ariel Bloch, and Chana Bloch, *The Song of Songs; a New Translation* (N.Y.: Random House, 1995), p. 55.

12. Michael Zohary, *Plants of the Bible,* (Cambridge: Cambridge University Press, 1982). p. 14.

13. Murphy, *The Song of Songs,* p. 136.

14. Francis Landry, *Paradoxes of Paradise: Identity and Difference in the Song of Songs* (Sheffield: The Almond Press, 1983), p. 83.

15. Northall, *English Folk-Rhymes,* p. 180.

16. *Ibid,* p, 143.

Part Four: Trade and Politics

1. Herodotus, *The Histories* Book 3, 110.

2. *Ibid,* Book 3, 111.

3. Theophrastus, *The Enquiry Into Plants* Vol. II, IX.

4. John Keay, *The Honourable Company, A History of the English East India Company* (London: HarperCollins, 1991), p. 4.

5. I Sam. 10:1.

6. Roy Strong, *The Renaissance Garden in England,* (London: Thames & Hudson, 1979), p.47.

7. *Ibid,* p. 46.

8. Judy Chard, "Primrose Harvest," *This England,* (Spring, 1983), p. 32.

9. John McCrae, "In Flanders Fields," verse1, lines 1-5.

BIBLIOGRAPHY

Addison, Josephine. *Love Potions, A Book of Charms and Omens.* London: Robinson Publishing, 1987.

Albertus Magnus. *The Book of Secrets.* ed. M. Best & F. Brightman. Oxford: Clarendon Press, 1973.

Allardice, Pamela. *A-Z of Companion Planting.* London: Cassell Publishers Ltd., 1993.

_____. *Love Potions, Charms and Other Romantic Notions.* Mosman, Australia: Pan Macmillan Publishers, 1991.

Alter, Robert. *The Art of Biblical Poetry.* N.Y.: Basic Books Inc. Publishers, 1985.

Anderson, A.W. *The Coming of the Flowers.* N.Y.: Farrar, Straus and Young, Inc. c. 1950.

Angeloglou, Maggie. *A History of Make-up.* London: Studio Vista Ltd., 1970.

Apicius. *The Roman Cookery of Apicius.* trans. and adapted by John Edwards. np. Vancouver, Hartley and Marks, 1984.

Arano, Luisa Cogliati. *The Medieval Health Handbook, Tacuinum Sanitatis.* N.Y.: George Braziller, 1976.

Ariès, Philippe. *The Hour of Our Death.* trans. Helen Weaver. N.Y.: Oxford University Press, 1991.

Asch, John. "Capitulare de Villis". *Garden Journal.* Sept/Oct. 1968. pp. 34-147.

Athenaeus. *The Deipnosophists.* trans. Charles Burton Gulic. London: William Heinemann, Ltd., 1927. 7 vol.

Back, Philippa. *The Illustrated Herbal.* London: Octopus Books Ltd., 1987.

Baker, Margaret. *Wedding Customs and Folklore.* London: David & Charles, 1977.

Baring-Gould, William S. and Baring-Gould, Ceil. *The Annotated Mother Goose.* N.Y.: Clarkson N. Potter, Inc., 1962.

Beals, Katharine M. *Flower Lore and Legend.* N.Y.: Henry Holt & Co., 1917.

Beckles, Gordon. *Coronation Glory: A Pageant of Queens, 1559-1953.* London: The London Express Newspaper Ltd., 1953.

Bennett, Jennifer. *Lilies of the Hearth, The Historical Relationship Between Women and Plants.* Camden East, Ontario: Camden House Publishing, 1991.

191

Black, Virgina. "Blessing the Bride". *This England*. Summer, 1981. p. 22.

Bloch, Ariel and Bloch, Chana. *The Song of Songs, A New Translation*. N.Y.: Random House, 1995.

Blundell, Sue. *Women in Ancient Greece*. London: British Museum Press, 1995.

Blunt, Wilfrid and Raphael, Sandra. *The Illustrated Herbal*. Toronto: Oxford University Press, 1979.

Briggs, K.M. *The Fairies in Tradition and Literature*. London: Routledge and Kegan Paul, 1967.

Brown, Alice Cooke. *Early American Herb Recipes*. N.Y.: Bonanza Books, 1966.

Carroll, Lewis. *Through the Looking Glass and What Alice Found There*. 1st ed., 1871. reprint ed. N.Y.: Smithmark Pub., 1995.

Castleman, Michael. *The Healing Herbs*. N.Y.: Bantam Books, 1991.

Clarkson, Rosetta E. *Magic Gardens. A Modern Chronicle of Herbs and Savory Seeds*. London: Macmillan Publishing Co., 1939, reprint 1992.

Coats, Alice M. *Flowers and Their Histories*. London: Hulton Press Ltd., 1956.

_____. *The Book of Flowers*. London: Phaidon Press Ltd., 1973.

Coats, Peter. *Flowers in History*. London, Weidenfeld & Nicolson, 1970.

_____. *Roses*. London: Weidenfeld & Nicolson, 1962. 3rd ed. 1970.

Coon, Nelson. *The Complete Book of Violets*. N.Y.: A.S. Barnes 7 Co., 1977.

Corson, Richard. *Fashions in Makeup*. London: Peter Owen, 1972.

Cosman, Medeleine Pelner. *Fabulous Feasts, Medieval Cookery and Ceremony*. N.Y.: George Braziller, 1976.

Culpeper, Nicholas. *Complete Herbal. Ware*. Hertfordshire: Omega Books Ltd., reprint 1985.

_____. *Culpeper's Book of Birth. A Seventeenth Century Guide to Having Lusty Children*. ed. Ian Thomas. London: Grange Books, 1985. reprint 1993.

Davies, Jennifer. *The Victorian Flower Garden*. London: BBC Books, 1991.

Dawson, Thomas. *The Good Huswifes Jewell*. London, 1596.

Detienne, Marcel. *The Gardens of Adonis, Spices in Greek Mythology*. trans. Janet Lloyd. New Jersey: The Humanities Press, 1977.

Dodge, Bertha S. *Quests For Spices and New Worlds*. Hamden Conn.: Archon Books, 1988.

El Mahdy, Christine. *Mummies, Myth and Magic in Ancient Egypt*. London: Thames and Hudson, 1989.

Evans, Mark. *Herbal Plants*. History and Uses. London: Studio Editions, 1991.

Evelyn, John. *Acetaria, The Grand Salad*. 1st ed. 1699. compiled and ed. Madeleine Masson. Bonchurch, Isle of Wight: Peacock Vane Publishing, 1984.

Field, Mary Anne. "Centenary of Cicely Mary Barker, the Artist Who Created the Flower Fairies". *This England*. Winter, 1995. pp. 35-37.

Fisher, John. *The Companion to Roses*. Harmondsworth: Penguin Books, 1986.

_____. *The Origins of Garden Plants*. London: Constable & Co., 1982. revised 1989.

Flint, Valerie I.J. *The Rise of Magic in Early Medieval Europe*. Princeton: Princeton University Press, 1991.

Flowerdew, Bob. *Good Companions, A Guide to Gardening With Plants That Help Each Other*. N.Y.: Summit Books, 1991.

Forbes, Leslie. *Recipes From the Indian Spice Trail*. London: BBC Books, 1994.

Fraser, Fir James George. *The Illustrated Golden Bough*. abridged Robert K.G. Temple. N.Y.: Simon & Schuster, 1996. originally published 1890 in 2 vol.

Friend, Rev. Hilderic. *Flowers and Flower Lore*. London: George Allen & Co. Ltd., 1883. 2 vol.

Genders, Roy. *Flowers and Herbs of Love*. London: Darton, Longman & Todd Ltd., 1978.

Gerard, John. *Gerard's Herball*. abridged Marcus Woodward. London: Bracken Books, 1985. original 1636.

Goody, Jack. *The Culture of Flowers*. Cambridge: Cambridge University Press, 1993.

Gordon, Lesley. *Green Magic.* Exeter: Ebury Press, 1977.
_____ *A Country Herbal.* London: Webb & Bower Ltd., 1980.

Grandville, J.J. *The Court of Flora, Les Fleurs Animées.* N.Y. George Braziller, 1981.

Greenaway, Kate. *Language of Flowers.* London: Frederick Warne & Co. Ltd., reprint 1979.

Hale, Sarah Josepha. *Flora's Interpreter and Fortuna Flora.* Boston: Benjamin B. Mussey & Co., 1858.

Hall, Manly P. *The Mystical and Medical Philosophy of Paracelsus.* Los Angeles. The Philosophical Research. 1964.

Hatfield, Audrey Wynne. *Pleasure of Herbs.* London: Museum Press Ltd., 1964.

Hayes, Elizabeth. *Spices and Herbs, Lore and Cookery.* N.Y.: Dover Publications, Inc., 1961.

Hendrickson, Robert. *Ladybugs, Tiger Lilies and Wallflowers.* N.Y.: Prentice Hall, 1993.

Hepper, F. Nigel. *Pharaoh's Flowers, The Botanical Treasures of Tutankhamun.* London: HMSO, 1990.

Herlihy, David. *Medieval Households.* Cambridge: Harvard University Press,1985.

Herodotus. *The Histories.* trans. David Grene. Chicago: The University of Chicago Press, 1987.

Herrick, Robert. *The Poems of Herrick.* ed. Henry Newbolt. London: Thomas Nelson & Sons, Ltd.

Hieatt, Constance B. and Butler, Sharon. *Pleyn Delit. Medieval Cookery for Modern Cooks.* Toronto: University of Toronto Press, 1976.

Hill, Thomas. *The Gardener's Labyrinth.* ed. Richard Mabey. Oxford: Oxford University Press, 1987. original 1577.

Hollingsworth, Buckner. *Flower Chronicles.* New Jersey: Rugers University Press, 1958.

Howard, J.S. "15 Old English Garden Rhymes". *This England.* Winter 1969/70. p. 65.

James, Paul. "Queen Alexandra". *This England.* Summer, 1993. p. 36.

Johnston, Harold Whetstone. *The Private Life of the Romans.* 1903. revised Mary Johnston 1932, reprinted N.Y.: Cooper Square Publishers, Inc., 1973.

Jones, Julia and Deer, Barbara. *The Country Diary of Garden Lore.* Toronto: McGraw-Hill Ryerson, 1989.

Jones, William. *Crowns and Coronations.* London: Chatto & Windus, 1902.

Keats, John. *Selected Poems.* ed. John Barnard. London: Penquin Books, 1988.

Keay, John. *The Honourable Company. A History of the English East India Company.* London: HarperCollins, 1991.

Kennett, Frances. *History of Perfume.* London: Harrop, 1975.

Klaits, Joseph. *Servants of Satan; The Age of Witch Hunts.* Bloomington: Indiana University Press, 1985.

Latham, Minor White. *The Elizabethan Fairies; The Fairies of Folklore and The Fairies of Shakespeare.* 1930. reprint N.Y.: Octagon Books, 1972.

Lehner, Ernst and Johanna. *Folklore and Symbolism of Flowers.* N.Y.: Tudor Publishing Co, 1960.

Leopold, Allison Kyle. *The Victorian Garden.* N.Y.: Clarkson Potter, 1995.

Levi, d'Ancona Mirella. *The Garden of the Renaissance.* Florence: Leo S. Olschki, 1977.

_____ *Botticelli's Primavera.* Florence: Leo S. Olschki Editore, 1983.

Lorwin, Madge, *Dining with William Shakespeare.* N.Y.: Antheneum, 1976.

MacNicol, Mary. *Flower Cookery: The Art of Cooking with Flowers.* N.Y.: Fleet Press Corporation, 1967.

McBryde, Anne. "Regiments and Rosaries". *This England.* Summer, 1985. p. 9.

Maple, Eric. *The Secret Lore of Plants and Flowers.* London: Robert Hale Ltd., 1980.

Markham, Gervase. *The English Housewife.* ed. Michael R. Best. Kingston & Montreal: McGill-Queen's University Presss, 1986.

Marryatt, Captain. *The Floral Telegraph or Affection's Signals.* London: Saunders & Otley, c. 1850.

Martingale, James. "Faggies: Silken Beauty". *This England.* Summer, 1997, p. 27.

Mercante, Anthony. *The Magic Garden.* N.Y.: Harper and Row, 1976.

Miller, Thomas. *The Poetical Language of Flowers or the Pilgrimage of Love*. London: David Boque, 1847.

Miloradovich, Milo. *Growing and Using Herbs and Spices*. N.Y.: Dover Publication Inc., 1986.

Monger, George. "Marry in Haste". *This England*. Spring, 1980. pp. 32-33.

Mulherin, Jennier. *The Macmillan Treasury of Spices and Natural Flavourings*. N.Y.: Macmillan Publishing Co., 1988.

Murphy, Roland, E. *The Song of Songs. A Commentary on the Book of Canticles or The Song of Songs*. Minneapolis: Augsburg Fortress, 1990.

Nahmad, Claire. *Garden Spells. The Magic of Herbs, Trees and Flowers*. London: Pavilion books Ltd., 1994.

Noll, Gunter. "The Origin of the So-Called Plan of St. Gall". *Journal of Medieval History*. 8, 1982. pp. 191-240.

Northall, G.F. *English Folk-Rhymes*. London: Kegan Paul, Trench, Trubner and Co., Ltd., 1892.

Ovid. *The Metamorphoses of Ovid*. trans. David R. Slavit. Baltimore: The Johns Hopkins University Press, 1994.

Ozment, Steven. *When Fathers Ruled, Family Life in Reformation Europe*. Cambridge: Harvard University Press, 1983.

Packer, Alison; Beddoe, Stella; and Jarret, Lianne. *Fairies in Legend and the Arts*. London: Cameron & Tayleur, 1980.

Parkinson, John. *Paradisi in Sole*. N.Y.: Dover Publications, 1976.

Paxton, Joseph. *Paxton's Botanical Dictionary Comprising the Names, History,and Culture of all Plants Known in Britain*. new edition by Samuel Hereman. London: Bradbury, Evans and Co., 1868.

Pennick, Nigel. *The Pagan Book of Days*. Rochester, Vermont: Destiny Books, 1992.

Pliny the Elder. *Natural History*. Loeb Classical Library.

Pratt, Anne. *Flowers and Their Associations*. London: Charles Knight and Co., 1840.

Rätsch, Christian. *The Dictionary of Sacred and Magical Plants*. trans. John Baker. Santa Barbara, Ca: ABC Clio, 1992.

Rix, Martyn. *The Art of Botanical Illustration*. London: Bracken Books, 1989.

Rohde, Eleanour Sinclair. *The Scented Garden*. London: The Medici Society, 1st ed. 1931. reprint 1989.

Rosengarten, Jr, Frederic. *The Book of Spices.* Wynnewood, Pens.: Livingston Publishing Co., 1969.

Sanecki, Kay. *History of the English Herb Garden.* London, Ward Lock, 1992.

Schivelbusch, Wolfgang. *Tastes of Paradise, A Social History of Spices, Stimulants and Intoxicants.* trans. David Jacobson. N.Y.: Vintage Books, 1993.

Scourse, Nicolette. *The Victorians and their Flowers.* London: Crooom Helm, 1993.

Singleton, Esther. *The Shakespear Garden.* London: Cecil Palmer, 1922.

Smith, Mrs. E. *The Complete Housewife: or Accomplish'd Gentlewoman's Companion.* London: 1753.

Soranus. *Gynecology.* trans. Owsei Temkin. Baltimore: The Johns Hopkins Press, 1956. reprint, 1991.

Strabo, Walafrid. *The Hortulus of Walafrid Strabo.* trans. Raef Payne. Pittsburg: Carnegie Mellon Press, 1966.

Strong, Roy. *The Renaissance Garden in England.* London: Thames & Hudson, 1979.

Stuart, Malcolm, ed. *The Encyclopedia of Herbs and Herbalism. London: Orbis Publishing, 1989.*

Talbot, Rob and Whiteman, Robin. *Brother Cadfael's Herb Garden.* London: Little, Brown & Co., 1996.

Tannahill, Reay. *Food in History.* N.Y. Crown Publishers. 1st ed. 1973. reprint, 1988.

Tanner, Lawrence E. *The History of the Coronation. London: Pitkin, 1952.*

Theophrastus. *Enquiry into Plants and Concerning Odours.* trans Sir Arthur Hort. London, Heinemann, 1916, 2 vol.

Thorndike, Lynn. "A Mediaeval Sauce-Book". *Speculum* 9 (1934) pp. 183-190.

Toynbee, J.M.C. *Death and Burial in the Roman World.* London: Thames and Hudson, 1971.

Twamley, Louisa Anne. *The Romance of Nature.* London: Charles Tilt, 1839.

Tyas, Robert. *Flowers and Heraldry.* London: Houlston and Stoneman, 1851.

_____. *The Sentiment of Flowers or Language of Flora.* London: R. Tyas. 9th ed. 1842.

_____. *The Handbook of the Language and Sentiment of Flowers*. London: Houlston and Stoneman, 1845.

Westland, Pamela. *The Victorian Book of Flowers*. Godalming, Surrey: CLB Publishing, 1995.

Zohary, Michael. *Plants of the Bible*. Cambridge: Cambridge University Press, 1982.